DID GOD CHANGE HIS MIND?

POLYSEMANTIC WORDPLAY AND CONDITIONALITY IN JONAH

by
Joseph Parle, Ph.D.

Exegetica Publishing
2022

DID GOD CHANGE HIS MIND?
Polysemantic Wordplay and Conditionality in Jonah

Written by Joseph Parle Ph.D.

© Copyright 2022 by Joseph Parle
Published by Exegetica Publishing
Independence, Missouri
ISBN – 978-1-60265-090-9

All rights reserved. No part of this publication may be reproduced, stored in a retrieval system, or transmitted in any form or by any means – electrical, mechanical, photocopy, recording, or any other – except brief quotation in printed reviews, without the prior permission of the publisher.

All Scripture quotations, except those noted otherwise are from the New American Standard Bible, © 1960, 1962, 1963, 1968, 1971, 1972, 1973, 1975, 1977, and 1995, by the Lockman Foundation.

In this highly engaging and thought-provoking treatise, Parle surveys the most common interpretations of Jonah 3:4, thoroughly examining and evaluating each view. Parle convincingly offers an alternative explanation, one that effectively deals a knockout blow to those who use this verse to support open theism or the idea of fallible prophecy.

Israel Loken
Chair of Bible, Theology, and Ministry Skills
College of Biblical Studies

The apparent non-fulfilment of prophetic pronouncements in the Old Testament is a thorny problem. Dr. Parle demonstrates that in the case of Jonah, one of the most difficult cases in the Old Testament, the text itself gives ample evidence that the prophecy was intended to be conditioned upon the response of the Ninevites themselves. This work deserves careful attention and wide acceptance.

Dr. Alan D. Ingalls
Professor of Old Testament and Hebrew
Northeastern Baptist College, Bennington VT

Joe Parle's detailed work on the controversial passage of Jonah 3:4, especially in light of contemporary debates about open theism, is a significant defense of the view that God did not change his mind relative to the Ninevites. Parle argues (correctly in my view) that the book of Jonah linguistically and contextually teaches an implied conditionality. This removes one contested passage from the debate over God's openness to change. Did God Change His Mind? is a must read for those who desire to pursue this issue.

Dr. Mike Stallard
Director of International Ministries
Friends of Israel

This book is dedicated to two very special people in my life.
First and foremost, to my Lord and Savior Jesus Christ:
Thanks for giving me the grace to study Your Word.
And also, to my beautiful wife Suzan Parle, who has lovingly
supported me throughout my ministry.
Thanks for supporting me.

Soli Deo Gloria.

PREFACE

This book addresses the fulfillment of Jonah's prophecy to the Ninevites in Jonah 3:4. Scholars have proposed various explanations for whether and how the prophecy was fulfilled. This book makes a case for the view that Jonah 3:4 contains a polysemantic wordplay of נֶהְפָּכֶת which is one of the key indicators of implicit conditionality. The root word הָפַךְ can imply both destruction and repentance. As a result, the wordplay was used to indicate that destruction or repentance was available depending on how the Ninevites responded to the prophecy. Either way, the Ninevites would ultimately be transformed or changed by Jonah's prophecy.

This argument is proven by taking a holistic approach to the issue by evaluating the immediate context and linguistic indicators as well as the larger contexts. The polysemantic wordplay view is superior because the lexical evidence points to it; Jonah's reaction in Jonah 4 indicates it; as well as the fact that this view fits best with the overall message of the book. Jesus' description in the New Testament of the repentant response of the Ninevites to Jonah's preaching and the implications for the Israelites who refused to repent provides additional support for this view. Hence, the polysemantic wordplay of נֶהְפָּכֶת best explains the implicit conditionality and fulfillment of Jonah's prophecy to the Ninevites. Ultimately, what looked from the perspective of the narrator of the Book of Jonah as a change of God's mind was actually a preordained fulfillment of the prophecy once the implied condition of the Ninevites' repentance was fulfilled.

ACKNOWLEDGEMENTS

There are many people who deserve acknowledgement for their help on this project, but space only allows for me to acknowledge a few. First, I thank Dr. Christopher and Cathy Cone along with everyone at Exegetica Publishing for working so hard on this project.

Second, I thank the faculty and staff of the College of Biblical Studies for all of their assistance and support. I pray that I will make their investment in me pay great dividends. Seferino Esparza, Matias Perez and Artis Lovelady III in the CBS library assisted me in locating several sources. Dr. Paul Shockley helped me identify philosophical information on implicature. Dr. Steve Sullivan assisted me with my research on Vern Poythress. I owe a debt of gratitude to my coworker Dr. Israel Loken for first encouraging me to write on this topic in his class on the prophets at Dallas Theological Seminary and for his counsel. Finally, I thank our CBS President Dr. Bill Blocker for giving me the time to write this book.

Third, I value the work of various scholars whom I have depended on to make my arguments. Most notably, I thank Dr. Ken Gardoski, Dr. Mark McGinnis, Dr. JB Hixson, Dr. Gary Gromacki, Dr. Alan Ingalls and Dr. Michael Stallard for their valuable feedback. I appreciate Dr. Robert Chisholm of Dallas Theological Seminary. While he and I disagree on some of our conclusions, he has consistently responded to my emails and interacted with me on this topic. He is a model of what scholarly dialogue should look like. Dr. David Klingler, Jonathan Master and Dr. Jamie Johns have also given me helpful feedback throughout this process. I thank the scholars at the Council on Dispensational Hermeneutics for their input and critique as well.

Fourth, I thank Robert and Jan Benjamin for their support and encouragement. Thanks for taking a chance on me so God could make this possible. Additionally, I appreciate the assistance of Anita Carman of Inspire Women.

Fifth, I would not have accomplished this without the help of my family. Most importantly, words cannot express my appreciation for the support of my wife: Suzan Parle. Suzan has been a great source of help and strength for me. She has worked hard to raise our daughter Faith and son Joseph Jr. in a manner that glorifies God and she had to invest additional time with Faith in order to allow me to complete this work. I hope that one day Faith and Joseph Jr. will read this book and realize it could not have been written without the support of their mother. I also thank my parents (Dr. Dennis and Mrs. Bertha Parle) for instilling the value of education in me. I recognize that I spent a great deal of time studying for this goal and I only hope that it will prove worthwhile to you and God.

Finally, I proclaim my sincerest appreciation for my Lord and Savior Jesus Christ who is before all things and in Him all things hold together (Colossians 1:17). I hope my life and research will be a holy sacrifice that is acceptable to Him as my spiritual service of worship (Romans 12:1).

TABLE OF CONTENTS

CHAPTER 1
    Preliminary Considerations..1
CHAPTER 2
    Summary of Interpretive Options............................53
CHAPTER 3
    Polysemantic Wordplay of Jonah 3:4.......................137
CHAPTER 4
    Context as Evidence for Implicit Conditionality....157
CHAPTER 5
    Theological Analysis:
        Jesus' References to Jonah.................................227
CHAPTER 6
    Summary and Conclusion...245

APPENDIX A
    Interpretation of Prophecy..251
APPENDIX B
    Defense of Single Meaning..295
APPENDIX C
    Regarding Late Date of Jonah.................................303
APPENDIX D
    Alternative Views of the Sign of Jonah...................333

BIBLIOGRAPHY..341

CHAPTER 1

PRELIMINARY CONSIDERATIONS

Jonah's prophecy in Jonah 3:4 is a source of debate for both liberal and conservative scholars. Jonah 3:4 can be translated as follows, "And He caused Jonah to begin to go into the city for a one-day visit and He spoke, 'Yet in forty days and Nineveh will be overturned.'" This book explores the possible interpretive options for the fulfillment of Jonah 3:4 and argues that an implicit polysemantic wordplay of נֶהְפָּכֶת (niphal of הָפַךְ which means "to change, to overturn, to destroy, to repent, or to transform") is an interpretive key to identifying the implicit conditionality of Jonah's prophecy. This argument is proven by taking a holistic approach that performs a linguistic analysis, evaluates the immediate and larger contexts of Jonah, and even discusses implications of Christ's sermons regarding Jonah in the New Testament. This holistic approach demonstrates that the original author of Jonah intended an implicit polysemantic wordplay of נֶהְפָּכֶת which can imply both repentance and destruction in order to provide the Ninevites an opportunity to respond to the conditional nature of the prophecy. As a result, the prophecy was completely fulfilled when the Ninevites repented. This introduction discusses the purpose of the study, the need for this study, the approach to this study, and the methodology employed in this book. Special focus is on the method for detecting implicature as well as polysemantic wordplay in order to argue for implicit polysemantic wordplay in Jonah 3:4.

THE PURPOSE OF THIS STUDY

Jonah 3:4 has often baffled interpreters with respect to the nature of the prophecy and the extent of its fulfillment. Some accuse Jonah of being a false prophet because his prophecy was not fulfilled.[1] Others argue that the prophecy demonstrates that Biblical prophecies sometimes fail. For instance, in *Surprised by the Voice of God*, Jack Deere uses this passage as an example of a time when a prediction failed. He notes three instances when a prophecy will remain unfulfilled: (1) The Lord did not speak the prediction; (2) The Lord may have spoken the message but the human messenger misinterpreted the message; or (3) God spoke and the messenger understood His voice accurately but a response on the part of others kept it unfulfilled.[2] Advocates of the open view of God believe the prophecy supports their argument that God disclosed His conditional intention and God did not demonstrate foreknowledge that the actual event that would come to pass.[3] The purpose of this study is to prove that the prophecy in Jonah 3:4 was entirely fulfilled within the forty day time period prophesied by Jonah. A lexical analysis of הָפַךְ as well as an analysis of the immediate and larger context of the prophecy will demonstrate that Jonah 3:4 cannot be used to support the open view of God or any position that holds for a fallible form of prophecy.

---

[1] Donald E. Gowan, *Theology of the Prophetic Books: The Death and Resurrection of Israel*, 1st ed. (Louisville, KY.: Westminster John Knox Press, 1998), 138–39.
[2] Jack Deere, *Surprised by the Voice of God: How God Speaks Today through Prophecies, Dreams, and Visions* (Grand Rapids, MI: Zondervan, 1996), 326.
[3] Gregory A. Boyd, *Satan and the Problem of Evil: Constructing a Trinitarian Warfare Theodicy* (Downers Grove, IL: Intervarsity Press, 2001), 94–95.

DID GOD CHANGE HIS MIND? 3

THE NEED FOR THIS STUDY

Several scholars have already argued for a polysemantic wordplay of נֶהְפָּכֶת in Jonah 3:4. This book is the first to uniquely analyze this issue from a holistic, inductive, traditional, dispensational perspective. Some scholars have focused on the lexical aspects of the issue.[4] Others have focused on the rhetorical, theological, and/or literary aspects of the issue.[5] This book demonstrates how the linguistic evidence for polysemantic wordplay relates to the overall purpose and message of Jonah. Rather than emphasize the nature of Jonah's prophecy as related to other Old Testament prophecies,[6] this study focuses

---

[4] See Billy K. Smith and Frank S. Page, *Amos, Obadiah, Jonah*, vol. 19B, 37 vols., New American Commentary (Nashville, TN: Broadman & Holman, 1995), 259; Douglas K. Stuart, *Hosea–Jonah*, vol. 31, 52 vols., Word Biblical Commentary (Waco, TX: Word Books, 1987), 482. D.J. Wiseman, "Jonah's Nineveh," *Tyndale Bulletin* 30 (1979) 49. Baruch Halpern and Richard Elliott Friedman, "Composition and Paronomasia in the Book of Jonah," *Hebrew Annual Review* 4 (1980): 79–80. Phillip Cary, *Jonah*, Brazos Theological Commentary on the Bible, ed. R.R. Reno (Grand Rapids, MI: Brazos Press, 2008), 108–10. Richard D. Patterson and Andrew E. Hill, *Minor Prophets*, vol. 10, 18 vols., Cornerstone Biblical Commentary, ed. Philip W. Comfort (Carol Stream, IL: Tyndale House Publishers, Inc., 2008), 276. W. Dennis Tucker, *Jonah: A Handbook on the Hebrew Text*, Baylor Handbook on the Hebrew Bible Series (Waco, TX: Baylor University Press, 2006), 70–71. Joyce Baldwin, "Jonah," *The Minor Prophets: An Exegetical and Expository Commentary*, ed. Thomas Edward McComiskey (Grand Rapids, MI: Baker Academic, 2009), 577.
[5] See Edwin M. Good, *Irony in the Old Testament* (Philadelphia,: Westminster Press, 1965), 42. T.A. Perry, *The Honeymoon Is Over: Jonah's Argument with God* (Peabody, MA: Hendrickson Publishers), 168; Phyllis Trible, *Rhetorical Criticism*, Old Testament Series, ed. Gene M. Tucker (Minneapolis, MN: Fortress Press, 1994), 180.
[6] For an example of this see Steven C. Roy, *How Much Does God Foreknow?* (Downers Grove, IL.: IVP Academic, 2006), 131–33.

directly on how the fulfillment of Jonah's prophecy relates to the overall purpose of the book. This book espouses the traditional dispensational perspective that recognizes the separation of the church and Israel. As a result, this book emphasizes the fact that the author of Jonah wrote to the nation of Israel in order to encourage them to repent of their present rebellion against God (as the more wicked Ninevites had) in order to avoid the pending judgment of the nation because of their sin.

The following reasons demonstrate the need for this book: (1) to refute the use of Jonah 3:4 to support a view that the future is open depending on the response of human agents; (2) to overcome the accusation that Jonah is a false prophet or that God gave Jonah a false message in order to motivate the Ninevites to repentance; (3) to dispute the use of Jonah 3:4 to defend a claim that Old Testament prophecy usually has unstated conditions.

Rationalization #1: Refute the Use of Jonah 3:4 by Advocates of the Open View of God

Advocates of the open view of God often use Jonah's prophecy to the Ninevites to defend their claims. Richard Rice and Gregory Boyd use Jonah's prophecy to support the open view of God position. From an open view of God perspective, the prophecy of the Ninevites to Jonah serves as an example of "God's willingness to change his plans" and that this willingness is "one of his gracious attributes."[7]

This book differs from the open view of God in several significant ways. First, the polysemantic wordplay of נֶהְפָּכֶת counters the notion that the prophecy was seemingly unconditional as advocates for an open view of God would

---

[7] Gregory Boyd, "What is the Significance of Jeremiah 18:7–11?" Christus Victor Ministries, http://www.gregboyd.org/qa/open-theism/arguments-for-open-theism/what-is-the-significance-of-jeremiah-187%e2%80%9311/ (accessed November 22, 2008).

suggest. Even Jonah argues that God knew from the very beginning that He would relent from destruction (Jonah 4:2). Second, the book shows that Jonah 3 reveals God's accurate foreknowledge and not a prophetic model to defend the view that God does not know the future. Third, this book affirms the orthodox view of God's omniscience.

Rationalization #2: Counter the Argument That Jonah Was a False Prophet

As previously mentioned, Jack Deere uses Jonah's prophecy as proof that modern day prophets may also have unfulfilled prophecies. Furthermore, Berlin attributes Jonah's anger in Jonah 4 to her belief that when God changes His mind it inevitably makes Jonah a false prophet.[8] Gowan also considers Jonah's prophecy to be a false prophecy:

> God did change His mind, and the city was saved. So, when Jonah did obey God, he became a false prophet, for his words did not come true. Finally, he reveals why he ran away. He did not want to be forced to proclaim judgment when he knew God would probably change His mind and thus ruin Jonah's reputation (4:2).[9]

Gowan interprets the message of Jonah in light of his identification of Jonah as a false prophet.

The perspective espoused by these writers requires the utilitarian and expedient notion of the end justifying the means. However, generating a false message is inconsistent with Titus 1:2, which says that God cannot lie. God would not present a

---

[8] Adele Berlin, "A Rejoinder to John A. Miles, Jr., with Some Observations on the Nature of Prophecy," *The Jewish Quarterly Review* 66 (April 1976): 231.
[9] Gowan, *Theology of the Prophetic Books: The Death and Resurrection of Israel*, 139.

case for destruction only to trick Jonah into prophesying to encourage the Ninevites to repent.

Rationalization #3: Discuss the Argument That Prophecy Often[10] Has Unstated Conditions

Some scholars utilize Jonah 3:4 to argue that prophecy usually has unstated conditions. For instance, D. Brent Sandy argues that conditionality is inherent in the language of blessing and judgment because it is rooted in the language of the covenant.[11] Robert Chisholm argues this point because of his concern for those who "claim all realized prophecy pertains to the eschaton" and who over sensationalize prophecy by espousing an overly contemporized interpretation of prophecy.[12] Allis, a covenant theologian, writes:

> Jonah was commanded to preach judgment, unconditioned, unqualified: "Yet forty days, and Nineveh shall be overthrown." Yet Jonah later declares, in explanation and extenuation of his disgraceful conduct, that he had assumed from the very first that God would

---

[10] This terminology comes from Chisolm's view that "God sometimes makes unconditional pronouncements about the future, but often (usually?) his statements of intention are conditional. Sometimes conditions are explicitly stated (for example, Isaiah 1:19–20), but more often they are unstated and implicit." Robert B. Chisholm Jr., "Making Sense of Prophecy: Recognizing the Presence of Contingency," (paper presented at the Far West Regional Meeting of the Evangelical Theological Society, Sun Valley, CA, April 2007), 2.
[11] D. Brent Sandy, "*Plowshares and Pruning Hooks* and the Hermeneutics of Dispensationalism," (paper presented at the annual meeting of the Evangelical Theological Society, San Diego, CA, 14–16 November 2007), 7.
[12] Robert B. Chisholm Jr., "When Prophecy Appears to Fail, Check Your Hermeneutic," (paper presented at the annual meeting of the Evangelical Theological Society, Atlanta, GA, 19 November 2003), 1.

spare the city if the people repented (even at the cost of making Jonah appear to be a false prophet); and the outcome proved the surmise to be correct. The unstated condition was presupposed in the very character of God as a God of mercy and compassion (iv. 2).[13]

Allis uses Jonah to argue that unconditional covenants can have unstated conditions.

This book addresses the appeal to Jonah to support this view. While this book cannot thoroughly discuss all of the passages they cite, it distinguishes between unstated or inferred conditions and implicit ones. Implicit conditions are usually textually indicated. The original author must intend implicatures. The hearer normally deduces inferences. Chisholm and Sandy base their arguments for unspoken conditions on the fulfillment of the prophecies (which must be deduced by the reader) rather than textual indicators (which indicate authorial intention). In contrast to implicit conditions, explicit conditions are "fully revealed or expressed without vagueness, implication, or ambiguity: leaving no question as to meaning or intent."[14] While Jonah 3:4 textually indicates the implied condition, the nature of the polysemantic wordplay in Jonah 3:4 is ambiguous. *Webster's Collegiate Dictionary* defines the word "ambiguous" as "doubtful or uncertain especially from obscurity or indistinctness" and "capable of being understood in two or more possible senses or ways."[15]

---

[13] Oswald T. Allis, *Prophecy and the Church: An Examination of the Claim of Dispensationalists That the Christian Church Is a Mystery Parenthesis Which Interrupts the Fulfilment to Israel of the Kingdom Prophecies of the Old Testament* (Philadelphia, PA: Presbyterian and Reformed Publishing Co., 1972), 32.
[14] *Merriam-Webster's Collegiate Dictionary,* Eleventh ed., s.v. "explicit."
[15] Ibid., "ambiguous."

APPROACH TO THIS STUDY

Even though other scholars have argued for a polysemantic wordplay of נֶהְפָּכֶת in Jonah 3:4, this book is the first to uniquely analyze this issue from a holistic, inductive, traditional, dispensational perspective. This book employs a methodology that is exegetical, inductive, literary, consistent with Biblical theology, hermeneutical, rhetorical, as well as canonical in nature. Since this book proposes an implicit polysemantic wordplay in Jonah 3:4, this introductory chapter outlines a methodology for how to identify implicatures as well as polysemantic wordplay. The second chapter discusses the interpretive options for Jonah 3:4 proposed by various authors. The third chapter provides a lexical study of the Hebrew word הָפַךְ to demonstrate its polysemy. The fourth chapter discusses the way in which the implicit polysemantic wordplay view relates to the immediate context of Jonah chapters 3–4, and the historical background of Jonah as well as the purpose, message, and genre of the book of Jonah. The fifth chapter seeks input from the New Testament to demonstrate how Jesus' sermons on Jonah relate to his being a sign of both repentance to the Ninevites and destruction for the unbelieving Israelites. The final chapter summarizes the arguments made in this book and provide suggestions for additional research.

Following is the overall approach to this book:

(1) It is exegetical in nature. By exegetical, the emphasis is placed on identifying the original meaning of the text as intended by the original author as deposited in the original text that was written to the original audience.

(2) It is inductive and literary in nature. The study begins with the lexical evidence and then tests the thesis against the immediate context, historical context, purpose, message, and genre of Jonah in order to examine congruency.

(3) This book employs Biblical theology as appropriate.

Only after the exegetical, lexical, contextual, and inductive analyses are completed can the larger context of the references to Jesus' sermons on Jonah in the New Testament be explored. This analysis helps determine how the proposed meaning of Jonah 3:4 relates to the statements Jesus made about the sign of Jonah in Matthew 12:39 and 16:4 as well as Luke 11:29–32.

(4) This book also utilizes hermeneutical strategies and rhetorical analysis in order to demonstrate a polysemantic wordplay of *word* הָפַךְ in Jonah 3:4. The evaluation of a possible double meaning in Jonah 3:4 requires a method for identifying wordplay in the Old Testament. This method helps determine the frequency with which the author employs wordplay in Jonah. Implicit polysemantic wordplay is the specific type of wordplay that is discussed, in which a word is "used once with two senses implied."[16] The likelihood of the author utilizing wordplay in Jonah 3:4 increases if the author employs this technique in other parts of the book. Wordplay is common in the Old Testament and especially in Jonah.

As part of the process of proving polysemantic wordplay of הָפַךְ, a word study is undertaken in order to evaluate the semantic range of the word הָפַךְ. The analysis demonstrates that the semantic range of הָפַךְ includes both destruction and a change of heart. This book explores how the author employs irony in order to reveal his intended message to the audience.

(5) This book assumes the inerrancy,[17] historical

---

[16] Robert B. Chisholm Jr., "Wordplay in the Eighth-Century Prophets," *Bibliotheca Sacra* 144, no. 573: 44–53.
[17] For a defense of inerrancy see Robert Paul Lightner, *A Biblical Case for Total Inerrancy: How Jesus Viewed the Old Testament* (Grand Rapids, MI: Kregel Publications, 1998). Also see Norman L. Geisler, *Inerrancy* (Grand Rapids, MI: Zondervan Publishing House, 1979).

accuracy,[18] and eighth century BC composition of Jonah.[19] This book employs the final form of the text as the basis for interpretation and assumes that the text in its original autograph is inerrant and historically accurate. This work affirms the historicity of the events narrated in Jonah as well as an eighth century BC composition of Jonah (also known as the early date of Jonah). While some of these assumptions will be discussed in the following chapters, this book does not focus on defending these assumptions.

This multifaceted approach to this book enables successful accomplishment of the stated purpose and accurately reflects the original author's intended meaning of Jonah 3:4. From a theological perspective, this book provides a conservative dispensational basis to refute the use of Jonah 3:4 to argue for the open view of God and arguments for fallible modern day prophets.

METHOD FOR DETECTING IMPLICITLY CONDITIONAL PROPHECY

Implicitly conditional prophecy exists. The major challenge is detecting implicitly conditional prophecy. This book will demonstrate how to interpret prophecy and how to detect implicit conditions in prophecy.

Prior to discussing implicitly conditional prophecy, one must establish the rules for prophecy in general. Walvoord's

---

[18] For a defense of the historicity of Jonah see Leigh F. Koerbel, "The Historicity of the Book of Jonah" (Th.M. Thesis, Capital Bible Seminary, 1985).

[19] For a defense of the early date of Jonah see Appendix C as well as R. Reed Lessing, *Jonah*, Concordia Commentary (St. Louis, MO: Concordia Publishing House, 2007), 8–17. Also see David W. Baker, T. Desmond Alexander, and Bruce K. Waltke, *Obadiah, Jonah, Micah*, The Tyndale Old Testament Commentaries, ed. D.J. Wiseman (Downers Grove, IL: Inter-Varsity Press, 1988), 51–68.

article "Interpreting Prophecy Today Part 1: Basic Considerations in Interpreting Prophecy" gives sound principles for interpreting prophecy:

> 1. Words are to be understood in their normal, natural sense unless there is firm evidence in the context that the word is used in some other sense. 2. Each statement of Scripture should be interpreted in its context. 3. A text of Scripture must always be seen in its historical and cultural contexts, and the intended meaning of the author is important. 4. Scripture should be interpreted in the light of grammatical considerations including such important matters as tense and emphasis. 5. If the language of Scripture is figurative, as is sometimes the case, this should be clearly established by the context itself and not by a priori considerations.[20]

Walvoord rightly says that the interpreter of prophecy should prefer the natural sense unless there is firm evidence to the contrary.[21] He also argues that the context alone, and not a priori considerations, determines whether the language is figurative. However, he rightly notes that literal interpretation takes figures of speech into account. Since double entendre is a figure of speech, as per Walvoord's important admonition, the interpreter does not violate the principle of literal interpretation by taking this contextually indicated figure of speech into account.

Walvoord's rules should apply to detecting implicitly

---

[20] John F. Walvoord, "Interpreting Prophecy Today Part 1: Basic Considerations in Interpreting Prophecy," *Bibliotheca Sacra* 139, no. 553 (January 1982): 7–8.

[21] Appendix A discusses and evaluates other approaches to interpretation of prophecy.

conditional prophecy. The interpreter of prophecy must prioritize the historical grammatical method and the author's original intent. The interpreter should identify conditions through contextual indicators.

Implicitly conditional prophecy is a little more difficult to identify because the implicit aspects are not explicit in the text. Implicit conditions must be determined by recognizing the author's originally intended implicatures from the words, tone, shared cultural values and the context of the statements. In order to help identify implicature, this work will rely on the research of Paul Grice who is a recognized scholar on implicature.

In *Studies of the Way of Words,* Grice describes the relationship between assertion, implication, and meaning. Grice bases his analysis of implicature on what he calls the cooperative principle. According to Grice, the cooperative principle governs what participants in a conversation are expected to observe. This cooperative principle follows four categories of maxims: quantity, quality, relation, and manner. These categories reflect the normal rules that govern regular conversations. For instance, under quantity of information provided, Grice suggests that participants should make their conversation "as informative as is required (for the current purposes of the exchange)" but they should not make "their conversation more informative than is required."[22] The second category of quality focuses on truth. Generally participants in a conversation should not say what they believe to be false or do not have enough evidence to prove.[23] Grice's third category, relevance, deals with the participants' contributions being appropriate to the immediate needs at each stage of the conversation.[24] Grice's

---

[22] Paul Grice, *Studies in the Way of Words*, First Harvard University Press Paperback ed. (Cambridge, MA: Harvard University Press, 1991), 26.
[23] Ibid., 27.
[24] Ibid., 28.

fourth category, manner, is avoiding obscurity of expression, ambiguity, brevity, and orderliness of communication.[25] These maxims of communication govern most communication and are typically assumed by the participants.

According to Grice, what makes a conversational implicature unique is that the speaker usually intends to violate one of the maxims of conversation. The speaker may intentionally violate a maxim in order to mislead; to opt out of performing a maxim (Grice gives the example of someone saying "I cannot say more; my lips are sealed" here), avoid a clash of two maxims (for example, if the speaker provides enough quantity of information to be appropriately understood, he or she may violate the quality principle if he or she does not have enough information to make the statement), or flouting a maxim by exploiting it.[26] As a result, implicature typically requires a voluntary decision on the part of the speaker to not provide as much, as accurate, as relevant, or as clear of communication as possible in order to avoid violating a specific principle of speech or for ironic purposes. A rational agent normally intends to speak as clearly as possible unless there is a reason why one cannot speak clearly. For example, if a woman is trying to help her husband stick to his diet and she asks, "Did you eat anything sweet today?" He might respond "Nothing as sweet as you honey" in order to avoid having to answer the question directly (and provide too much information) while also trying to avoid lying to his wife. Grice asserts that in order to understand a conversational implicature the interpreter will often need to know the following:

> (1) the conventional meaning of the words used, together with the identity of any references that may be involved;

---

[25] Ibid., 27.
[26] Ibid., 30–31.

(2) the Cooperative Principle and its maxims; (3) the context, linguistic or otherwise, of the utterance; (4) other items of background knowledge; and (5) the fact (or supposed fact) that all relevant items falling under the previous headings are available to both participants and both participants know or assume this to be the case.[27]

Even though Grice's principles do not directly address Biblical interpretation, one should not be surprised that numbers one, three and four of Grice's methodology correspond nicely with Walvoord's five principles for interpreting prophecy.

Grice addresses ambiguity in his discussion of implicature. His discussion helps establish implicit polysemantic wordplay in Jonah 3:4. In order for ambiguity to be an implicature, it must be deliberate. The speaker must intend ambiguity, and he expects the reader to recognize the ambiguity. Grice writes, "The problem the hearer has to solve is why a speaker should, when still playing the conversational game, go out of his way to choose an ambiguous utterance."[28] Grice provides two types of cases. The first case, double entendre, is the most important for this study. In double entendre, the author "is conveying both what he would be saying if one interpretation were intended rather than the other, and vice-versa."[29] Grice argues that the author may imply two meanings of an utterance. This is often done by a sophisticated writer, speaker, or poet and should be determined by the use of internal evidence. Double entendre, as a figure of speech, does not violate the principle of single meaning since the author singularly means two things in one utterance.[30]

---

[27] Ibid., 31.
[28] Ibid., 35.
[29] Ibid.
[30] For a defense of single meaning see Appendix B. Also see E. D. Hirsch, *Validity in Interpretation* (New Haven, CT: Yale University Press, 1967). Hirsch recognizes this distinction in puns on page 232 of his book.

Grice describes a second category of ambiguity in which one interpretation may be less straightforward than another. In this situation, one might make a case for one meaning over the other. For instance, Grice argues that when other hearers are present, one might be intentionally obscure so that the intended hearer can understand what is being said while keeping the other hearers from understanding the communication. This is common when adults are having adult conversations in the presence of children. They may discuss sexual terms or otherwise unsuitable ideas for children by using vocabulary that may communicate something else to a child. This is also commonly used when a person is writing something in code so others will not understand.

One significant aspect of Grice's research is his arguments connecting implicature to the author's intended meaning. Grice distinguishes between "standard meaning" and "occasional meaning." Grice labels the standard meaning as the general meaning of a sign. One might understand this meaning by simply knowing what the words actually mean in their traditional definitions. However, Grice defines the occasional meaning as "what the sentence or expression means on *this* occasion in this speaker's mouth."[31] In Grice's view, the meaning of a sign "needs to be explained in terms of what users of the sign do (or should) mean by it on a particular occasion."[32] Grice accurately acknowledges that words can have varied meanings in expressions. This is true of implicature in which the standard meaning often does not give the whole picture of what the author is trying to communicate. The obscurity of some implicatures may cause the hearer to make conclusions that were not intended by the author or speaker. Consequently, the ultimate arbiter of what was actually implied must be the speaker or author. This is one reason why it is common to clarify

---

[31] Grice, *Studies in the Way of Words*, 352. Emphasis his.
[32] Ibid., 217.

implicatures by asking the speaker, "Are you implying...?" or "What are you implying by that?" Bach agrees with Grice's conclusion when he writes:

> That's why implicature is pragmatic in character, hence why in different situations one can utter a given unambiguous sentence and implicate different things. For example, you could say "John's command of English is excellent" to implicate, depending on the situation, that John is a mediocre student, that he would make a fine translator, that he understood something he heard, or that he had no excuse for the sloppy paper he wrote. Of course, what a speaker could, in a given situation, plausibly be taken to implicate will be constrained by the semantic content of the sentence — certainly it matters what the sentence means — but this doesn't make implicature a property of the sentence itself.[33]

Hence, Bach makes an important clarification. Implicatures are not the product of the meaning of sentences but instead the intended meaning of the speaker. Thus, if one is trying to detect implicature in prophecy, he must prove the implicature was intended by the author.

This brings up an important distinction between implicature and inference. This distinction is described in *The American Heritage Book of English Usage*:

> People sometimes confuse *infer* with *imply*, but the distinction is a useful one. When we say that a speaker or

---

[33] Kent Bach, "The Top 10 Misconceptions About Implicature," in *Drawing the Boundaries of Meaning: Neo-Gricean Studies in Pragmatics and Semantics in Honor of Laurence R. Horn*. Ed. Betty J. Birner and Gregory Ward (Philadelphia, PA: John Benjamins Publishing Company, 2006), 22.

sentence implies something, we mean that information is conveyed or suggested without being stated outright: *When the mayor said that she would not rule out a business tax increase, she implied* (not *inferred*) *that some taxes might be raised.* Inference, on the other hand, is the activity performed by a reader or interpreter in drawing conclusions that are not explicit in what is said: *When the mayor said that she would not rule out a tax increase, we inferred that she had been consulting with some new financial advisers, since her old advisers were in favor of tax reductions.*[34]

As previously mentioned, an author or speaker intends implicature. The reader or audience usually deduces an inference from what the speaker or author says. Sometimes the reader or audience rightly infers the implicature the speaker is expressing. Other times, the audience may infer more or less than what the author or speaker is implying.

Specific Examples of Implicit Conditionality

A discussion is needed here on two specific examples of implicit conditionality: one positive and one negative. We analyze these examples by using Walvoord's method of interpreting prophecy as well as Grice's emphasis on the cooperative principle and the author's intention. In order to provide specific comparisons to Jonah, all the prophecies discussed in this section come from Old Testament narrative portions of the Bible. Exodus 32:10 serves as an implicitly conditional example. The example of a prophecy that was not

---

[34] *The American Heritage Book of English Usage: A Practical and Authoritative Guide to Contemporary English* "Infer/Imply" (Boston, MA: Houghton Mifflin Company, 1996) 108–109. All emphasis in original text. Cited originally in Kent Bach, "The Top 10 Misconceptions About Implicature," 23.

implicitly conditional is from 2 Samuel 12:14.

Exodus 32:10

Exodus 32:10 is a controversial passage in the debate among advocates of the open view of God and conservative evangelical scholars.[35] The primary question is whether Moses' intersession changed God's planned course of action. The language of this passage relates to Jonah's prophecy in several ways. For instance, the decree of the king and the nobles in Jonah 3:9 is very similar to Moses' plea in Exodus 32:12b when he asks God[36] to "turn from Your burning anger and change Your mind about doing harm to Your people."[37] Jonah 3:10 is almost an exact quote of Exodus 32:14 which the NASB translates as, "So the LORD changed His mind about the harm which He said He would do to His people."[38]

If one applies Walvoord's methodology of interpreting the passage literally within its context, there are strong indicators of implicit conditionality. Walvoord suggests that "Words are to be understood in their normal, natural sense unless there is firm evidence in the context that the word is used in some other sense" and "Scripture should be interpreted in the light of grammatical considerations including such important matters

---

[35] See, for example, the use of the passage by an advocate of the open view of God position in John Sanders, *The God Who Risks: A Theology of Providence* (Downers Grove, IL: InterVarsity, 1998) 66. Also see Richard Rice, "Biblical Support for a New Perspective," in *The Openness of God: A Biblical Challenge to the Traditional Understanding of God* (Downers Grove, IL: InterVarsity, 1994), 27–29.

[36] Unless otherwise noted, all scriptural quotes are from the *New American Standard Bible* (La Habra, CA: Lockman Foundation, 1995). Unless otherwise indicated, all emphasis is in original translation.

[37] R. Reed Lessing, *Jonah*, Concordia Commentary (St. Louis, MO: Concordia Publishing House, 2007), 368.

[38] Ibid., 368.

as tense and emphasis."[39] For instance, Exodus 32:10 begins with an imperative and cohortative that are connected by a simple vav which "are greatly used to express *design* or purpose; or, according to our way of thought, sometimes effect."[40] As others have argued, the command by God to be left alone is likely an ironic invitation for Moses to intercede on behalf of the nation. Stuart writes:

> For God to announce to a prophet (Moses being the paradigm for all future prophets) his intention to do something as a way of inviting intercession has many parallels, the most famous perhaps being those of Amos 7:1–6, where God showed Amos things he was planning to do by way of judgment upon Israel and then, in response to Amos' intercession, relented. In that context he was clearly inviting Amos to intercede so that He (God) might relent. A similarly prominent example is found in Jonah's required announcement that Nineveh would be destroyed in "forty days" (Jonah 3:4), a message Jonah reluctantly gave because he knew that it represented an invitation to repent and not an irreversible condemnation.[41]

As Stuart argues, God's invitation to Moses to intercede shows that God did not intend an irreversible condemnation. If God planned on destroying them, one must wonder why He would not have simply destroyed them without stating His

---

[39] Walvoord, "Interpreting Prophecy Today Part 1: Basic Considerations in Interpreting Prophecy," 7.
[40] A. B. Davidson, *Introductory Hebrew Grammar Hebrew Syntax*, 3d ed. (Edinburgh, Scotland: T. & T. Clark, 1902), 90. Emphasis his.
[41] Douglas K. Stuart, *Exodus*, vol. 2, 37 vols., New American Commentary (Nashville, TN: Broadman & Holman Publishers, 2006), 670.

intentions.[42] This event served as a test to determine if Moses would put the needs of his people above his own self-interest. Hence, Exodus 32:10 would probably fall under the category of quantity of information rather than quality or truthfulness of the information.

Furthermore, the Hebrew word וַאֲכַלֵּם ("may destroy") is likely cohortative in meaning although there is no unique form for the cohortative. The cohortative can express a contingent condition.[43] Here, the cohortative following the imperative indicates purpose.[44] God asks Moses to leave Him alone so He may destroy rebellious Israel. One may infer from this dialogue that if Moses does not leave Him alone, He may not destroy them. This may be why several English translations translate this word as "may destroy them" or "may consume them" (cf. ESV, KJV, NASB, NIV, et al.).

Additionally, as Walvoord has noted, context is key to interpretation of prophecy. He says, "Each statement of Scripture should be interpreted in its context" and "a text of Scripture must always be seen in its historical and cultural contexts, and the intended meaning of the author is important."[45] Thus, the context of the book is important for identifying implicit conditions. Jonathan Master has effectively demonstrated implicit conditionality of Exodus 32 through various textual indicators which include the overall argument of

---

[42] In a similar vein, one must wonder why God would call Jonah to prophesy to the Ninevites if His sole intention was to destroy them.
[43] Friedrich Wilhelm Gesenius, *Gesenius' Hebrew Grammar.*, 2nd English ed., ed. E. Kautzsch and Sir Arthur Ernest Cowley (London, England: Oxford University Press, 1909), 320.
[44] For more information see Bruce K. Waltke and Michael Patrick O'Connor, *An Introduction to Biblical Hebrew Syntax* (Winona Lake, IN: Eisenbrauns, 1990), 577.
[45] Walvoord, "Interpreting Prophecy Today Part 1: Basic Considerations in Interpreting Prophecy," 7.

the book.[46] He does this by showing God's sovereign calling of Moses, his pattern of dialogue with Moses in which he reveals His character and His willingness to sovereignly keep His promises to Moses and Israel despite their disobedience. Master writes:

> Finally, a biblical theology of Moses' dialogue with God establishes what the context of Exodus and the language of Exodus 32 have already made plain: God's words to Moses were not to be viewed as unchanging promises, but rather as expressions of divine displeasure and righteous anger. Moses was invited to dialogue; he was expected to remember the revelation of God in the past; he was responsible to remember God's promises to the nation.
> Therefore, although Exodus 32 does raise difficult questions about the nature of forgiveness and the expression of divine grace, it does not promote a theology which sees God as responding to the whims of man, being won over by a good argument, or surprised by something which had not yet entered his mind. Rather, the picture is of a God who is justifiably angry. It is of a God who forgives, remembering his unwavering promises and responding in accord with his unchanging perfection.[47]

Master's holistic approach is important for setting an understanding of context for identifying implicit conditions in prophecy. One must not only explore the immediate lexical context but also the message and purpose of the book as a whole. This is one reason why chapter four of this book will explore the immediate context of Jonah 3:4 in Jonah 2–4, the historical

---

[46] Jonathan Master, "Exodus 32 as an Argument for Traditional Theism," *Journal of the Evangelical Theological Society* 45, no. 4 (2002): 585–98.
[47] Ibid., 598.

background of Jonah, and the purpose and message of Jonah. The larger context of the book helps to identify conditions.

Another key textual indicator for implicit conditionality is the covenantal basis of the prophecy. As Walvoord and Grice point out, one must properly identify the original author's intended meaning of the prophecy in order to find implicit conditions. One must also understand the antecedent covenantal theology that the author may be assuming in his prophetic assertions. As Master notes, God's promise to Moses to be made a great nation contains similarities to His promise to Abraham in Genesis 12:2. This provides a strong hint for God's preferred basis for intercessory appeal: the Abrahamic Covenant.[48] In fact, in Exodus 6:8, Yahweh communicates His promise of the land to Abraham and He puts His name on it, "I will bring you to the land which I swore to give to Abraham, Isaac, and Jacob, and I will give it to you for a possession; I am the LORD."[49] The whole basis for the compassion of God and subsequent deliverance of the Israelites was the Abrahamic Covenant (Exodus 2:24, 6:4–8 and 33:1). In fact, it is on this same basis that Moses himself appeals to Yahweh in Exodus 32:13. Moses urges God to remember (זְכֹר) Abraham, Isaac, and Jacob and the promise of the land to their offspring. The unconditional nature of the Abrahamic Covenant, as well as the focus on deliverance of the Israelite people as a result of the Abrahamic Covenant, lends further credibility to the implicit conditionality of Exodus 32:10.[50]

---

[48] Ibid., 593.

[49] Ibid., 587.

[50] In response to the argument that God could have still fulfilled the Abrahamic Covenant through the descendants of Moses, Barrick rightly refers to the promises to all of the tribes of Israel in Genesis 49. If God rebuilt the nation through Abraham, only the Levites would benefit from the promises of Genesis 49. For more information see William D. Barrick, "The Openness of God: Does Prayer Change God?," *Master's Seminary Journal* 12, no. 2 (2001): 159.

Finally, Master appeals to other passages in the Bible that discuss this event. In particular, he disputes the argument that Yahweh responded to Moses' intercession as a result of God's care and friendship with Moses. As Master notes, this reason is never given in the Bible. Instead, God acts on the basis of His covenantal promise and repentance. Master appeals to Deuteronomy 9 to defend this assertion. He rightly notes that the basis for their entrance into the land is due to God's promise to Abraham. He also states that God did not destroy them completely because of the acts of repentance that Moses demonstrated in his appeal to God (Deuteronomy 9:16–21).[51] Thus, the lexical context, the argument of Exodus and the Biblical theology all point to implicit conditionality of Exodus 32:10.

Consequently, this analysis (based on the work of Master) demonstrated the implicit conditionality of Exodus 32:10 based on the lexical context, the immediate context, the literary context of the argument and message of the book as well as other Biblical examples. I take a similar approach in this book. The lexical context is evaluated through a word study of הָפַךְ in chapter three. This word study takes into account usage as well as grammatical situations as recommended by Walvoord. Chapter four focuses on the immediate context, the historical context, as well as the purpose, message, and genre. Chapter five consults other passages related to Jonah 3.

2 Samuel 12:14

Exodus 32:10 was an example of a textually indicated implicitly conditional prophecy. 2 Samuel 12:14 serves as an example of a prophecy that was not implicitly conditional. The

---

[51] It is important to note that God did in fact punish some of the Israelites for their sin (see Exodus 32: 34–35). This indicates that some level of repentance was likely required for deliverance from judgment.

same method used to identify textually indicated conditions in Exodus 32:10 will eliminate the probability of implicit conditionality in 2 Samuel 12:14.

First, following Walvoord's method, one must begin by evaluating this prophecy at the lexical level. In response to David's repentance in 2 Samuel 12:13, Nathan prophesies deliverance from death for David despite the fact that David should die as a murderer (cf. Genesis 9:6, Exodus 21:14, Leviticus 24:17, Numbers 35:31, *et al.*) and an adulterer (cf. Leviticus 20:10). Since this was a defiant sin (Numbers 15:30–31), the appropriate punishment was death. As a result, Yahweh's forgiveness of David under the circumstances is remarkable and gracious.

However, there is a key textual indicator that he will experience consequences. Verse fourteen begins with the contrastive word אֶפֶס. This word typically means extremity or end, but in this context, it probably functions as a limiting word meaning nevertheless.[52] Omanson and Ellington make the following statement regarding the extent of contrast implied by the use of the word אֶפֶס here:

> The transition word here is unusual but clearly introduces something that is contrary to expectation. In spite of the fact that David is promised that he will not die because of his sin with Bathsheba, their child will be taken from them. A rather strong contrastive conjunction will probably be required in the receptor language.[53]

The strong contrast indicates that God does not intend to show more grace in this prophecy.

---

[52] Ludwig Köhler *et al.*, *The Hebrew and Aramaic Lexicon of the Old Testament*, Study ed., vol. 1, 2 vols. (Boston, MA: Brill, 2001), 79.
[53] Roger L. Omanson and John Ellington, *A Handbook on Second Book of Samuel*, UBS handbook series (New York, NY: United Bible Societies, 2001), 849.

In addition, 2 Samuel 12:10 contains two strong statements that match the severity of the sin with the severity of the punishment. Nathan states that because David's deed revealed utter scorn (נִאֵץ נִאַצְתָּ) then David's son will surely die (מוֹת יָמוּת). The Hebrew repeats the term for scorn and death twice together for emphasis.[54] The certainty of the death of the child is stated in the strongest terms of certainty.

The larger context of the prophecy also points to the lack of implicit conditionality in the prophecy. The prophecy is attributed to Yahweh in no uncertain terms (כֹּה אָמַר יְהוָה). Whereas Exodus 32:10 utilized the imperative and cohortative strings to emphasize conditionality, this prophecy is given in far more certain terms. David is told in no uncertain terms that the sword will never depart from his house (2 Samuel 12:10) and that another man will lie with David's wives in daylight (2 Samuel 12:12).

Furthermore, the context of David's reaction to the parable points to the lack of conditionality of the prophecy. David states that as the Lord lives (חַי־יְהוָה), the person responsible must pay back fourfold (cf. Exodus 22:1). In effect, David lost four of his sons: his first son from Bathsheba, Amnon, Absalom, and Adonijah. His fate was secured by his own judgment.

The purpose of 1 and 2 Samuel is "to trace the move of the nation from a theocratic judgeship to a theocratic monarchy."[55] As Loken notes, the book consistently contrasts the superiority of David as Yahweh's choice for king over Saul. It also emphasizes the role of the prophets in David's life. This situation emphasizes both. David is superior to Saul because he repents upon hearing of his disobedience from the prophet Nathan. However, he experiences the consequences of Yahweh's

---

[54] Ibid., 848–49.
[55] Israel Loken, *The Old Testament Historical Books: An Introduction* (Longwood, FL: Xulon Press, 2008), 123.

discipline even though his life is spared.

Other portrayals in the Bible also point to the lack of implicit conditionality. In Psalm 51:4, David acknowledges the justness of God's judgments when he says, "You are justified when You speak And blameless when You judge." David never complains about God's decision to not spare this son. The rest of Nathan's prophecy regarding the sword never departing from David's house and his secret acts occurring publicly against him are reported in other books in the Bible. Every aspect of this prophecy is literally fulfilled.

There is also no strong covenantal basis for an implicitly conditional prophecy in 1 Samuel 12:14. Prior to the birth of this unnamed son, David already had at least six sons who could have become king (1 Chronicles 3:1–4). At some point, David received the revelation that he would have a son named Solomon who would build the Lord's temple and reign over the Davidic Kingdom (1 Chronicles 22:9–11). The fact that Solomon was not born yet is one strong explanation for why Yahweh spared David and not the child. If David happened to know that Solomon would be the king at this point, he probably would not have assumed that this child born to Bathsheba must be preserved by God in order to build the temple.[56]

All David could rely on at this point was the merciful character of God. He hopes against all hope that Yahweh would be gracious (חָנַן) to him and spare his son. Of course, as 2 Samuel 12:5–6 indicates, David himself lacked compassion (חָמַל) and essentially judged himself. Thus, it seems unlikely in the context that he would receive such grace.

In the end, when the child dies in 2 Samuel 12:18, it is

---

[56] It is difficult to ascertain whether the first child born to Bathsheba is the Shimea who is mentioned in 1 Chronicles 3:5. Shimea is never mentioned as having descendants so he might be this son. Of course, if David had not received the revelation that Solomon would build the temple, he might have assumed that this child could potentially fulfill 2 Samuel 7 and might have hoped God would spare him for that reason.

clear that Nathan's prophecy was not as implicitly conditional as David had hoped. As a result, Chisholm concludes:

> Most divine statements of intention are unmarked. In these cases, one cannot be sure from the form of the statement whether it is conditional or unconditional. For this reason, the recipient of such a message sometimes does what is appropriate, declaring, "Who knows? The Lord may be gracious/turn/relent" (cf. 2 Samuel 12:22; Joel 2:14; Jonah 3:9). These ambiguous statements of divine intention sometimes prove to be decrees. For example, when Nathan declared that the son conceived from David's adulterous encounter with Bathsheba would die (2 Samuel 12:14), David was unsure if the statement was unconditional. He prayed and fasted until the child died, hoping that God might take pity on him and spare the child's life (v. 22). God's refusal to respond to David's acts of repentance shows that Nathan's declaration was unconditional.[57]

God's lack of response to David's acts of repentance to save the life of the child help prove that Nathan's declaration was unconditional. However, it is not the only evidence. As the process for detecting implicit conditions (or the lack thereof) in prophecy has shown, there are plenty of textual indications aside from the lack of fulfillment that Nathan's prophecy in 2 Samuel 12:14 was not implicitly conditional.

Summary

This section summarizes the methodology for detecting implicit conditionality by utilizing the methodology of Walvoord

---

[57] Robert B. Chisholm Jr., "Does God 'Change His Mind'?" *Bibliotheca Sacra* 152, no. 608 (1995): 390–91.

and Grice. When an author implies something, he typically utilizes shared conventional meanings of linguistic expressions (which may include ambiguous elements such as puns). Normally the author violates conversational maxims such as quality, quantity, relevance and manner as part of the implicature. In other words, the author may have a purpose in not explicitly stating all conditions in the prophecy but there should be textual indicators that help identify implicit conditionality. In order to demonstrate this, two prophecies were assessed: Exodus 32:10 and 2 Samuel 12:14. The methodology espoused in this book demonstrates the implicit conditionality of Exodus 32:10 and the lack of implicit conditions in 2 Samuel 12:14.

METHOD FOR DETECTING IMPLICIT POLYSEMANTIC WORDPLAY

Definition and Categories of Wordplay

Wordplay is defined by Petrotta as "a sophisticated linguistic and literary endeavor that collates sound, sense, and syntax in such a way as to exploit similarities and ambiguities in an effort to suggest relationships, both cognitive and affective, that go beyond the ostensive reference of the individual phonological, semantic and syntactical units."[58] As Petrotta observes, wordplay includes utilizing similar sounds (for example, alliteration), sense (repetition and visual similarities), as well as syntax. In general, wordplay connects people, ideas, and words together, so that the reader evaluates the connection between the two. He also states, based on the work of Kelly, that wordplay often leads the reader to take a second look at the material. In the case of puns, double meaning occurs and one or the other meaning comes to the forefront. However, he sets the

---

[58] Anthony J. Petrotta, *Lexis Ludens: Wordplay and the Book of Micah* (New York, NY: P. Lang, 1991), 25.

stipulation that both must be evident in the text itself.[59] Petrotta is correct that one must be able to establish that both meanings were intended by the original author himself, and the contextual clues make this intention evident.

As a result, wordplay is categorized in many different ways.[60] Time and space do not allow for an in-depth analysis. In this section, I will focus on the classifications provided by Chisholm because of its simplicity and direct application to prophetic literature. Chisholm describes his overall perspective in classifying wordplay as, "Wordplay can be based on repetition, various meanings expressed by an individual word (polysemy), identity in sound between two or more words (homonymy), or similarity in sound between two or more words (paronomasia)."[61] Chisholm classifies wordplay according to wordplay involving a single word and wordplay involving two or more words.

The first category includes single words that are repeated in the same semantic sense, repeated with a different sense (explicit polysemantic wordplay) and words that are used once with two senses implied (implicit polysemantic wordplay).[62] The author of Jonah utilizes repetition of the same word with different nuances in order to highlight the relationships of the main characters. Some cases, such as the use of הָפַךְ in Jonah 3:4, involve implicit polysemantic wordplay. This category is occasionally called double entendre or pun. Watson prefers

---

[59] Ibid., 29.
[60] For example see I.M. Casanowicz, "Paronomasia in the Old Testament," *Journal of Biblical Literature* 12 (1893). For poetic aspects of wordplay see Wilfred G. E. Watson, *Classical Hebrew Poetry: A Guide to Its Techniques*, 2nd ed. (Edinburgh, Scotland: T & T Clark, 2005), 239–50. For a history of the classification of wordplay and an in-depth discussion of different linguistic theories regarding wordplay see Petrotta, *Lexis Ludens: Wordplay and the Book of Micah*, 1–58.
[61] Chisholm Jr., "Wordplay in the Eighth-Century Prophets," 44.
[62] Ibid.

labeling it as polysemantic pun because it "denotes a word which can have two or more meanings."[63] He describes their function as follows, "Such puns are the most effective kind because they demand quick-wittedness from both poet and audience since the operative word occurs once only. They exemplify the principle of thrift operative in oral poetry—although many polysemantic puns are strictly literary in nature."[64] Watson rightly argues that the pun is in the quick-witted mind of the author.[65] Puns can be an efficient, sometimes ironic, and artful way of making a point by using a few words.

According to Watson, "It took a skilled poet to exploit multiple meaning."[66] While polysemantic wordplay was commonly understood and appreciated by the ancient Hebrews, it is often missed by contemporary scholars who insist that a word must only have one meaning in a given context. However, singular meaning does not exclude the possibility that the original author was meaning to use more than one meaning of a word as part of the original meaning in order for his work to have more meaning for his audience (puns intended). Even the English phrase "pun intended" shows that our culture accepts the fact that occasionally a speaker intends to use a word in multiple ways at the same time for ironic purposes. In his dissertation entitled "Polysemy in the Hebrew Bible" Walter Herzberg evaluates the traditional approach to polysemy as follows:

> Words often have more than one meaning, resulting from the fact that languages contain many homonymous and

---

[63] Watson, *Classical Hebrew Poetry: A Guide to Its Techniques*, 241.
[64] Ibid.
[65] Although Watson's work *Classical Hebrew Poetry: A Guide to Its Techniques* is focused on poetry, he makes a strong argument for the fact that prose uses poetry as a stylistic device, especially in prophecy (see 48–60).
[66] Watson, *Classical Hebrew Poetry: A Guide to Its Techniques*, 242.

polysemous words. Scholars throughout the ages have pointed out words in the Hebrew Bible capable of two meanings. However, the traditional approach to solving the problem of translating these ambiguous polysemous words has been to choose one meaning and eliminate the other in any given passage. Therefore, the researcher decided to examine a select group of polysemous words to show that often the best solution is double meaning."[67]

As previously mentioned, implicit conditionality requires shared usage of cultural and linguistic conventions. Herzberg's dissertation proves that polysemantic wordplay was common enough in the Hebrew Bible to be understood by the original audience of Jonah.

Chisholm describes a second category of wordplay that involves two or more words. His subcategories include those that are identical in sound (homonymy) and similar in sound (paronomasia). According to Chisholm, paronomasia includes similarity in consonants (alliteration) and/or vowels (assonance).[68] While the author of Jonah uses some examples of wordplay that involves similarities in sound, this study will not focus on this function as extensively as implicit and explicit polysemantic wordplay.

Purpose of Wordplay

According to Petrotta, the primary function of wordplay is to "hook the audience."[69] Watson concurs when he argues that wordplay requires quick-wittedness on the part of both the author and audience in order to expose the underlying relationships that are connected through wordplay. He gives

---

[67] Walter Herzberg, "Polysemy in the Hebrew Bible" (Ph.D. Dissertation, New York University, 1978), abstract.
[68] Chisholm Jr., "Wordplay in the Eighth-Century Prophets," 44.
[69] Petrotta, *Lexis Ludens: Wordplay and the Book of Micah*, 20.

several general functions of wordplays in oral poetry (some of which can apply to prophetic literature): to amuse and sustain interest, to assist composition, to lend authenticity, to link a poem or its parts, to denote reversal of fortune, to show appearance can be deceptive, to equate two things, as well as other functions (for example,, to distract mourners in lament psalms, to assist in audience memory, etc).[70] The most significant for the study of Jonah are: equating two things, denoting reversal of fortune, as well as showing that appearance can be deceptive. For instance, while the use of רָעָה in Jonah 4:6 may initially indicate a cure for Jonah's discomfort, the analysis in the next section will show that it really is intended to reveal Jonah's evil or sin.

Casanowicz argues that wordplay occurs most frequently in prophetic literature:

> Plays upon words are especially frequent in the prophets. As an element of the daily speech, with their biting, ironical, or sarcastic force, they are best suited to the prophetic sermons, which adhere closely to living speech and aim to reach the mind and conscience of the hearer, and to bring home to him directly and vividly a truth or fact.[71]

Casanowicz rightly argues that the nature of the prophetic genre makes wordplay more frequent.[72] He says that it most likely occurs in prophetic sermon (which Jonah 3:4 is) because of the desire of the prophet to bring home a truth or fact. These

---

[70] Watson, *Classical Hebrew Poetry: A Guide to Its Techniques*, 245–46.
[71] Casanowicz, "Paronomasia in the Old Testament," 121.
[72] The forthcoming section on Biblical examples of implicit polysemantic wordplay includes two examples in prophetic literature from Ezekiel 37:9–10 and Isaiah 30:1. Also see pages 108–109 in this book for an example of wordplay in Hosea 11:8 that uses the same Hebrew root word הָפַךְ that was used in Jonah 3:4.

observations increase the likelihood that wordplay is being used in Jonah 3:4.

Chisholm makes some very important observations about the use of wordplay in prophetic literature when he writes:

> While wordplay has numerous functions, its most exegetically significant uses are to indicate correspondence and contrast (or reversal). The prophets frequently used wordplay to bring out the relationship between events that on the surface might seem unrelated or only loosely connected. This is especially true with respect to the themes of sin and judgment. The prophets used wordplay to draw attention to the appropriate or poetic nature of divine justice.[73]

It is important to note that wordplay often indicates contrast or reversal. Jonah 3 and 4 employ wordplay to describe the reversal of fortunes of the Ninevites in light of the possibility of both repentance and destruction because of Yahweh's divine justice. It connects the seemingly unrelated events of Jonah's experiences with the sailors, his experience in the large fish, the Ninevite repentance, and Jonah's anger with God in Jonah 4. Yahweh's willingness to offer both repentance and destruction to the Ninevites (and by implication the Israelites) provides the irony that the reader recognizes throughout the book. Rather than utilizing a long discourse by the narrator on how this was possible, the author of Jonah uses repetition of key words and polysemantic wordplay to cause the reader to make connections between situations and circumstances. These connections enable the narrator to evaluate the characters of the book according to the divine and human authors' intention.

Youngblood also notes that ambiguity had a specific

---

[73] Chisholm Jr., "Wordplay in the Eighth-Century Prophets," 52.

purpose within prophetic literature when he writes:

> Ambiguity is not unknown in Israelite prophetic literature and it was occasionally used to ensnare those who had turned their hearts against God (cf. Judges 18:6; 1 Kings 22:15). In other examples, the ambiguity is primarily directed to the recipient of the prophecy as a means of exposing recalcitrance toward God. In Jonah 3:4c, however, the ambiguity appears to be aimed at the prophet himself, in order to expose Jonah's bitterness towards Assyria.[74]

Youngblood's argument for the polysemantic wordplay of הָפַךְ is an interesting one. Not only was the message likely ambiguous for the original Assyrian audience (as well as the Israelite audience reading Jonah) but it may have also been employed because Jonah may have been too resistant to proclaim a more direct explicit prophecy of repentance to avoid destruction.

Chisholm also cites a theological purpose for wordplay:

> Theologically speaking, wordplay often highlights the sharp distinction between the divine and human perspectives. God's erring people fell short of His holy standard (Amos 5:10, 15) and failed to evaluate properly His sovereign actions (Micah 6:3–4). Consequently, they failed to achieve their own ambitions (Amos 3:12; Micah 2:5, 10). In spite of His people's sin, which brings harsh divine judgment, God still promised to restore Israel and reverse their situation, a fact highlighted by wordplay (Hosea 13:7; 14:9, Eng. v. 8; and Isaiah 32:9, 11, 18). In this way one gains insight into the gracious character of divine

---

[74] Kevin J. Youngblood, *Jonah: God's Scandalous Mercy*, ed. Daniel Block (Grand Rapids, MI: Zondervan, 2013), 132.

salvation. The same God who appropriately judges sin promises to reverse completely the effects of that judgment.[75]

This same statement could have been made about the book of Jonah. This statement shows that wordplay is often used in prophetic literature in order to indicate contrast or reversal in judgment oracles. Jonah 3:4 occurs in the midst of a contrast between the heart of God and the heart of Jonah as revealed in his response to the repentance of the Ninevites. Jonah is filled with contrasts between Jonah and the Gentile sailors and Ninevites. The Gentiles fear God and repent in light of his impending judgment while Jonah (representing the Israelite nation) pridefully gloats in his covenant position and prefers death over adopting the character of Yahweh.

Biblical Examples of Implicit Polysemantic Wordplay

Herzberg's dissertation entitled "Polysemy in the Hebrew Bible" categorizes several instances of implicit polysemantic wordplay (i.e. double entendre) in the Hebrew Bible. As part of the validation for polysemantic wordplay in Jonah 3:4, I will cite a few instances of polysemantic wordplay in the Old Testament in order to demonstrate instances in which the same Hebrew word can have two meanings at the same time.

One of the most notable examples of implicit polysemantic wordplay occurs in Song of Songs 2:12. Commentators and translators have often struggled with how to translate הַזָּמִיר. The Hebrew root זמר can either refer to a song (cf. Job 35:10, Psalm 95:2, Psalm 119:54, etc.) or pruning (cf. Leviticus 25:3, Isaiah 5:6, etc.). As a result, the English Standard Version, the New King James Version and the New International version translate הַזָּמִיר as singing while the New

---

[75] Chisholm Jr., "Wordplay in the Eighth-Century Prophets," 52.

American Standard (NASB) translates it pruning. What makes this somewhat problematic is that both translations fit well in the context. The translation of pruning would fit well with the agricultural context of the rains being gone, the flowers springing up, the fig trees forming fruit and the grapevines blossoming. However, the idea of singing would correspond well with the voice of the turtledove being in the land.

Herzberg's admonition to avoid the either/or fallacy of assuming one definition should apply here. Instead, the reader should admire the artistry of the author of the Song of Song's utilization of a double entendre to illuminate both aspects of the word. Garrett writes:

> This portion of the man's canto is a beautiful account of the coming of spring. The link between springtime and romance is natural and universal.... It is difficult to decide if זָמִיר (v 12) means "song" or "pruning." Context could incline one in either direction; the flowering of the plants in 12a favors "pruning" while the cooing of the doves in 12c favors "song." Keel ([1994] 101) contends that the pruning of vines takes place between January and March before the sap begins to rise but that the winter rains can last until the end of April. He also argues that the flowering of the plants and the emergence of young figs takes place in April or May, too late for the pruning season. Thus, he contends that זָמִיר means "song" here. On the other hand, it is difficult to imagine that no pruning at all took place while plants were in flower and beginning to bear fruit. In fact, Isaiah 18:5 explicitly asserts that the pruning and cutting of vines occurred while they were in flower. The term זָמִיר also appears in line 6 of the Gezer Calendar (see Gibson, *Textbook of Syrian Semitic Inscriptions,* 1.1–4), and it may be that the two occurrences illuminate one another (Lemaire, *VT* 25 [1975] 15–26). However, the meaning of the Gezer Calendar is unclear here, and it is difficult to correlate

the two. The ancient versions unanimously take the word to mean "pruning" (for example, the LXX καιρὸς τῆς τομῆς ἔφθακεν). The meaning "pruning" cannot be excluded on horticultural grounds. At the same time, זָמִיר routinely means "song" (for example, Isaiah 24:16; Psalm 95:2; Job 35:10), and the reference to the cooing of doves is suggestive of singing. We probably have here a case of deliberate ambiguity or double meaning. The text demonstrates this with a form of Janus parallelism; it is a time both of pruning (with 12a) and of singing (with 12c). He is continuing to woo her and to appeal to her to come out to him; spring is the time when the earth awakens, and he is seeking to awaken love in her.[76]

Gordon agrees as he remarks that forcing one definition of הַזָּמִיר may make one miss the artistry of the passage:

The commentators insist that while either meaning is conceivable, the author could have intended only one or the other. But this misses the point. The poet knew how to exploit the double meaning of zāmîr. Retrospectively it parallels the first member of the tristich pertaining to the growth of the soil; proleptically it parallels the final member pertaining to the song. The skillful exploitation of twin meanings, providing through a single word twofold parallelism, is artistry of the highest order.[77]

Gordon's analysis shows why it would be important for the author to utilize polysemantic wordplay in Song of Songs 2:12. The wordplay beautifully connects the two surrounding tristiches and it shows the artistic value of wordplay.

---

[76] Duane A. Garrett and Paul R. House, *Song of Songs* (Nashville, TN: Thomas Nelson Publishers, 2004), 159.
[77] Cyrus H. Gordon, "New Directions," 59–60.

Another example of polysemantic wordplay occurs in Ezekiel 37:9–10. Chapter 37 employs three different uses of the polysemantic term רוּחַ. This word can mean breath, wind, and spirit. The chapter involves the Spirit of God breathing in the breath of life by the four winds. There is some question on how to translate the first part of Ezekiel 37:9. Is Ezekiel commanded to prophesy to the wind, breath, or Spirit? Once again, an either/or distinction may be ignoring the overall polysemantic wordplay that the author is using there with רוּחַ. Some even argue that the Gospel of John picks up on this wordplay in John 3:5.[78] Polysemantic wordplay is found in the Book of John as often Jesus speaks about spiritual things to individuals who are focused on earthly matters and do not comprehend is meaning.

The translator notes of the *NET Bible* and Watson both identify implicit polysemantic wordplay in Ecclesiastes 12:4, "and the doors on the street are shut as the sound of the grinding mill is low, and one will arise at the sound of the bird, and all the daughters of song will sing softly." The *NET Bible* says:

> The noun טַחֲנָה (takhanah) refers to a "grinding-mill" where grain is ground into flour (*HALOT* 374 s.v. טַחֲנָה). The term is here used as a double entendre, figuratively describing the loss of one's teeth at the onset of old age. The figurative usage also draws upon the polysemantic nature of this noun; the related Arabic root *tahinat* means "molar tooth" (*HALOT* 374 s.v. *טַחֲנָה).[79]

Once again, the poetic use of polysemantic wordplay combines the idea of a grinding mill with teeth in order to illustrate the loss of teeth at old age.

In his book *Classical Hebrew Poetry*, Watson provides

---

[78] Zane C. Hodges, "Problem Passages in the Gospel of John Part 3: Water and Spirit—John 3:5," *Bibliotheca Sacra* 135, no. 539 (1978): 217.
[79] Biblical Studies Press, *The NET Bible*, first edition (Biblical Studies Press, 2005), 1222.

examples of what he prefers to call polysemantic puns. He cites Proverbs 28:23, Judges 14:14, Isaiah 29:4, Isaiah 30:1, Isaiah 57:6, Job 7:6, Lamentations 2:13, Isaiah 29:15, and Song of Songs 8:1–2 as examples of polysemantic puns in the Hebrew Bible. This analysis will focus on two of the examples he provides: Proverbs 28:23 and Isaiah 30:1. For instance, Watson refers to the use of חָלַק in Proverbs 28:23 which can mean "to be smooth" or "to destroy."[80] Hence, the proverb is likely referring to both a smooth/slippery/flattering and a destructive tongue. Another example of a polysemantic pun Watson discusses is Isaiah 30:1. The NASB translates the passage as, "Woe to the rebellious children," declares the LORD, "Who execute a plan, but not Mine, And make an alliance, but not of My Spirit, In order to add sin to sin." Instead of translating וְלִנְסֹךְ מַסֵּכָה as "make an alliance" the King James Version translates it as "cover with a covering." Watts says it can refer to "a cognate usage which has four possible meanings (BDB, 650–51): (1) 'pour out a libation' (as in 48:5); (2) 'cast a molten image' (30:22; 42:17); (3) 'weave a web' (25:7); (4) 'negotiate an alliance.'"[81] The idea is that they are committing idolatry by covering themselves in an alliance. The wordplay helps the reader understand the ironic message that Yahweh intends to portray.

Another example occurs in Exodus 32:6. This passage is translated by the New American Standard as "So the next day they rose early and offered burnt offerings, and brought peace offerings; and the people sat down to eat and to drink, and rose up to play." Rather than translating לְצַחֵק as "play" the NIV translates it as "to indulge in revelry." The root word צחק can refer to a form of laughing as when Abraham and Sarah laughed to themselves (cf. Genesis 17:17, 18:12–13, 18:15) or jesting as describing Lot's sons in laws (Genesis 19:14). However, the word

---

[80] Watson, *Classical Hebrew Poetry: A Guide to Its Techniques*, 241.
[81] John D. W. Watts, *Isaiah 1–33* (Waco, TX: Word Books, 1985), 391.

can also contain sexual connotations as when Abimelech sees Isaac caressing his wife in a way that a brother would not normally caress his sister (Genesis 26:8). It can also refer to the type of entertainment that is done at a pagan ritual (Judges 16:23). Hence, it appears that the idea of play in Exodus 32:6 may not only imply involvement in a form of pagan ritual but also sexual activity. Paul seems to pick up on this in 1 Corinthians 10:7–8 when he calls the Israelites idolaters and individuals who commit ἐπόρνευσαν or sexual immorality. Durham also acknowledges a wordplay in Exodus 32:6:

> There can be little surprise, therefore, that they rise from their communion meal to frivolity. לְצַחֵק "to laugh, make fun" has a connotation also of sexual play (Genesis 26:6–11; 39:6c–20). The contrast with the ritual and the communion meal of chapter 24, which may originally have immediately preceded the narrative of 32:1–6, is devastating and must not be lost with the insertion of the instruction narratives of chaps. 25–31. The celebration of an obligating relationship in Exodus 24 becomes in Exodus 32 an orgy of the desertion of responsibility.[82]

This brief survey provided examples of implicit polysemantic wordplay in the Old Testament. Implicit polysemantic wordplay is common in Old Testament prophetic literature because of the tendencies towards using powerful and symbolic language to drive home a point. Examples of wordplay were provided from historical narrative, wisdom, and prophetic literature in the Old Testament.

The Frequency of Wordplay as Used by the Author of Jonah

The author of Jonah uses wordplay frequently. In

---

[82] John I. Durham, *Exodus*, vol. 3, 59 vols., Word Biblical Commentary (Dallas, TX: Thomas Nelson, 2002), 422.

"Composition and Paronomasia in the Book of Jonah" Halpern and Friedman argue that the book of Jonah is "replete with word-play" that can serve as a "sampler of paronomastic techniques" and it is a "unique example of the contribution that formal artistry makes to the impact of the final work."[83] Magonet says that the author of Jonah uses wordplay in order to draw out "dimensions of meaning in a single root by varying the context and the subject, thus allowing once again the contrasting aspects of his characters to emerge, and deepening the nature of their interrelationships."[84] Other commentators have also argued that the author of Jonah skillfully uses wordplay throughout Jonah in order to contrast characters and provide implicit evaluation of their actions. The author's frequent use of wordplays lends greater probability that the author intended a polysemantic wordplay of הָפַךְ in Jonah 3:4.

Specific Examples of Wordplay in Jonah

Magonet describes the author of Jonah's strategy of using words with multiple meanings as follows, "Although the author could have chosen a different word each time to express different shades of meaning, by retaining this one, he allows each usage to interact with the other, multiplying levels of correspondence and contrast between the respective subjects and contexts related to the word."[85] One example is the word קָרָא. In Jonah 3:2 קָרָא is used by the command of God for Jonah to call out or proclaim. While this proclamation may imply a certain level of confidence, it is also used in the book to describe crying out to God. Jonah was called to cry against (וּקְרָא עָלֶיהָ) the city of

---

[83] Halpern and Friedman, "Composition and Paronomasia in the Book of Jonah," 79–80.
[84] Jonathan Magonet, *Form and Meaning: Studies in Literary Techniques in the Book of Jonah* (Heidelberg, Germany: Herbert Lang, 1976), 28.
[85] Ibid., 22.

Nineveh in Jonah 1:2, but he left his calling. However, the sailor instructs Jonah to cry out to his God (קְרָא אֶל־אֱלֹהֶיךָ) in Jonah 1:6 and the sailors cry out to God in prayer (Jonah 1:14). The Ninevites perform the same task in Jonah 3:5 and 8. Jonah did so in his psalm in Jonah 2:3. Thus, the same word is used in two ways in Jonah: 1) a proclamation as a representative on behalf of God 2) a cry from a disobedient individual who is crying out to God for mercy.

Magonet also provides examples of wordplay of יָדַע in Jonah. While it is a relatively common word, it provides an interesting interchange between the Gentiles and Jonah throughout the book. In Jonah 1:7, יָדַע is used to describe the process the sailors undertook to identify the individual who brought the calamity upon them. They then come to know that it is Jonah who was fleeing from God (1:10). Jonah himself knows that he is responsible for this great tempest coming upon them (1:12). However, in Jonah 3:9, the Ninevites ask "who knows?" (מִי־יוֹדֵעַ) whether God will relent from the promised destruction. Magonet writes:

> With this statement he [the king of Nineveh] goes one step further than the captain of the ship, whose parallel perhaps (1:6) is limited to a hope that God will "think of them." The king speculates on the inner workings of the mind of God, which as a pagan in this story, he can only guess at. We are thus ready for the next transition of meaning, when Jonah speaks yet again of what he knows (4:2).[86]

Ironically, Jonah, who represents Israel, has all the knowledge of God but he does not reflect the character of God. The Gentiles, who have little or no knowledge of God, seem to know the right responses that God is requiring in order to avoid

---

[86] Ibid., 27.

destruction. Both the Ninevites and sailors repent and pray to Him. While Jonah does not want to see Nineveh spared, the Gentile sailors attempt to row back to land in order to save Jonah's life from God's judgment. They instinctively know the possibility of perishing is due to their disobedience of Yahweh, but they also recognize the possibility of repentance. Jonah, on the other hand, praises God for his deliverance from the fish but later requests death. As chapter four of this book will show, the Israelites in Jonah's time experienced great deliverance from God, but they were not willing to repent in order to avoid His judgment. Thus, the Israelites ironically needed to imitate the actions of the wicked Ninevites. It is interesting that wordplay is used throughout Jonah to mark this contrast.

In Jonah 4:2, Jonah proclaims his knowledge of God's gracious and compassionate character. Rather than praising God for that, he justifies his fleeing to Tarshish because of God's character. Magonet remarks on the irony of this knowledge:

> Thus here the root ידע takes on the peak of its meaning, the transcendent knowledge of the nature of God, obtained through revelation, and confirmed in the experience of Israel—and at the same time in the mouth of Jonah, that knowledge becomes absurd! Because it is spoken in the middle of Jonah's complaint about the very qualities of God, and, in addition, because of the ironic fact that but for this very patience and compassion of God, Jonah himself would not be alive to complain about them![87]

This ironic wordplay points to a key theme in the book of Jonah. The Israelites, represented by Jonah, who have the very revelation of God and claim to know God, are unwilling to repent and turn to God in order to avoid the imminent destruction that

---

[87] Ibid., 28.

awaits them. However, the worst of Gentile nations, who received less revelation, repented at the first prophetic warning of destruction. Wordplay helps highlight this contrast.

Halpern and Friedman also describe many instances of word repetition and wordplay throughout Jonah. For instance, they note the repeated use of the words קוּם and עָלָה ("go up") as well as יָרַד ("go down") throughout Jonah. In Jonah 1:2 Yahweh commands Jonah to arise (קוּם) because the sins of the Ninevites have arisen (עָלְתָה) to Him. Instead, Jonah got up (וַיָּקָם) and went down (וַיֵּרֶד) to Joppa and later descended into a boat. In Jonah 1:6 the sailors told Jonah to arise (קוּם) and call out to his God. Eventually, by Jonah's own admission, he later descended (יָרַדְתִּי) to the bottom of the mountains into a pit. However, Yahweh brought him up (וַתַּעַל) from there. In Jonah 3:2, God reiterated His command for Jonah to arise (קוּם) and go to Nineveh. Jonah did arise and go to Nineveh (וַיָּקָם) as God requested. When the king of Nineveh heard Jonah's prophecy, he arose from his throne (וַיָּקָם) and sat in the ashes in repentance. Later God appointed a plant that came up over Jonah (וַיַּעַל) as well, and the worm attacked the plant as the dawn came up (בַּעֲלוֹת).[88]

What is the significance of this wordplay? Halpern and Friedman write:

> It is worth noting that the term [יָרַד] surfaces again in Jonah's metaphor of his distraint in the fish's belly ('I went down to the bases of the mountains' —2:7); this represents both his deliberate and his enforced alienation from the deity, a fact that is obvious from the sequence, but it can be drawn out more objectively from a structural analysis of the book."[89]

They later say, "Lexically, then, it is as though descent

---

[88] Halpern and Friedman, "Composition and Paronomasia in the Book of Jonah," 80–81.
[89] Ibid., 80.

represents distance from YHWH, ascent movement toward him."[90] This point reflects the beauty of the use of wordplays in the Hebrew Old Testament. Through the use of repetition of key words, one notes the author's evaluation of the actions of the characters without the narrator actually having to make formal declarations of his evaluation of the characters. Thus, the words serve the purpose of describing the situation and giving the narrator's analysis of the actions at the same time.

Halpern and Friedman also find irony in the use of the word גָּדוֹל which occurs thirteen times in the book of Jonah. The word is used to describe the great city Nineveh (1:2 and 3:2–3 and 4:11), the great wind (1:4), the great storm (1:4), the great fear of the sailors (1:10, 16), the big fish (2:1), the largest Ninevite who is contrasted to the smallest (3:5), etc. Regarding the use of this word Halpern and Friedman state:

> Everything that is "big" in the story is produced by YHWH, or by YHWH's deeds. The implication is that Nineveh's grandeur stems from YHWH as well, a point made directly in 4:10–11. YHWH raises; YHWH enlarges. This dovetails so fully with the use of the ascent/descent terminology in the story that it becomes difficult to regard the pattern as accidental.[91]

Perhaps one notable exception from Halpern and Friedman's point is the reaction of Jonah (which technically could be classified under something that is produced by Yahweh's deeds). In 4:1, Jonah experiences extreme displeasure or evil (רָעָה גְדוֹלָה) in reaction to Yahweh's mercy. He also experiences extreme joy (שִׂמְחָה גְדוֹלָה) when God graciously provides the plant. Thus, while Yahweh is doing big things, Jonah is having big reactions. While Jonah has great anger

---

[90] Ibid., 81.
[91] Ibid., 82.

against the Lord, the Gentile sailors in Jonah 1:16 fear Him greatly (יִרְאָה גְדוֹלָה) and the Ninevites great and small repent in Jonah 3:5. The likelihood of this ironic use of גָּדוֹל being purely coincidental is greatly remote.

Another interesting wordplay occurs in Jonah 4:10–11. The *NET Bible* discusses the irony of the contrast between Jonah's concern (חַסְתָּ) over the little plant (the diminutive use of הַקִּיקָיוֹן in 4:10 emphasizes this) as contrasted with God's concern (אָחוּס) over the great (הַגְּדוֹלָה) city of Nineveh. This wordplay uses the two possible meanings of חוס which can mean upset/troubled and show compassion in order to contrast Jonah and Yahweh. The *NET* Bible says, "Jonah's misplaced priorities look exceedingly foolish and self-centered in comparison with God's global concern about the fate of 120,000 pagans."[92]

According to Halpern and Friedman, two specific words in Jonah call attention to Yahweh's sovereignty: מָנָה and אָבַד. The Hebrew word מָנָה is used to describe Yahweh's sovereign preparation of the large fish (2:1), the gourd (4:6), the worm (4:7), and the east wind (4:8). In all of these passages, the word is used to describe Yahweh's "manipulation of phenomena in the account."[93] The word אָבַד, which is translated as perish, is used by the sailors (1:6 and 1:14), the king of Nineveh (3:9), and of the destruction of the gourd (4:1). The same word is consistently used to describe "perishing at YHWH's hand."[94] The purpose of this consistent repetition is to "reinforce the important theme of YHWH's control of objects and events, his mastery of fate."[95]

---

[92] Biblical Studies Press, *The NET Bible*, 1739.
[93] Halpern and Friedman, "Composition and Paronomasia in the Book of Jonah," 82.
[94] Ibid.
[95] Ibid. It is ironic that some use Jonah to argue that God does not know or chooses not to control the future when there are such clear instances by the use of certain words that He is in absolute control in the book. Even when Jonah chooses to run from God's calling, God sovereignly prepares a large fish to bring him back to shore to do God's will. If Jonah

The point of emphasizing the wordplay within Jonah is to demonstrate the strong likelihood of a polysemantic wordplay in Jonah 3:4. The polysemantic wordplay in Jonah 3:4 does not escape Halpern and Friedman's notice either:

> Apart from meaning "physical overthrow," the verb *hpk* denotes a change of character (1 Samuel 10:6, 9; cf. Exodus 14:5; Hosea 11:8; Lamentations 1:20; and the nuance of transformation in Deuteronomy 32:6; Jeremiah 31:13; Amos 5:7; Psalm 30:12; Nehemiah 13:2, for example,). Nineveh's transformation fulfills profoundly Jonah's prophecy.[96]

Jonah is also one of the books featured in Good's monograph *Irony in the Old Testament*. Good describes several ironic wordplays within Jonah. In Jonah 1:1, Jonah is described as "the son of Amittai" which literally means "son of faithfulness" or "truth" (and can sometimes mean "son of valor") even though Jonah "abandons faithfulness at the first opportunity and speaks truth only under duress, even then not understanding it."[97] Similar to Halpern and Friedman, Good finds irony in the fact that Jonah is told to arise and go to Nineveh (קוּם), and instead Jonah rose up to flee to Tarshish (וַיָּקָם) in 1:3.[98] Jonah claims to fear the Lord (יָרֵא) in 1:9 even though the sailors were the ones who knew what fearing the Lord was truly about in 1:10 and 1:16. Good also recognizes the polysemantic wordplay in Jonah 3:4 when he argues that the threat "has double meaning," that the "city is doomed," and that

---

learns anything in the book, it is that He can't escape God's sovereign control.

[96] Ibid., 87. Emphasis in quote.
[97] Good, *Irony in the Old Testament*, 42.
[98] Ibid., 47.

it can be changed "from something bad to something good."⁹⁹

Page also recognizes wordplay in Jonah. For instance, he says:

> The word "blazed" is the same Hebrew word translated "chewed" in v. 7. It is a general word (נָכָה) meaning to "strike." Having been deliriously happy, Jonah was being struck down by a series of natural "calamities" until his misery was complete. The blazing sun beat down on Jonah's head, which was lacking any helpful shade. The verb translated "grew faint" (עָלַף) is almost identical in form and meaning to the word Jonah used in 2:7 (עָטַף, Heb 2:8) of his life "ebbing away." Jonah probably felt that God was finally answering his prayer in 4:3 by taking his life. So, since nothing has changed, he repeated the prayer. At his wits' end, Jonah was completely exhausted; the text says literally, "He asked his life to die."¹⁰⁰

One can see how the wordplays in Jonah 4 provide a startling contrast to his poem of deliverance in Jonah 2. Whereas he once praised God from delivering him from the pit and the certain death of the surrounding water, now Jonah asks for death.

Additionally, the author of Jonah repeatedly utilizes different meanings of the word רָעָה to make ironic comparisons. Magonet notes that this word is used in relationship to all three main characters of the book: God, Jonah, and the pagans.¹⁰¹ In one instance, the author makes a play on words on two different occasions in the same verse. Page writes regarding Jonah 4:6, "The verb for 'deliver,' נצל, is a play on the word for 'shade,' צל.

---

⁹⁹ Ibid., 48–49. Good argues that the positive meaning of the prophecy may not have been in Jonah's mind. I believe Jonah understood both meanings and I will discuss that in more detail in chapter four.
¹⁰⁰ Smith and Page, *Amos, Obadiah, Jonah*, 280.
¹⁰¹ Magonet, *Form and Meaning: Studies in Literary Techniques in the Book of Jonah*, 22.

There also is intentional ambiguity in the use of רָעָה, for while God's immediate purpose for the vine was to relieve Jonah's discomfort, his real purpose was to deliver Jonah from his sinful attitude."[102] Once again, the concept of calamity and deliverance is contrasted. However, on this occasion, Jonah is the recipient of mercy as a potential object lesson to reveal his evil.

Page describes the relationship between Jonah's sinful attitude and comfort as follows, "The phrase 'to ease his discomfort' is literally 'to deliver him from his evil' (רָעָה). The latter word is the term occurring throughout the book with its two senses, 'wickedness' or 'trouble, calamity.'"[103] Page's assertion regarding the use of רָעָה in Jonah 4:6 is critical for the argument of this book because it is an example of implicit polysemantic wordplay by the author of Jonah. Regarding the larger context of the book, the word does occur in several circumstances throughout the book (Jonah 1:2, 7–8; 3:8, 10; 4:1–2, 6). In some cases, it does carry the sense of calamity or trouble (cf. Jonah 1:7–8), while in others it means evil (Jonah 1:2 and 3:8). In one case, both uses are found in the same verse (Jonah 3:10). In this passage, the Ninevites repented of their evil and God relented on the calamity they deserved. One can see the irony in Jonah 4:1 when the same word that described the evil of the Ninevites now describes Jonah. Page writes:

> The NIV speaks of Jonah's great displeasure and great anger. The literal translation is, "It was evil to Jonah with great evil." There is a play on words here with the root רָעָה, which can refer to wickedness on the one hand (see 1:2) or to disaster, trouble, or misery as here. The evil that was characteristic of the people of Nineveh here described the prophet of God.[104]

---

[102] Smith and Page, *Amos, Obadiah, Jonah*, 278.
[103] Ibid.
[104] Ibid., 271.

Chisholm also identifies this instance as an example of polysemantic wordplay:

> An initial reading of the statement [in Jonah 4:6a] suggests that רָעָה, "distress," refers to Jonah's physical discomfort, caused by the hot sun beating down on his head. Jonah is happy about the plant, but God quickly destroys it, prompting one more complaint from Jonah and the book's final dialogue, which is designed to show Jonah why God has been merciful to Nineveh. At this point, the statement in verse 6a takes on deeper meaning. If God were just concerned about Jonah's physical comfort, he would not have destroyed the plant he made. Through the object lesson of the plant, he really wants to purge Jonah of his morally wrong attitude. One can detect a double meaning in the word רָעָה. On the surface, it means "physical discomfort," but it also has a deeper meaning. God made the plant grow to give Jonah some temporary relief from his physical discomfort, but his larger purpose in making the plant was to use it as an object lesson in ridding Jonah of his moral "evil," another attested nuance of this noun.[105]

Chisholm's arguments are very helpful. Once again, polysemantic wordplay must be intended by the author and that the use of a phrase like "deeper meaning" does not imply an allegorical method of interpreting the passage. If the author intends the polysemantic wordplay, then a literal interpreter must interpret it as such. Having said that, Jonah lacks an understanding of the deeper purposes of God throughout the book. The polysemantic wordplay in Jonah 4:6 demonstrates the

---

[105] Robert B. Chisholm Jr., *From Exegesis to Exposition: A Practical Guide to Using Biblical Hebrew* (Grand Rapids, MI: Baker Books, 1998), 52.

contrast between Jonah's selfish focus and Yahweh's justice in judging sin in order to eliminate it.

Not only this, but while God is slow to anger and relents from calamity (for instance, the use of רָעָה in Jonah 3:10 and 4:2 to describe what God relents from), Jonah angrily becomes displeased in an evil way (4:1) because of God's mercy (Jonah 4:1–2). The very mercy that the Ninevites hoped to see was resented by Jonah. Page writes, "As God's anger and judgment were averted in chapter 3, Jonah's anger was incited."[106] The ironic contrast brought about by the wordplay of רָעָה in Jonah 4 is inescapable.

Hence, רָעָה is often used in Jonah to describe a disastrous situation that God has brought upon a group of individuals to lead them to His gracious deliverance through repentance. The fact that God brings these situations about indicates they are not necessarily evil. Instead, they are intended to purge people of their evil. Much to the reader's surprise, in Jonah's case, the situation Jonah faces in chapter four is far less disastrous than the ones that the sailors and the Ninevites face; yet while the sailors and Ninevites repent and plead for their life, Jonah refuses to repent and pleads for his death! Jonah thinks his problem is his discomfort from losing his shade when his real problem is his evil and unrepentant heart.

The frequency of wordplays in Jonah help demonstrate that God commanded Jonah to use the word הָפַךְ in 3:4 in a way which, as Good argues, means to be changed in a positive sense from something bad to good[107] or a city that is doomed or overthrown.[108] This is not to say that a text can have multiple

---

[106] Smith and Page, *Amos, Obadiah, Jonah*, 271.
[107] Good., *Irony in the Old Testament*, 48–49. As evidence, Good points to the Qal form used in Zephaniah 3:9, 1 Samuel 10:9, Jeremiah 31:13, Nehemiah 13:2, and the niphal in Hosea 11:8 and Exodus 14:5.
[108] Ibid., 48. For evidence on this translation, Good cites Genesis 19:25, 29, Amos 4:11, and Isaiah 1:7.

meanings, but that the intended meaning of the passage was an ironic polysemantic wordplay that God intended from the lips of Jonah to the Ninevites.

SUMMARY

This chapter establishes the purpose of the study, the need for this study, the approach to this study as well as the methodology employed in this book. The purpose of this study is to demonstrate that the author of Jonah uses an implicit polysemantic wordplay of הָפַךְ in order to provide the possibility of both repentance and destruction for the Hebrews. The implicit polysemantic wordplay view helps overcome arguments by those who consider Jonah to be a false prophet or advocates of the open view of God who use Jonah 3:4 to defend the notion that the future is uncertain to God. The method for interpreting prophecy and implicature was then defended by explaining the contributions of Walvoord and Grice respectively. Finally, wordplay was defined as "a sophisticated linguistic and literary endeavor that collates sound, sense, and syntax in such a way as to exploit similarities and ambiguities in an effort to suggest relationships, both cognitive and affective, that go beyond the ostensive reference of the individual phonological, semantic and syntactical units."[109] Two categories of wordplay were described: wordplays involving a single word or wordplays involving two or more words. The first category was emphasized due to its relationship with Jonah 3:4. After categorizing the forms of wordplays, I elaborated on the purpose of wordplays and gave specific examples in the Bible and Jonah. The author of Jonah used wordplays in judgment oracles to indicate reversal of fortune as well as to direct the reader's attention to God's divine justice.

---

[109] Petrotta, *Lexis Ludens: Wordplay and the Book of Micah*, 25.

CHAPTER 2

SUMMARY OF INTERPRETIVE OPTIONS

This chapter reviews differing views on the fulfillment of Jonah 3:4, including the critical view, the open view of God, the unstated condition view, the false message from God intended to generate Ninevite repentance view, the altered or distorted message view, and the latter fulfillment view. Since R.J. Lubeck has discussed several of the views in his article entitled "Prophetic Sabotage: A Look at Jonah 3:2–4," some of his analysis will be used as a framework for discussing these views. After evaluating these views, the implicit polysemantic wordplay view will be presented in more detail.

R. J. Lubeck identifies the principal options for this problem when he writes:

> (1) Jonah did deliver Yahweh's message exactly as he received it, but both he, Yahweh, the Ninevites, and we readers are meant to understand it as something else, namely, that it is a conditional threat which will not be carried out if Nineveh repents.
> (2) Jonah delivered the message as given, but he knew beforehand that it was false. Yahweh never intended to execute it, but his posturing is justifiable on the grounds that it achieved a higher good, the repentance of the Ninevites.
> (3) Jonah conveyed the message accurately, but it was fulfilled at a later time when the Assyrian empire was destroyed by the Babylonians; i.e. the destruction did

take place as prophesied, although the timing was off. (4) Jonah did *not* [emphasis his] utter the message Yahweh gave him, but either altered or abbreviated it to suit his own purposes. Instead of delivering the original, conditional message, he distorted it so that the Ninevites would understand it as a pronouncement of irrevocable judgment.[1]

Lubeck himself concludes:

We observed that Jonah only begins to fulfill his task and that he may have prematurely walked off the job. Jonah utters a truncated, highly irregular oracle which implies certain upheaval, yet offers no reasons, no hope, makes no reference to God, and contains no call for a response; furthermore its formal structure is unlike any other (legitimate) prophetic speech...Ironically, the oracle, altered as it was by Jonah, nevertheless proved to be true, though not in the sense that Jonah had wished. Nineveh was overturned, not by annihilation, but by experiencing a unanimous change of heart. And Yahweh sovereignly and ironically overturned Jonah's perverted proclamation in a way that accomplished his divine purpose (the repentance of Nineveh) while safeguarding from falsity the very letter of Jonah's utterance.[2]

This chapter discusses all four of Lubeck's options prior to implicit polysemantic wordplay view of the prophecy in Jonah 3:4.

---

[1] R. J. Lubeck, "Prophetic Sabotage: A Look at Jonah 3:2–4," *Trinity Journal* 9:1 (1988): 38.
[2] Ibid.

THE CRITICAL VIEW

Many critical scholars argue against the historicity of Jonah. They believe that the prophecy in Jonah 3:4 is conditional but there would be no literal fulfillment to be expected since Jonah is primarily didactic in nature.

Implicitly Conditional but Not Historical

The common critical view is that the prophecy was conditional but the fact that the book is not historical basically makes the question a moot point. For instance, although he ultimately denies the historicity of the book of Jonah, Fretheim writes:

> The book was thus intended to make clear that God's actions are finally impenetrable to human insight, a situation with which the community of faith must learn to live.... But the issue for Jonah is not so much *that* God repents, but *for whom* God repents. Jonah is certainly aware that Israel's very life depended upon God's willingness to change his mind, to be merciful rather than simply just. Jonah's problem is the *indiscriminate* extension of God's repentance to other people.[3]

Thus, Fretheim considers the book of Jonah to be about the nature of God's mercy which causes Him to repent. In Fretheim's view, the prophecy is an example of a situation in which God changes His mind. Jonah is not so much upset about the fact that God changes His mind, but for the fact that He would do so by sparing the sinful Ninevites.

Adele Berlin has a similar position on the prophecy. She considers the book of Jonah to be a theoretical and hypothetical

---

[3] Terence E. Fretheim, *The Message of Jonah: A Theological Commentary* (Minneapolis, MN: Augsburg Publishing House, 1977), 23. Emphasis his.

case as contrasted with historical prophecy.[4] In Berlin's view, the Book of Jonah is "completely a-historical" but it "captures the essence of Israelite prophecy."[5] However, in a slight variation to Fretheim's view, Berlin believes that Jonah is mainly upset in Jonah 4 because when God changes His mind it inevitably makes Jonah a false prophet.[6] Berlin cites other Biblical examples of false prophecy such as Isaiah 38:1–8, Jeremiah 22:19 and Ezekiel 26:7–14. Ultimately, Berlin believes that the key lesson God is trying to teach Jonah is that the change in the prophecy brought about by the Ninevite repentance is a sign of His compassion, which is more important than Jonah's self-image.[7]

Trible acknowledges that "*hpk* holds opposite meanings of destruction and deliverance."[8] However, she also concludes, "Nowhere in the story has Yhwh given Jonah these exact words to speak. Is his prophecy, then, true or false? A contrast by omission also feeds doubt about the authenticity of the utterance."[9] Hence, she recognizes the double entendre in Jonah 3:4 but also questions the historicity of the event. This view is characteristic of several critical scholars who acknowledge the possibility of double entendre, but they ultimately deny the historicity of the event.[10]

---

[4] Adele Berlin, "A Rejoinder to John A. Miles, Jr., with Some Observations on the Nature of Prophecy", *The Jewish Quarterly Review* 66 (April 1976), 230.
[5] Ibid., 235.
[6] Ibid., 231.
[7] Ibid., 233.
[8] Phyllis Trible, *Rhetorical Criticism*, Old Testament Series, ed. Gene M. Tucker (Minneapolis, MN: Fortress Press, 1994), 180. Emphasis hers.
[9] Ibid. The section on the Word of the Lord given to Jonah in chapter four of this book addresses the argument that the book of Jonah never claims that the prophecy actually was from YHWH. Evidence from Jonah 3:4 and 3:10 is provided to counteract this claim.
[10] T. A. Perry, *The Honeymoon Is Over: Jonah's Argument with God* (Peabody, MA: Hendrickson Publishers), 168. Rosemary A. Nixon, *The*

Evaluation of the Critical View

This book strongly affirms the historicity of Jonah and will defend it on several fronts.[11] First, the statements by Christ about Jonah confirm the circumstances portrayed in Jonah actually occurred. Secondly, God's role in Jonah provides evidence of the historicity of Jonah. Thirdly, the historicity of Jonah was assumed by early Jewish and Christian interpreters. Finally, similar occurrences of individuals surviving in large fish will be explored as well.

The first and most obvious reason to affirm the historicity of Jonah is the perspective of Jesus Christ. In the NASB of Matthew 12:39–41, Jesus compared Jonah's experience in the large fish to his death, burial, and resurrection when He said:

> But He answered and said to them, "An evil and adulterous generation seeks after a sign, and no sign will be given to it except the sign of the prophet Jonah. For as Jonah was three days and three nights in the belly of the great fish, so will the Son of Man be three days and three nights in the heart of the earth. The men of Nineveh will rise up in the judgment with this generation and condemn it, because they repented at the preaching of Jonah; and indeed something greater than Jonah is here."

It is important to note that Jesus not only affirmed the historical validity of the event itself but also the response of the Ninevites. Jesus argued that the Ninevites repented at hearing His preaching and responded to His sign. Even if one could argue that Jesus was referring to a legendary story of Jonah's experience in a fish, how could Jesus refer to the Ninevites repenting if they never actually did? Furthermore, this story

---

Message of Jonah: Presence in the Storm (Leicester, England; Downers Grove, IL: InterVarsity Press, 2003), 165.

[11] For a more extensive discussion see Leigh F. Koerbel, "The Historicity of the Book of Jonah" (Th.M. Thesis, Capital Bible Seminary, 1985).

illustrated the present resistance of the Jewish people to repent even when one who was greater than Jonah was in their presence. If the Ninevites did not repent, would not Jesus' opponents have mentioned that it was not a historical event and thus an invalid argument?

Allen responds to the appeal to Matthew 12 as evidence of the historicity of Jonah:

> Essentially, Jesus referred to Jonah and the fish as a means of communicating the significance of his own mission. His fundamental concern was not to expound the book of Jonah but to reveal truth concerning himself in terms his Jewish audience acknowledged and could understand. The best of teachers, he argued from what was accepted and what was as yet unknown. He turned to good use the current interpretation of Jonah 2 and made it the vehicle of vital truth. A greater phenomenon than that of Jonah was here. Prophet par excellence, he was to conquer death in a reality that transcended the symbolic shadow of Jonah's survival.[12]

He scoffs at Western literalists who do not make room for the figurative element in the teaching of Jesus when he says, "If a modern preacher would not be at fault if he challenged the congregation with a reference to Lady Macbeth or Oliver Twist, could not Jesus have alluded in much the same manner to a well-known story to reinforce his own distinctive message?"[13] Alexander provides a good response to this reasoning:

> As the narrative [of Jonah] now stands, God is the central character in all that takes place; we are informed not only of his actions but also of his words. This, however, raises

---

[12] Leslie C. Allen, *The Books of Joel, Obadiah, Jonah and Micah* (London, England: Hodder and Stoughton, 1976), 196–97.
[13] Ibid., 180.

an important question: given Jewish attitudes concerning God, in particular prohibitions against the making of idols and the improper use of the divine name, is it not highly improbable that a Jewish author of the period 780 to 350 BC would have dared create a fictional account with God as a central character? Would not this have been viewed by devout Jews of that time as tantamount to blasphemy?[14]

These two quotations show a key difference between the assumptions about a Jewish perspective of the book of Jonah. Prior to the time of Christ, a significant quotation that affirms the historicity of Jonah is found in Tobit 14:4–8 in the KJV with Apocrypha:

Go into Media my son, for I surely believe those things which Jonas the prophet spake of Nineve, that it shall be overthrown; and that for a time peace shall rather be in Media; and that our brethren shall lie scattered in the earth from that good land: and Jerusalem shall be desolate, and the house of God in it shall be burned, and shall be desolate for a time; And that again God will have mercy on them, and bring them again into the land, where they shall build a temple, but not like to the first, until the time of that age be fulfilled; and afterward they shall return from all places of their captivity, and build up Jerusalem gloriously, and the house of God shall be built in it for ever with a glorious building, as the prophets have spoken thereof. And all nations shall turn, and fear the Lord God truly, and shall bury their idols. So shall all nations praise the Lord, and his people shall confess God, and the Lord shall exalt his people; and all those which

---

[14] T. Desmond Alexander, "Jonah and Genre," *Tyndale Bulletin* 36 no. 1 (1985): 58.

love the Lord God in truth and justice shall rejoice, shewing mercy to our brethren. And now, my son, depart out of Nineve, because that those things which the prophet Jonas spake shall surely come to pass.

Thus, a Jew who was writing around 200 BC considered the events described in the book of Jonah to be actual events and he expected for Jonah's prophecies to be literally fulfilled.

Another testimony of the Jewish view of Jonah comes from Josephus when he said:

> Now I cannot but think it necessary for me, who have promised to give an accurate account of our affairs, to describe the actions of this prophet, so far as I have found them written down in the Hebrew books. Jonah had been commanded by God to go to the kingdom of Nineveh; and, when he was there, to publish it in that city, how it should lose the dominion it had over the nations. But he went not, out of fear; nay, he ran away from God to the city of Joppa, and finding a ship there, he went into it, and sailed to Tarsus, to Cilicia, and upon the rise of a most terrible storm, which was so great that the ship was in danger of sinking, the mariners, the master, and the pilot himself made prayers and vows, in case they escaped the sea. But Jonah lay still and covered [in the ship], without imitating anything that the others did; but as the waves grew greater, and the sea became more violent by the winds, they suspected, as is usual in such cases, that some one of the persons that sailed with them was the occasion of this storm, and agreed to discover by lot which of them it was. When they had cast lots, the lot fell upon the prophet; and when they asked him whence he came, and what he had done? He replied, that he was a Hebrew by nation, and a prophet of Almighty God; and he persuaded them to cast him into the sea, if they would escape the danger they were in, for that he was the

occasion of the storm which was upon them. Now at the first they durst not do so, as esteeming it a wicked thing to cast a man, who was a stranger, and who had committed his life to them, into such manifest perdition; but at last, when their misfortunes overbore them, and the ship was just going to be drowned, and when they were animated to do it by the prophet himself, and by the fear concerning their own safety, they cast him into the sea; upon which the sea became calm. It is also related that Jonah was swallowed down by a whale, and that when he had been there three days, and as many nights, he was vomited out upon the Euxine Sea, and this alive, and without any hurt upon his body; and there, on his prayer to God, he obtained pardon for his sins, and went to the city Nineveh, where he stood so as to be heard; and preached, that in a very little time they should lose the dominion of Asia; and when he had published this, he returned. Now, I have given this account about him, as I found it written [in our books].[15]

Thus, the affirmation of both Josephus and Tobit show the early Jews considered the book of Jonah to be a historical record of a true prophet.

The early church also affirmed the historicity of Jonah. Justin the Martyr said:

But when Jonah was grieved that on the (fortieth) third day, as he proclaimed, the city was not overthrown, by the dispensation of a gourd springing up from the earth for him, under which he sat and was shaded from the heat (now the gourd had sprung up suddenly, and Jonah had neither planted nor watered it, but it had come up all at

---

[15] Josephus, Flavius, and William Whiston. *The Works of Josephus: Complete and Unabridged.* Includes index., Ant 9.208–14. Peabody, MA: Hendrickson, 1996, c1987.

once to afford him shade), and by the other dispensation of its withering away, for which Jonah grieved, [God] convicted him of being unjustly displeased because the city of Nineveh had not been overthrown[16]

For Methodius, Jonah's sign was assurance of resurrection for Christians:

> As, then, Jonah spent three days and as many nights in the whale's belly, and was delivered up sound again, so shall we all, who have passed through the three stages of our present life on earth—I mean the beginning, the middle, and the end, of which all this present time consists—rise again. For there are altogether three intervals of time, the past, the future, and the present. And for this reason the Lord spent so many days in the earth symbolically, thereby teaching clearly that when the fore-mentioned intervals of time have been fulfilled, then shall come our resurrection, which is the beginning of the future age, and the end of this.[17]

Some have argued for the impossibility of Jonah's survival in the belly of the fish. This is a major argument for the symbolic interpretation. For instance, Brevard Childs considers the literal perspective to be "almost universally rejected as untenable."[18] Despite the doubts, there is ample evidence to support the literal interpretation of the Biblical account. Ambrose John Wilson discussed this issue in "The Sign of the

---

[16] Alexander Roberts, James Donaldson, and A. Cleveland Coxe, *The Ante-Nicene Fathers Vol.I: Translations of the Writings of the Fathers Down to AD 325* (Oak Harbor, WA: Logos Research Systems, 1997) 252–53.
[17] Ibid., 378.
[18] Brevard Childs, "Jonah: A Study in Old Testament Hermeneutics," *Scottish Journal of Theology* 11 (1958): 53.

Prophet Jonah and Its Modern Confirmations."[19] He addressed the common argument that the whale's gullet is too small by saying that the whale's gullet is able to expand like a serpent to swallow large prey (even sometimes prey as large as it is).[20] He gives the example of James Bartley who in 1891 survived in a whale for three days. After exiting the whale, he spent two weeks as a raving lunatic but then his senses returned at the end of the third week. By his own estimation, he could have lived inside until he starved. He was easily able to breathe and the temperature inside was approximately 104 degrees Fahrenheit. The blubber of the whale would enable Jonah to survive even the coldest conditions in the ocean. Another account in 1771 reports that Marshall Jenkins was swallowed by a whale and survived with bruises but no serious injuries.[21] Stanton also defends the accuracy of the Jonah account:

> Although it is true that the Greenland whale has a throat so small that he would probably choke to death on an orange, there are many other species of whales which can swallow men. The mouth of the sperm whale is very large and wide; and the throat, unlike that of the Greenland whale, is very wide—sufficiently so to admit the body of a man. Horses, large sharks, and other objects have been found in the stomach of whales, and it is evident from that angle how the Jonah account is at least plausible. Frank Bullen, an experienced whale-fisher, says in "The Cruise of the Cachalot"—a book to be found in every respectable library—that one piece of matter, of which there were several, ejected from the stomach of a whale he had helped to kill was estimated to measure "8 feet x 6 feet x

---

[19] Ambrose John Wilson, "The Sign of the Prophet Jonah and Its Modern Confirmations," *The Princeton Theological Review* 25, no. 25 (1927): 630–42.
[20] Ibid., 633.
[21] Ibid., 636–37.

6 feet." That is to say, it was much longer than a tall man, and in girth equal to twelve men in one body. And, says the same witness, "a shark 15 feet long has been found in the stomach of a Cachalot (sperm-whale)...An English sailor was swallowed by another Rhinodon in the English Channel, and after the capture of the giant fish two days and nights later he was found inside, unconscious but alive, and lived to advertise himself as the Jonah of the Twentieth Century."[22]

Thus, there is sufficient historical evidence to support the validity of the Biblical account.

Furthermore, it must be remembered that Jonah 1:17 says in the King James Version, "Now the LORD had prepared a great fish to swallow up Jonah. And Jonah was in the belly of the fish three days and three nights." The Lord specifically created a fish that would be capable of swallowing Jonah. Stanton says with respect to this fact, "If man can devise a metal fish, that is, a submarine capable of submerging for several days with a crew of fifty or more men, who are we to deny God the Creator the power of preparing a great fish capable of playing host to a disobedient prophet for three days and three nights?"[23]

Finally, there is nothing in the original that says that Jonah was swallowed by a whale. Stanton said it well when he wrote:

> The Hebrew word is דג and means "fish," and is so translated in Jonah 1:17. The New Testament Greek word is κῆτος which means a "sea monster." Since a whale is not a fish but is properly classified as a mammal, it is evident that most of the ridicule on this point conveys empty words, reflecting prejudice rather than

---

[22] Gerald B. Stanton, "The Prophet Jonah and His Message: Part 1," *Bibliotheca Sacra* 108, no. 430 (1951): 241–42.
[23] Ibid.

scholarship. It may have been a Rhinodon shark or some other great fish now extinct. The point is that it was "prepared by God," and that God was dealing with Jonah and preserving him that he might yet fulfill his mission. The miraculous element is everywhere seen in this book, and the question is not "From whence came the storm?" or "How big was the whale?" but it is "How big is your God?" The God who made both heaven and earth is abundantly able to control the affairs of a man and a fish.[24]

Thus, by all accounts, it is entirely possible for a human to be swallowed by a large fish like a sperm whale or a Great White shark or a large fish that was specifically created for this purpose. The major point of this sign is not to focus on how this can be naturally explained but the greatness of the God who accomplished such an amazing task.

In a similar vein, after exploring similar issues, Stuart concludes:

It is important to note that there is ample evidence to support the historicity of the book, and surprisingly little to undermine it. The style, as noted above, is neutral; sensationalism can never be equivocated with a lack of factuality. A true story may be told in a host of ways, from dull to sensational, as may a false story, as may a fictional story. Style is largely irrelevant to factuality; guilt by association (sensational equals fictional) is an inadequate basis for rejecting historicity. The usual mustering of "improbabilities," moreover, is hardly adequate to suggest a lack of historicity.[25]

---

[24] Ibid., 242–43.
[25] Douglas K. Stuart, *Hosea–Jonah*, vol. 31, 52 vols., Word Biblical Commentary (Waco, TX: Word Books, 1987), 440.

Thus, the style of Jonah does not disprove the historicity of Jonah. Hence, this view does not adequately explain the fulfillment of the prophecy in Jonah 3:4.[26]

THE OPEN VIEW OF GOD

Advocates of the open view of God use Jonah's prophecy to the Ninevites to support their position. Richard Rice and Gregory Boyd espouse this view. From an open view of God perspective, the prophecy of the Ninevites to Jonah is one example of "God's willingness to change his plans" and this willingness is "one of his gracious attributes."[27]

Richard Rice in his book *God's Foreknowledge and Man's Free Will* argues that Jonah's conditional prophecy to the Ninevites was intended to lead them to repentance:

> Indeed, this is the only way to make sense out of it. For if God intends to destroy Nineveh, willy-nilly, there was no reason to send Jonah with his announcement. What would that have accomplished? If, however, God intended to destroy Nineveh only if its citizens failed to change their ways, then Jonah's mission becomes intelligible. God wanted to enable and encourage the Ninevites to avert their impending destruction.[28]

Rice argues from a Ninevite-centric perspective. However, the

---

[26] For archaeological discoveries that confirm Jonah's portrayal of Nineveh see D.J. Wiseman, "Jonah's Nineveh," *Tyndale Bulletin* 30 (1979): 45–51. Chapter 3 of this book discusses Wiseman's research.

[27] Gregory Boyd, "Is the Open View the Only View Compatible with the Incarnation?" Christus Victor Ministries, http://www.gregboyd.org/qa/jesus/is-the-open-view-the-only-view-that-is-compatible-with-the-incarnation/ (accessed November 15, 2008).

[28] Richard Rice, *God's Foreknowledge & Man's Free Will* (Minneapolis, MN: Bethany House, 1985), 80.

book of Jonah was not written to the Ninevites but to the Israelites. It is more likely that Jonah's prophecy was intended to be an example to the Israelites that they too had the choice to repent or be destroyed.

Gregory Boyd also utilizes Jonah's prophecy to the Ninevites to defend his view. He writes concerning this prophecy:

> The Lord instructed Jonah to proclaim, "Forty days more, and Nineveh will be overthrown!" (Jonah 3:4). This sounds like an unconditional declaration of a future event.... If Nineveh had not repented, of course, the inspired decree that Nineveh would perish in forty days would have been fulfilled. This would have undoubtedly made it *look like* God had declared an unconditional prediction about the future; a number of prophecies *seem* unconditional for this reason: the conditions for God to alter his plans are not met. In this instance, however, the Ninevites repented, so God changed his mind, clearly demonstrating that God was declaring to Jonah his conditional *intention* to overthrow Nineveh (3:4), not disclosing his *foreknowledge* about Nineveh...Passages such as this not only show that the open view of the future is compatible with biblical prophecy; they also challenge the classical view of foreknowledge. If God knew with certainty that Nineveh was going to repent, then his prophecy that the city would be destroyed in forty days seems disingenuous—it does not express a real intention. And if God didn't really change his mind regarding the future of Nineveh; then the explicit biblical teaching that 'God changes his mind about the calamity' is misleading. If we concede that the future can to some extent be open,

however, the text can be understood straightforwardly.[29]

Hence, Boyd considers Yahweh's prophecy to the Ninevites to be a model for which all prophecy can be evaluated. He argues that the prophecy is implicitly conditional even though it may appear unconditional and Jonah's prophecy disproves the argument that the open view of God does not adequately explain fulfilled prophecy. According to Boyd, if the Ninevites would have repented it would have appeared that God foreknew the future but the Ninevite repentance and subsequent response from God show God did not foreknow the future. Furthermore, Boyd considers Jeremiah 18:1–12 to be a key passage in the debate:

> The Lord states that "if that nation, concerning which I have spoken, turns from its evil, I will change my mind about the disaster that I intended to bring on it." But if a nation which he has declared he will bless "does evil in my sight…I will change my mind about the good that I had intended to do to it."
>
> If the Lord exhaustively foreknows what will definitely transpire in the future, it is impossible for him to genuinely intend to curse or bless a nation and then later genuinely reverse his plan. In other words, it's difficult to avoid denying the premise of this entire passage, and all passages like it. If the classical understanding of God's foreknowledge is correct, God eternally knows exactly what he will and will not do and what every nation will and will not do. There can be no authentic reversal.
>
> Yet the Bible depicts God's willingness to change his mind as one of his attributes of greatness (Jonah 4:2; Joel 2:12–13). And, as we have seen, there are a wealth of

---

[29] Gregory A. Boyd, *Satan and the Problem of Evil: Constructing a Trinitarian Warfare Theodicy* (Downers Grove, IL: InterVarsity Press, 2001), 94–95. All emphasis his.

biblical examples in which the Lord demonstrates this attribute. Dare we hold any view which requires us to conclude that such a magnificent aspect of the biblical portrait of God is merely anthropomorphic and not depicting God as he actually is? ....

In contrast to this, if we agree with Scripture that this fatalistic attitude is wrong, then shouldn't we conclude that the future is *not* exhaustively settled? Shouldn't we conclude that it is, to some degree, open to our decisions as free agents? Shouldn't we conclude that, to some extent, the future is not definitely this way or definitely that way, but rather possibly this way or possibly that way? And since God knows reality perfectly, shouldn't we conclude that God knows the future as being, in part, a realm of possibilities, not only definite certainties?

Only when we accept this, I submit, can passages like Jeremiah 18:7–11 be cleared of any hint of disingenuousness. The verse speaks about God as he truly is: He plans, he responds, he changes.[30]

Boyd considers Jonah's prophecy to be an indication of God's lack of exhaustive foreknowledge of the future as well as His willingness to change His plans. The implicit polysemantic wordplay view provides strong evidence to dispute that assertion.

Evaluation of the Open View of God Interpretation

The polysemantic wordplay of נֶהְפָּכֶת provides a textual basis for an implicit condition in the prophecy that counters Boyd's notion that the prophecy was unconditional. This is not

---

[30] Gregory Boyd, "What is the significance of Jeremiah 18:7–11?" Christus Victor Ministries, http://www.gregboyd.org/qa/open-theism/arguments-for-open-theism/what-is-the-significance-of-jeremiah-187%e2%80%9311/ (accessed November 22, 2008). Emphasis his.

only supported by the lexical evidence but also the context. Jonah does not argue that God changed His mind due to a lack of foreknowledge. Instead, he charged God with wanting to relent concerning calamity all along. Is it not possible that Jonah knew God's intentions because he was the bearer of the prophetic word? Furthermore, he had his own experience in Jonah 2 as well as the experience with the sailors in Jonah 1 to evaluate God's response to repentance. Apart from his own experience, Jonah could have reflected on Exodus 34:6–7 to substantiate his suspicions that God would be compassionate. Not only that, but Good points out that Jonah spoke a formula that is used almost verbatim at least six other times in the Old Testament (Exodus 34:6, Psalm 86:15, Psalm 103:8, Psalm 145:8, Joel 2:13, and Nehemiah 9:31).[31] Good writes, "Jonah is mouthing—not for the first time—a liturgical cliché, a rote theology. He had spouted another such phrase to the sailors (Jonah 3:9)."[32] Thus, Jonah 4:2 demonstrates Jonah's recognition of the implicitly conditional nature of the prophecy he delivered rather than evidence that God changed His mind on something He already announced or was in the process of doing. Jonah is disappointed with God because of His unwavering character that always responds the same to those who repent.

Jonah 3:9 shows that the Ninevites understand more about the divine grace than Jonah does.[33] Good compares Jonah's wish for God to take his life with Elijah's request in 1 Kings 19:4. Good says, "But where Elijah is in genuine despair over his failure to turn the hearts of idolatrous Israel, Jonah's despair rises out of his vexation at God's acceptance of pagan Nineveh. And his sullen death wish is surely a parody of Elijah's

---

[31] Edwin M. Good, *Irony in the Old Testament* (Philadelphia, PA: Westminster Press, 1965), 50.
[32] Ibid.
[33] Ibid.

profound discouragement."³⁴ Thus, the ironic nature of Jonah's complaint towards God demonstrates that he understood God's desire to provide an opportunity to the Ninevites for repentance. He also knew that his message was the main vehicle for doing that. Consequently, this prophecy does not reveal a last-minute change of mind on God's part but an intentional plan which Jonah sought to avoid.

Second, Boyd's conclusion that the divine repentance illustrated in Jonah shows a result of a lack of knowledge about God. John Piper accurately argues that the anthropomorphic view is not the only explanation for passages suggesting that God changes His mind or repents. He writes:

> I say that there is a real change in God's mind, but that this does not imply a lack of foreknowledge. God can express an intention or a resolve toward a people that accords with what is true now, all the while knowing that this condition will not be true in the future, and that his resolve will also be different when their condition is different. That an [sic.] future-knowing God speaks this way is owing to the fact that he really means for his word to be the means of bringing about changes in people to which he himself responds in a way that he knows he will.³⁵

As Piper points out, the prophecy itself secured the reaction of the people that was necessary to allow Him to change from a

---

[34] Ibid., 51.
[35] John Piper, "Answering Greg Boyd's Openness of God Texts," Desiring God, May 11, 1998,
http://www.desiringgod.org/ResourceLibrary/Articles/ByDate/1998/1548_Answering_Greg_Boyds_Openness_of_God_Texts/ (accessed November 28, 2008). Also cited in Michael Stallard, "A Dispensational Critique of Open Theism's View of Prophecy," *Bibliotheca Sacra* 161, no. 641 (January–March 2004): 30.

position of inflicting calamity on them to showing mercy.

Piper distinguishes between the way humans repent and God repents when he makes the following three observations in his comparison of 1 Samuel 15:11 and 15:28–29:

1. A natural reading of 1 Samuel 15 would seem to imply that there is a way that God does "repent" and a way that he does not. That is what I am arguing in the texts that Boyd puts forward. He insists that God repents in a way that implies lack of foreknowledge of what is coming. I think this is the kind of "repentance" that would fall under Samuel's criticism: "God is not a man that he should repent."
2. In other words, God does not have the human limitations of knowledge that would involve him in repenting *that way*. Rather his repentance is an expression of a resolve or an attitude that is fitting in view of new circumstances. That God is ignorant of what will call for that new resolve or attitude is not necessarily implied in the change.
3. So the repentance over Saul means not that he did not know what Saul would be like, but that he disapproves of what Saul has become and that he feels sorrow at this evil in his anointed king and that he looks back on his making him king with the same sorrow that he experienced at that moment when he made him king, foreknowing all the sorrow that would come…For God to say, "I feel sorrow that I made Saul king," is *not* the same as saying, "I would not make him king if I had it to do over knowing what I know now." God is able to feel sorrow for an act that he does in view of foreknown evil and pain, and yet go ahead and will to do it for wise reasons. Later, when he looks back on the act, he can feel the sorrow for the act that was leading to the sad conditions, such as Saul's

disobedience.[36]

Piper's approach is helpful because he does not explain away the literal statements that God does repent through the use of anthropomorphic language. However, Piper also reconciles God's repentance with other passages that state that His repentance is not like that of human beings. Stallard agrees with this distinction and writes:

> In other words, Piper is saying that Boyd and other open theists have mishandled the verses that refer to God repenting, and thus they wrongly view prophecy as conditional. Piper warns that Bible interpreters should be "slow to attribute human-like repentance to God," as open theists do. Verses that speak of God's "repenting" cannot be used to suggest that most prophecies of the Bible are conditional in nature.
>
> Boyd's response to 1 Samuel 15:28–29 is that classical theists take all the other "repentance" texts in a nonliteral sense while taking this one literally. He prefers to say that God is sometimes willing to change His mind and sometimes He is not (as in this passage). He also argues that because of His perfection, God is not human-like in His repentance. That is, He repents perfectly and not deceitfully or arbitrarily as people sometimes do. However, Boyd still views God's repentance as similar to human repentance, though 1 Samuel 15:29 categorically states that God is not like humans at this point. Piper correctly notes that the passage is not placing God and humans as two points on a continuum of comparison. Instead it affirms the uniqueness of God.[37]

---

[36] Ibid.
[37] Stallard, "A Dispensational Critique of Open Theism's View of Prophecy," 30–31.

Stallard accurately asserts that the Biblical statements that God does repent do not mean that all or most prophecy has unstated conditions. In fact, his comparison between 2 Samuel 7 and Psalm 89 shows how God cannot change His mind regarding His promise to David because that would make Him a liar (cf. Psalm 89:35). Psalm 89 shows that even the disobedience of David's descendants will not invalidate the promise that God made. He will ensure fulfillment based on His holiness as Psalm 89:35 indicates.[38] Stallard also agrees with Piper that God's response in Jeremiah 18 is not due to unforeseen developments. Instead, according to Stallard and Piper, Jeremiah 18 shows that God intends for His Word to bring about the change in people that allows for Him to relent concerning calamity.

Furthermore, the alleged change in God is not due to a lack of foreknowledge on His part but part of His consistent response to repentance. Chafer says:

> God though immutable, is not immobile. If He consistently pursues a righteous course, His attitude must be adapted to every moral change in men. God's unchanging holiness requires him to treat the wicked differently from the righteous. When the righteous become wicked, his treatment of them must change. The sun is not fickle or partial because it melts the wax but hardens the clay...the change is not in the sun, but in the objects it shines upon.[39]

Chafer rightly argues that while God's treatment of men may change, His sovereign plan does not. God always prophesies judgment on the wicked and grace for the repentant. His attitude towards these two groups does not change. Gaebelein adds:

---

[38] Ibid., 32.
[39] Lewis Sperry Chafer, "Part 3 Biblical Theism: The Attributes of God (Concluded)," *Bibliotheca Sacra* 96, no. 381 (1939): 30.

> Helpful also is the analogy of the thermometer. Is it changeable or unchangeable? The superficial observer says it is changeable, for the mercury certainly moves in the tube. But just as certainly it is unchangeable, for it acts according to fixed law and invariably responds precisely to the temperature.[40]

Berkhof explains it this way, "The Bible teaches that God enters into manifold relations with man and, as it were, lives their life with them. There is change round about Him, change in the relations of man to Him, but there is no change in His Being, His attributes, His purposes, His motives of action or His promises."[41] As Berkhof notes, God does not change even though the situations around Him change. Because He has chosen to reveal Himself to man, who is limited in time and understanding, certain things may appear to change in God's mind even when they were part of His original intention.

Some may argue that a change of attitude would still disprove the immutability of God. However, the change of God's attitude is a result of the change in relationship with another individual. This does not emphasize a change on God's part but a result from a change on the individual's part. Erickson writes:

> Some cases of relational change are really not changes at all in the subject. The other, the object to which the subject is related, may have changed, thus changing the relationship. So for example, if I am taller than my teenage friend and I remain the same height but he grows taller than me, I am now shorter than him, but this is not

---

[40] Frank Ely Gaebelein, *Four Minor Prophets: Obadiah, Jonah, Habakkuk, and Haggai; Their Message for Today* (Chicago, IL: Moody Press, 1970), 111.
[41] Louis Berkhof, *Systematic Theology*, 4th rev. and enl. ed. (Grand Rapids, MI: Wm. B. Eerdmans Publishing Co. 1986 c1941.), 59.

really a change in me."⁴²

Another illustration may help better explain the significance of the nature of this change of relation. In this illustration, Norm the Ninevite is at a connection point in the conditional prophecy train station. There are two choices to make. One choice is the repentance train which has a final destination at compassion. The second train is the guilty train which has a final destination at punishment. This punishment destination can represent the temporal discipline or eternal punishment depending on whether one is part of the covenant community. Norm initially boards guilty train and is headed to punishment. If he chooses to get off the train at one of the stops and board repentance train, he certainly will not go to punishment. This change does not represent a change in the train station or its plan, but a change in Norm's choice. When the Ninevites chose to repent, they boarded God's train that was destined for compassion. This did not reflect a change in God or His plan but a change in the choice that the Ninevites made.

Therefore, use of Jonah 3 by advocates of the open view of God as evidence that God does not know the future is inadequate because the implicitly conditional prophecy was consistent with God's unwavering character towards those who repent. This change of relationship is a result of a change in humanity, not a change in God. None of God's attributes, decrees, promises, or plans are affected by this human change. Instead, God sovereignly uses these changes within man to accomplish His eternal purposes for His glory.

THE UNSTATED CONDITIONAL VIEW

Lubeck describes this option as follows, "The first of our

---

⁴² Millard J. Erickson, *God the Father Almighty: A Contemporary Exploration of the Divine Attributes* (Grand Rapids, MI: Baker Books, 1998), 101.

options maintains that while Jonah spoke God's precise words of unconditional judgment, the unstated *intent* of those words was conditional."[43] Lubeck points out that the vast majority of the evidence for this view comes from Old Testament passages that point to the conditionality of God's judgment. Some conservative advocates argue for the historicity of Jonah but also believe that prophecy often contains implicit conditions due to the functional nature of language.[44] Advocates of this view usually appeal to Jonah 3 to defend this position.

D. Brent Sandy

One representative of this view of prophecy is D. Brent Sandy. Sandy and others who espouse this view believe that prophecy is often implicitly conditional, but they do accept the historicity of the events themselves. While discussing the conditional nature of prophecy Sandy writes, "Unfortunately it is not always clear even in retrospect what parts of the covenant were unconditional, what parts conditional, and what parts hyperbolic. At least from the surface level of the text, God can appear to change his mind, but conditionality is not always stated."[45] He even raises the question of whether all prophecy may be considered conditional. Rather than answering the question he simply concludes, "Actually it [prophecy] would be less of a problem if we could determine when promises of blessing were subject to being conditional, if we knew when

---

[43] Lubeck, "Prophetic Sabotage: A Look at Jonah 3:2–4," 39. Emphasis his.
[44] An excellent summary of the current debate on this can be found in Michael A. Grisanti's, "Conditional and Hyperbolic Language in the OT Prophets: Where Are We Now?" (paper presented at the annual meeting of the Evangelical Theological Society, Washington, D.C., 15–17 November 2007), 1–9.
[45] D. Brent Sandy, *Plowshares & Pruning Hooks: Rethinking the Language of Biblical Prophecy and Apocalyptic* (Downers Grove, IL: InterVarsity Press, 2002), 46–47.

prophecies were given in hyperbole, if we knew when to take the words at face value."⁴⁶ While choosing to avoid taking sides on the debate of the open view of God, he says, "Unexpressed conditions are common in human communication. Is that true for divine communication as well?"⁴⁷

Sandy's belief in the metaphorical nature of prophecy affects his view of fulfillment of prophecy. He considers prediction to be only one type of prophecy, and the most important function of a prophet was to enforce the covenant between God and the Israelites:

> If the primary point of prophecy is that God's patience has a breaking point and his wrath has a beginning point, how much of prophecy is really predictive? Though the ferocity of God's wrath is incomprehensible, the prophets sketched ways in which the teeth of his wrath would take savage bites out of the disobedient. Since the intent of the sketches was striking prosecution rather than interesting information, perhaps the lead in prophets' pencils was too thick to spell out details about the future.⁴⁸

While researching prophecy that has already been fulfilled, Sandy concludes:

> The already fulfilled prophecies demonstrate a pattern of translucence rather than transparency. The intent was apparently not to give specific information about the future. Rather than predict with precision, the prophets sought to prosecute with power. In some cases, pronouncements were fulfilled explicitly. But even then, it had not been possible to know before fulfillment what

---

⁴⁶ Ibid., 47.
⁴⁷ Ibid.
⁴⁸ Ibid., 133.

would be fulfilled transparently.[49]

This issue is addressed in the evaluation, but for now it is important to note that Sandy does not think that prophecy primarily gives details about the future; hence, fulfillment may not be expected to be in kind and extent according to the explicit details of the prophecy.

Sandy's emphasis of the performative nature of language[50] leads him to argue that the majority of prophecies in the Bible are implicitly conditional. According to Sandy, human language is often implicitly conditional, so one should not be surprised that God makes similar statements. He also describes a tension between some of the covenantal promises and some of the prophets' declarations of judgment. According to Sandy, the Abrahamic covenant promised that the Israelites would be in the land forever and the Davidic covenant promised everlasting reign in the Davidic dynasty. He says Jeremiah believed that God was deceiving them in making these promises. Sandy resolves this by arguing that some aspects of the covenant were conditional and that God could change His mind.[51]

In contrast to a traditional dispensational view of this issue, Stallard addresses the fulfillment of the covenant promises of the Old Testament:

> In other words, God is saying that his prior unconditional and absolute promise to David could not be changed, altered, or annulled by the later free actions of the various Davidic kings. God knew ahead of time that many of them would fail but asserted that He was not open to the

---

[49] Ibid., 146.
[50] The performative nature of language is a view that language does more than inform but it often intends to produce an action on the part of the hearer. For more information on Sandy's view of Ibid., 81.
[51] Sandy, *Plowshares & Pruning Hooks: Rethinking the Language of Biblical Prophecy and Apocalyptic*, 46.

cancellation of the entire covenant package. Only the individual's participation in the experience of blessing under the covenant would be cancelled. The significance of this truth for the present debate is no small matter in light of the fact that the covenant promises (especially Abrahamic, Davidic, and New Covenants) are interconnected and that the vast majority of prophetic details in the Old Testament text relate to these same covenant promises.[52]

The interconnectedness of the promises is critical for a future fulfillment for national Israel. Sandy treats individual prophecies as if they were divorced from the unconditional royal grant covenants they were based on. Within those covenants were conditions for the individual enjoyment of the blessings, yet the promises of those covenants were reaffirmed (cf. Jeremiah 32:37–44; Isaiah 55:3; Ezekiel 16:60–63, 37:26–28; Psalm 89:3–4, etc.).

D. Brent Sandy also argues that Jonah 3:4 has unstated conditions. He believes that conditionality is inherent in the language of blessing and judgment because it is rooted in the language of the covenant.[53] Regarding Jonah 3:4, he writes:

> Illocution is especially pertinent to stereotypical language in the prophets. Using virtually identical language announcing the destruction of city after city suggests formulaic terms designed for their effect (cf. Amos 1:3–2:16). In the case of Jonah, he should not be

---

[52] Mike Stallard, "The Open View of God and Prophecy" (paper presented at the annual meeting of the Conservative Theological Society, Fort Worth, TX, August 2001), 6.
[53] D. Brent Sandy, "Plowshares and Pruning Hooks and the Hermeneutics of Dispensationalism," (paper presented at the annual meeting of the Evangelical Theological Society, San Diego, CA, 14–16 November 2007), 7.

considered a false prophet because he announced the destruction of Nineveh in forty days. The illocution of his language was to call for repentance.[54]

Sandy argues that the nature of the speech act makes the prophecy conditional. Regarding the nature of fulfillment Sandy writes:

> How will prophecies be fulfilled? Are the detailed theories of the twentieth century (of premillennial dispensationalism in particular) valid interpretations of prophecy and apocalyptic? While many have assumed that prophecy reveals specific scenarios of future events, we may need to rethink those approaches. Futurespeak is rich in poetic imagery. Its function transcends the surface meaning of its words. Reading and hearing the words of prophecy and apocalyptic should thrill every faithful follower with a hope focused on the Christ of prophecy.[55]

Sandy seems to miss the overall connectedness of the dispensational system. It is not that everything is postponed to the future in dispensationalism. Dispensationalism argues for unity in God's overall prophetic plan. Stallard writes:

> Admittedly, this great volume of prophetic teaching is not all about end-time events such as the tribulation, Second Coming, and the eschatological kingdom. However, the interconnectedness of areas of theology show that prophetic passages relative to the end-time days fit within a larger scheme of God's overall plan. In the history of dispensationalism, this has been called the panorama of the ages or the picture of the biblical

---

[54] Ibid., 11.
[55] Sandy, *Plowshares & Pruning Hooks: Rethinking the Language of Biblical Prophecy and Apocalyptic*, 188.

purposes of God in history. Oftentimes it is presented through the lens of the various dispensations. These dispensations culminate in the final kingdom age and demonstrate that history is going somewhere. Thus, the eschatological kingdom age is seen from this angle as a part within a whole. Dispensationalists have not ignored the other parts, but they have exercised some excitement about their place within the flow of God's work leading up to the final stages of the divine plan: "One of the distinctives of biblical Christianity is that God knows and reveals the future (Isaiah 46:8–11). Only God can do that. Thus, the future is settled, and not open to change…We can have confidence that God will continue to carry out His plan for the ages, and we who are Christians have a significant part in that plan."[56]

Stallard's analysis is critical for understanding the overarching dispensational framework. It is not that dispensationalists are solely focused on charting the future, but they are interested in connecting God's inerrant and inspired Word in the past, present, and future to see His ultimate plan. Not only does dispensationalism have a hope focused on the Christ of prophecy, but it also encourages a hope in God's faithfulness to fulfilling His promises.

Sandy's work indicates a tendency to view most prophecy as implicitly conditional. He bases his view on the performative nature of language and a more translucent perspective to prophetic fulfillment than a transparent one. While this is an interesting proposal, it remains unconvincing on both a Biblical

---

[56] Mike Stallard, "Why are Dispensationalists so Interested in Prophecy?" (paper presented at the annual meeting of the Conservative Theological Society, Fort Worth, TX, August 2005) 3. The quotation within Dr. Stallard's quote comes from Tim LaHaye and Thomas Ice, *Charting the End Times* (Eugene, OR: Harvest House, 2001), 25.

and theological level.⁵⁷ This is discussed in the evaluation of both Chisholm and Sandy's views in this chapter.

Robert B. Chisholm, Jr.

Chisholm is a strong advocate of the view that prophetic language is functional and that prophecies usually have implicit conditions. He discusses Jonah 3 in two main areas. In his article "Does God Change His Mind?"⁵⁸ Chisholm uses Jonah 3:4 as an example of a time when God retracts an announcement. In his paper entitled "When Prophecy Appears to Fail, Check Your Hermeneutic,"⁵⁹ Chisholm uses Jonah 3:4 as an example of a contingent prophecy that has unstated conditions.

Chisholm's View of Whether God Changes His Mind

In Chisholm's article "Does God Change His Mind?" he states his thesis as follows:

> The thesis of this article is that the question, "Does God change His mind?" must be answered, "It all depends." This study begins with a lexical survey of the Niphal and Hithpael stems of נחם. The article then defines and illustrates the four kinds of forward-looking divine statements in the Old Testament: (a) marked or formal decrees, (b) unmarked or informal decrees, (c) marked or explicitly conditional statements of intention, (d)

---

[57] For a good review of Sandy's view of prophecy see Mike Stallard, "Response to D. Brent Sandy's Paper: *Plowshares and Pruning Hooks* and the Hermeneutics of Dispensationalism," (paper presented at the annual meeting of the Evangelical Theological Society, San Diego, CA, 14–16 November 2007), 1–11.
[58] Robert B. Chisholm Jr., "Does God 'Change His Mind'?," *Bibliotheca Sacra* 152, no. 608 (1995): 387–400.
[59] Robert B. Chisholm Jr., "When Prophecy Appears to Fail, Check Your Hermeneutic," (paper presented at the annual meeting of the Evangelical Theological Society, Atlanta, GA, 19 November 2003), 1–12.

> unmarked or implicitly conditional statements of intention. The article then argues that if God has issued a decree, He will not change His mind or deviate from it. However, the majority of God's statements of intention are not decrees. And God can and often does deviate from such announcements. In these cases, He "changes His mind" in the sense that He decides, at least for the time being, not to do what He had planned or announced as His intention.[60]

Chisholm provides an important distinction between a decree and an announcement. He also argues that the majority of God's statements of intention are announcements and not decrees.

Chisholm argues that the traditional anthropomorphic view of the passages that seem to suggest that God has changed His mind is "an arbitrary and drastic solution that cuts rather than unties the theological knot."[61] In this article, he interprets Jonah 3:4 as follows, "Jonah's seemingly uncompromising declaration ('Yet forty days and Nineveh will be overthrown,' Jonah 3:4) remained unfulfilled when the people of that pagan city repented."[62] He notes that although Jonah's announcement of judgment on Nineveh "sounded unconditional, it was accompanied by no formal indication that it was a decree (3:4)."[63] In contrast, I argue that Jonah 3:4 was fulfilled and the conditions were indicated in the passage.

Furthermore, Chisholm theologically distinguishes a decree from an announcement by saying that a divine decree (or oath) is "an unconditional declaration" that is "certain to come to pass" and "the response of the recipient cannot alter it" even though "the exact timing of its fulfillment can be conditional."[64]

---

[60] Chisholm Jr., "Does God 'Change His Mind'?" 387–88.
[61] Ibid., 387.
[62] Ibid., 391.
[63] Ibid., 398.
[64] Ibid., 389.

According to Chisholm, a decree is usually marked as such. In contrast, an announcement is "a conditional statement of divine intention which may or may not be realized, depending on the response of the recipient or someone else whose interests it affects."[65] As a result, since it was not a decree, Chisholm believes God could change His mind in response to the Ninevite repentance. Jonah did anticipate this change and he fled as a result of this. He then writes, "With words almost identical to those of Joel 2:13, he observed that God is 'a gracious and compassionate God, slow to anger and abundant in lovingkindness; and one who relents concerning calamity' (4:2)."[66]

Chisholm then evaluates the reason for the prophecy in Jonah 3 and the subsequent change of mind. He writes, "As Rice argues, this passage makes it clear that many warnings of judgment, rather than being unalterable decrees, are actually designed to motivate repentance and in turn, enable God to retract the announced punishment (Richard Rice, *God's Foreknowledge and Man's Free Will* [Minneapolis, MN: Bethany House, 1985], 79–80)."[67] Thus, Chisholm agrees with Richard Rice that the purpose of Jonah's prophecy is to motivate the Ninevites to repent so God can retract the punishment. It is the same effect as a parent who yells "Don't make me come up there" to discipline his child when he has no intentions of going up to the child's room. Chisholm believes that this ability to change His mind is one of God's "fundamental attributes."[68] He reiterates the importance of the label of Jonah 3 as an announcement, "In every case where such a change is envisioned or reported, God had not yet decreed a course of action or an outcome. Instead He chose to wait patiently, hoping His warnings might bring people to their senses and make judgment

---

[65] Ibid.
[66] Ibid.
[67] Ibid.
[68] Ibid., 399.

unnecessary."[69]

Chisholm's View of Implicitly Conditional Prophecy

In a similar vein, in his article entitled "When Prophecy Appears to Fail, Check Your Hermeneutic," Chisholm considers Jonah's prophecy in Jonah 3 to be an example of the functional nature of implicitly conditional prophecy. In this category of language, Chisholm argues that God announces judgment in vivid, seemingly uncompromising language in order to evoke a response of repentance. The implications for prophecy according to Chisholm are:

> The language is not simply informative, but motivational. When the intended response comes, God relents and does not bring the judgment. In other words, the prophecy, rather than being a fixed decree of what the future holds, is really a conditional threat or warning. God mercifully shows the addressees what the future will look like if the situation addressed, which usually involves moral and ethical failure, does not change. This is how "foretelling" and "forthtelling," traditionally thought to be the two primary functions of prophecy, are linked. The foretelling of a conditional future (consisting of announcements of judgment) supports forthtelling (consisting of accusations and calls for repentance) by motivating the addressees to change their ways and escape the threatened disaster…. However, one must not think that once disaster was averted these prophecies were no longer relevant. Though these prophecies were contingent, they reflect God's unchanging moral standards and demands.[70]

Chisholm seems to argue that the details of the prophecy are not

---

[69] Ibid.
[70] Chisholm Jr., "When Prophecy Appears to Fail," 5.

DID GOD CHANGE HIS MIND? 87

as important as the effect. In a sense, God uses prophecy in order to motivate His audience to repentance so that He will not have to act upon the prophecy that He gave.

Chisholm points out how this works with respect to Jonah 3 as follows:

> The Book of Jonah illustrates this. Jonah announced in seemingly unconditional terms that Nineveh would be destroyed in forty days (3:4). Uncertain if the message was unconditional or not (3:9), the king and the entire city repented. After all, the inclusion of a time limit might imply a window of opportunity for repentance. Sure enough, Nineveh's response prompted God to withhold the threatened judgment. Jonah pouted about this; he explained that this was why he had refused to go to Nineveh in the first place. He knew that God is merciful and that he characteristically relents from sending judgment when people repent of their sin (4:2).[71]

Some of the disagreement with respect to Jonah 3:4 may be a matter of semantics. Although Chisholm considers the prophecy in Jonah 3:4 to be "seemingly unconditional," he acknowledges some key textual indicators that point to why the text may be implicitly conditional. Chisholm acknowledges that the Ninevites were uncertain of the conditionality of the prophecy. According to Chisholm the time limit might leave open the possibility of repentance. Additionally, he acknowledges the fact that even Jonah recognized the possibility of the Ninevite repentance prior to going to Nineveh.

Based on Jonah 3 and other verses, Chisholm concludes that prophecy is often implicitly conditional, "God sometimes makes unconditional pronouncements about the future, but often (usually?) his statements of intention are conditional.

---

[71] Ibid., 4.

Sometimes conditions are explicitly stated (for example, Isaiah 1:19-20), but more often they are unstated and implicit."[72] This quote demonstrates that Chisholm believes that a condition can be unstated and implicit at the same time. Chisholm also argues that an implicitly conditional view of prophecy will help interpreters avoid two extremes: the modern critical approach that discounts the supernatural revelatory nature of Old Testament prophecy or the typical popular approach that places fulfillment of all Old Testament prophecy in the eschaton.[73]

Chisholm cites Richard L. Pratt, Jr. as a main supporter of his view. Pratt gives evidence of his support when he writes:

> As we have seen, with rare exception, OT prophets did not speak of what *had* to be but what *might* be. Even the few prophecies that guaranteed fulfillment did not address their timing or manner of realization. Therefore, prophetic predictions were not designed to be building blocks of a futuristic scheme into which current events fit in particular ways. To approach biblical prophecies in this manner is to misuse them.[74]

Pratt cites Jonah 3 as an example of when prayer or repentance had the potential to change the predicted outcome.[75]

Both Pratt and Chisholm base their view on the

---

[72] Robert B. Chisholm Jr., "Making Sense of Prophecy: Recognizing the Presence of Contingency," (paper presented at the Far West Regional Meeting of the Evangelical Theological Society, Sun Valley, CA, April 2007), 2.
[73] Chisholm Jr., "When Prophecy Appears to Fail," 1.
[74] Richard L. Pratt, Jr., "Historical Contingencies and Biblical Predictions," in *The Way of Wisdom: Essays in Honor of Bruce K. Waltke*, ed. J. I. Packer and Sven K. Soderlund (Grand Rapids, MI: Zondervan, 2000), 195. Emphasis his.
[75] Ibid., 187.

foundational nature of Jeremiah 18. For instance, Chisholm says:

> As Pratt observes, Jeremiah 18 is a foundational text in this regard. The Lord sent Jeremiah to the potter's house for an object lesson (vv. 1–2). As the potter shaped his pot according to a specific design, the clay proved to be unpliable, so the potter reshaped it into a different type of pot (vv. 3–4). Just as the potter improvised his design for the unpliable clay, so the Lord could change his plans for Israel (vv. 5–6). If the Lord intends to destroy a nation, but it repents when warned of impending doom, the Lord will relent from sending judgment (vv. 7–8). Conversely if the Lord intends to bless a nation, but it rebels, the Lord will alter his plan and withhold blessing (vv. 9–10). God makes plans and announces his intentions, but a nation's response can and often does impact God's decision as to what will actually take place. To use the language of the Confession, God makes room in his decree for second causes to operate freely and/or contingently. In doing so, God's omniscience (defined in the classical sense), sovereignty, and immutability are not compromised. God fully knows what will transpire because he has decreed the future. But this decree, by God's sovereign decision, accommodates the choices and actions of creatures to whom God imparts a degree of freedom. It also makes room for God to respond to these choices and actions. This relational flexibility is a corollary of his immutability, which encompasses both his justice and compassion.[76]

While Jeremiah 18 is an important text regarding the potentially contingent nature of prophecy, it should not drive the discussion of Jonah 3 for several reasons. First, if one assumes

---

[76] Chisholm Jr., "When Prophecy Appears to Fail," 4.

that the events in Jeremiah 52 were part of the original text, then the date of the book is in the sixth century BC. If one accepts the early date of Jonah as being written in the eighth century BC, then the book of Jonah was probably written nearly two centuries before Jeremiah. Thus, Jeremiah 18 cannot be the interpretive key to Jonah 3:4 because the original audience of Jonah would not have been familiar with it.[77]

Evaluation of the Unstated Conditional View

This writer agrees with Sandy and Chisholm on the following:

1. Implicitly conditional prophecies do exist in the Bible.
2. Some prophecies assume a background of conditionality as a result of their relationship with the conditional Mosaic covenant.
3. Consistent with Exodus 34:6–7 and Jeremiah 18:7–10, God is compassionate, and He relents regarding calamity for the repentant and does not leave the guilty unpunished.

Having said that, there are some significant areas of disagreement that require elaboration. The primary areas of disagreement are:

1. The method by which they determine that most prophecies are implicitly conditional.
2. Their use of the term implicit.

---

[77] In defense of Pratt and Chisholm they are not arguing that Jeremiah 18 is central for interpreting Jonah 3. They are arguing that it is foundational for interpreting all implicitly conditional prophecy. However, Jonah 3 should not primarily be interpreted in light of Jeremiah 18 at the exegetical level. Jeremiah 18 can be helpful for understanding Jonah at a theological level though.

3. Chisholm's terminology.

This evaluation begins with areas of agreement and then discusses areas of disagreement.

Areas of Agreement
Chisholm and Sandy rightly conclude that there are implicitly conditional prophecies in the Old Testament. Chisholm rightly acknowledges that the timing of unconditional decrees may be conditional. Chisholm and Sandy rightly label Jonah 3:4 as an implicitly conditional prophecy. Linguistic and contextual clues seem to demonstrate this. In fact, Chisholm recognizes a textual indicator in his discussion of the forty-day period.

This writer disagrees with them regarding how one detects implicitly conditional prophecy. Sandy and Chisholm equate unstated conditions with implicit ones. Nevertheless, as Grice indicates, an implicature must be intended by the speaker or author (who indicates intention in the text). When an author is implying something, it is usually because he is choosing to violate an aspect of the cooperative principle. Nevertheless, both Sandy and Chisholm seem to argue that unstated conditions are more common in written and spoken language than explicit ones. Grice's arguments from the cooperative principle (that are primarily based on the common rules that apply to communication) would seem to argue otherwise.

While this author does not entirely agree with Chisholm's assertions, one of Chisholm's statements seems to make a great deal of sense: "While prophecy may be contingent, God's standards pertaining to covenantal loyalty and justice remain firm."[78] In this regard, Chisholm has a point. Rather than appealing to the functional nature of prophetic language, one might identify some aspect of contingency in prophecy based

---

[78] Ibid., 5.

on the nature of the covenants. Even the unconditional covenants of the Old Testament had inherent stipulations on which generations would enjoy the benefits of the covenant. The fulfillment of these covenants would occur in kind and extent, but the enjoyment of the covenant blessing or experience of covenant curses was contingent on covenant loyalty by the one who entered into the covenant. This seems especially relevant in the case of Jonah who struggles in Jonah 4:2 to understand God's covenant application of Exodus 34:6–7 to the pagan Ninevites.

Chisholm is also accurate in stating that God does in fact change His mind, as the Bible seems clear on that point. However, it seems better to define that change in the same way Piper and Stallard do. God's repentance is completely distinct from the repentance of man. Exodus 34:6–7 and Jeremiah 18 describe God's response to repentance. It is very likely that Jonah had Exodus 34:6–7 in mind in Jonah 4:2. As an overall principle, God does punish the guilty and He forgives the repentant. However, this is part of His immutable character as expressed in the illustration of the trains presented in the evaluation of the open view of God.

Areas of Disagreement

The Normalizing Principle

Of particular concern is the process by which Sandy and Chisholm come to their conclusions. They argue that prophecy is usually conditional based on certain narrative texts. The cooperative principle by Grice suggests that implicature falls outside of the normal rules of communication. To a certain degree, implicature is the exception to the general rules of speech rather than the normal form of speech. However, arguing that prophecy is often conditional (especially implicitly conditional) seems to be at odds with most of the linguistic research on the nature of implicature. Furthermore, the passages they rely on for their conclusion seem to be at odds with more prescriptive, earlier, and foundational texts in the Old Testament on prophecy. Thus, this review of Sandy and Chisholm's methodology will raise questions on how they determine that prophecy is usually conditional.

While Sandy and Chisholm emphasize the relationship between Jonah 3 and Jeremiah 18, the greater likelihood is that the author of Jonah depended on antecedent theology in Exodus 34:6–7. It would be a logical deduction based on Exodus 34:6–7 that God would show mercy to repentant people. This antecedent theology contained in Exodus would also be a strong reason to support an implicitly conditional view of Jonah 3:4.

The audience would also have greater familiarity with Deuteronomy 18 which set the norms for the true prophet instead of Jeremiah 18. Chisholm says regarding Deuteronomy 18:

> In Deuteronomy 18:21–22 Moses gives a criterion by which the people can determine whether or not a prophet has truly spoken the word of the Lord. The test seems to be quite simple: If a prophetic word does not come to pass, then one can safely assume that it was not from the Lord. One may assume that the opposite is true (if the word does come to pass, it is from the Lord), though other texts suggest this may not necessarily be the case (see Deuteronomy 13:1–3). At any rate, this criterion would seem to leave no room for contingency in prophecy. After all, if a contingent prophecy spoken in seemingly unconditional terms did not come to pass, the prophet, though called by the Lord and commissioned to preach the message, could be labeled an imposter. Yet the evidence for contingent prophecy seems incontrovertible (see the classic texts discussed in the paper—Jeremiah 18; Jonah 3–4; Micah 3:12/Jeremiah 26:17–19—as well as many others, including 1 Samuel 2:30 and Isaiah 38). So how does one resolve the problem? Can the criterion of Deuteronomy 18:21–22 be harmonized with texts

> demonstrating that genuine prophecy is sometimes (usually?) contingent? .... The briefly stated test of Deuteronomy 18:21–22 must be qualified in light of common sense and the totality of biblical evidence. The test must apply to short range prophecies, not prophecies of the distant future. Otherwise, it would have been irrelevant to those who needed to know now, not later, if a prophet could be trusted. The biblical evidence supports this. In texts where the Deuteronomic test seems to be in the background, a true prophet is in conflict with false prophets. He puts his authority to the test by making a short-range prediction (1 Kings 22:28; Jeremiah 28). In qualifying the Deuteronomic test, one must also make room for essential, as opposed to exact, fulfillment. Analysis of prophetic fulfillment in Kings shows that a prophecy could be understood as fulfilled even if some details were not realized exactly (for example, compare 1 Kings 21:19 with 22:38).[79]

There are several problems with this argument regarding Deuteronomy 18. First, one must question why Chisholm chooses to submit the Deuteronomy 18 passage to a qualification in light of "common sense and the totality of Scripture." First, with respect to common sense, one would imagine that Chisholm's own application of Deuteronomy 18 would be extremely difficult for the original audience to apply. Wouldn't it be possible for every prophet who had been accused of a false prophecy to state that there were unstated conditions in their prophecy in order to escape stoning? How would the original audience know when to stone a prophet? While Chisholm notes that Deuteronomy 18 might be a test to distinguish true from false prophets, many of the false prophets in the Old Testament were disqualified by Deuteronomy 18:9–14 because they

---

[79] Ibid., 12.

DID GOD CHANGE HIS MIND? 95

attempted to encourage the Israelites to follow false gods. The test of Deuteronomy 18:15-22 seems to apply to individuals who claim to be true prophets of Yahweh. The only possible test in that case is to test the complete fulfillment of the words of their prophecy.

Methodologically speaking, Deuteronomy 18 is prescriptive in nature, and it is directly related to testing of a prophet. Most of Chisholm's examples are descriptive in nature and not as helpful for deriving prescriptive principles. Hence, one must question some of the methodological assumptions Chisholm relies on while making his claim. One would think that several of the passages Chisholm refers to should be interpreted in light of the earlier and foundational work of Deuteronomy rather than reinterpreting Deuteronomy 18 in light of later narrative writings that the original audience of Deuteronomy 18 would not be familiar with. The following survey will show that much of his "incontrovertible" evidence does not seem to be sufficient to make the argument that most prophecy is inherently contingent.

For instance, he discusses Malachi 3:12 and Jeremiah 26:17-19:

> Another classic example of an implicitly conditional prophecy is Micah's warning that Jerusalem would be left a heap of ruins (Micah 3:12). Despite the seemingly unconditional tone of the prophecy, this did not happen because Hezekiah repented, prompting God to relent from sending the calamity (Jeremiah 26:17-19). An examination of Micah's prophecy shows that he revised his vision of the future in light of Hezekiah's response. In chapter four he predicted that Jerusalem would be delivered from the Assyrian threat in the immediate future (vv. 11-13), only to be conquered at a later time by Babylon (v. 10)....
>
> However, one must not think that once disaster was averted these prophecies were no longer relevant.

> Though these prophecies were contingent, they reflect God's unchanging moral standards and demands. Micah's prophecy of Jerusalem's demise, though unrealized in the historical context in which it was given (Jeremiah 26:17–19), was essentially fulfilled at a later time, when the Babylonians destroyed the city, an event anticipated by Micah in the revised version of his prophetic message (Micah 4:10). The sin denounced by Micah reappeared, making Micah's ancient prophecy relevant again. In resurrecting their sin, as it were, the people resurrected God's response to it. This time no Hezekiah interceded to prevent disaster and the prophecy was fulfilled in its essence. One sees from this example that a prophecy, even when it has been seemingly rendered obsolete, can reappear when the conditions that originally prompted it resurface. While prophecy may be contingent, God's standards pertaining to covenantal loyalty and justice remain firm.[80]

First of all, Chisholm's argument assumes a revision of the prophecy within Micah's writing that is exegetically difficult to prove from the book of Micah. Secondly, he seems to argue for the necessity of an immediate fulfillment in the immediate historical context. The prophecy itself was general in nature and could be fulfilled at any time according to the obedience or disobedience of the people. Thus, as Chisholm acknowledges in his definition of decrees, the fact of fulfillment is not contingent, but the timing of the fulfillment is. The main question is why he limits this principle to unconditional decrees and does not apply it to prophecies he labels as announcements. If this logic could apply to the Davidic Covenant, why can it not be applied to Micah's prophecy? In fact, if one sees Micah 4 as being related to Micah 3 and not a revision of Micah 3 (if the prophecy was

---

[80] Ibid., 5.

revised one must wonder why Micah still kept the original prophecy in Micah 3), then the author of Micah accurately predicted the fulfillment. Thus, one cannot use this passage to argue for the contingent nature of all Old Testament prophecy in the way that Chisholm is defining it.

One may note a similar challenge in Chisholm's appeal to Huldah's prophecy to Josiah to support his view:

> The prophetess Huldah, having announced the downfall of Jerusalem, commended Josiah for his efforts and assured him that he would die in peace and not have to witness the devastation of the city (2 Kings 22:15–20). However, the next chapter tells how Josiah attempted to prevent Pharaoh from marching to the aid of the Assyrians. Josiah was killed in battle (2 Kings 23:29–30), seemingly contradicting what Huldah had promised. If one views prophecy as fixed, we are faced with a serious problem and forced to conclude, with Cogan and Tadmor, that "these words of Huldah remain a striking example of unfulfilled prophecy." However, if we view the prophecy as implicitly conditional to begin with and make room for human freedom in the equation, we can conclude that Josiah's decision to become embroiled in international politics compromised God's ideal. Even so, the promise was fulfilled in its essence for Josiah went to the grave without having to see Jerusalem's downfall.[81]

It is important to note Chisholm's tendency to detect implicit conditionality by the results of the prophecy as opposed to looking for textual indicators.

The problem with Chisholm's argumentation is his assumption that the promise of peace was individual and not national. A similar use of the word is found in 2 Kings 20:19,

---

[81] Ibid., 5–6.

"Then Hezekiah said to Isaiah, 'The word of the LORD which you have spoken is good.' For he thought, 'Is it not so, if there will be peace and truth in my days?'" The *International Standard Bible Encyclopedia* defines what happened after this:

> That was also the year of Hezekiah's deadly illness (2 Kings 20; Isaiah 38), when for a time we know not how long he would be incapacitated for active administration of affairs. Not unlikely on his recovery he found his realm committed beyond withdrawal to an alliance with Egypt and perhaps the leadership of a coalition with Philistia; in which case personally he could only make the best of the situation. There was nothing for it but to confirm this coalition by force, which he did in his Philistine campaign mentioned in 2 Kings 18:8. Meanwhile, in the same general uprising, the Chaldean Merodach-baladan, who had already been expelled from Babylon after an 11-year reign (721–710), again seized that throne; and in due time envoys from him appeared in Jerusalem, ostensibly to congratulate the king on his recovery from his illness, but really to secure his aid and alliance against Assyria (2 Kings 20:12–15; Isaiah 39:1–4). Hezekiah, flattered by such distinguished attention from so distant and powerful a source, by revealing his resources committed what the Chronicler calls the one impious indiscretion of his life (2 Chronicles 32:31), incurring also Isaiah's reproof and adverse prediction (2 Kings 20:17 f; Isaiah 39:6 f). The conflict with Sennacherib was now inevitable; and Hezekiah, by turning the water supply of Jerusalem from the Gihon spring to a pool within the walls and closing it from without, put the capital in readiness to stand a siege. The faith evoked by this wise work, confirmed by the subsequent deliverance, is reflected in Psalm 46. That this incurring of a hazardous war, however, with its turmoils and treacheries, and the presence of uncouth Arab mercenaries, was little to the

king's desire or disposition, seems indicated in Psalm 120, which with the other Songs of Degrees (Psalms 120 through 134) may well reflect the religious faith of this period of Hezekiah's life.[82]

Hezekiah did have individual battles in his time of prophesied peace. However, he would not be alive when the nation experienced the national curses of the loss of land or to his seed on the throne who would be overtaken by a foreign power due to national disobedience according to Deuteronomy 28. In a similar way, this prophecy to Josiah guaranteed that he would go to the grave without seeing Jerusalem's downfall. This was not an example of contingent unfulfilled prophecy but of prophecy that was completely fulfilled in its original intended meaning.

Chisholm's analysis of Elijah's prophecy of Ahab's death has a similar problem:

> In this case we have both the prophecy (1 Kings 21:19) and a narrative of its fulfillment (1 Kings 22:38). By comparing the two, we can gain insight into how the biblical author viewed the nature of prophetic fulfillment and in this way validate our proposal about the nature of prophetic language. Elijah warned that dogs would lick up Ahab's blood in the very spot where they had licked up Naboth's shed blood. According to 1 Kings 22:38, the prophecy was fulfilled when dogs licked up Ahab's blood at a pool where his bloodstained chariot was cleaned following his death in battle. The author unreservedly states that this was "according to the word of the LORD which he spoke." Yet the prophecy was partially, not completely fulfilled. Dogs licked up Ahab's blood at a pool in Samaria, not in Jezreel, the site of Naboth's execution

---

[82] James Orr, John L. Nuelson, and Edgar Y Mullins, eds., *The International Standard Bible Encyclopedia*, Fully rev. ed., 4 vols., vol. 3 (Grand Rapids, MI: W.B. Eerdmans, 1960), 1386.

(1 Kings 21:1–14). One could argue that the prophecy was, subsequently to 1 Kings 21:19, revised but not preserved in the canonical text, creating an apparent tension in the text. But one wonders why an editor would allow such a discrepency [*sic*] to stand.[83]

Contra Chisholm's argument, this prophecy was actually fulfilled twice (and hence the author did not allow this alleged discrepancy to stand). 2 Kings 9:25–26 and 28–37 say:

> Then Jehu said to Bidkar his captain, "Pick him up, and throw him into the tract of the field of Naboth the Jezreelite; for remember, when you and I were riding together behind Ahab his father, that the LORD laid this burden upon him: 'Surely I saw yesterday the blood of Naboth and the blood of his sons,' says the LORD, 'and I will repay you in this plot,' says the LORD. Now therefore, take and throw him on the plot of ground, according to the word of the LORD ...."
>
> And his servants carried him in the chariot to Jerusalem, and buried him in his tomb with his fathers in the City of David. In the eleventh year of Joram the son of Ahab, Ahaziah had become king over Judah. Now when Jehu had come to Jezreel, Jezebel heard of it; and she put paint on her eyes and adorned her head, and looked through a window. Then, as Jehu entered at the gate, she said, "Is it peace, Zimri, murderer of your master?" And he looked up at the window, and said, "Who is on my side? Who?" So two or three eunuchs looked out at him. Then he said, "Throw her down." So they threw her down, and some of her blood spattered on the wall and on the horses; and he trampled her underfoot. And when he had gone in, he ate and drank. Then he said, "Go now, see to this accursed

---

[83] Chisholm Jr., "When Prophecy Appears to Fail," 8–9.

woman, and bury her, for she was a king's daughter." So they went to bury her, but they found no more of her than the skull and the feet and the palms of her hands. Therefore, they came back and told him. And he said, "This is the word of the LORD, which He spoke by His servant Elijah the Tishbite, saying, 'On the plot of ground at Jezreel, dogs shall eat the flesh of Jezebel; and the corpse of Jezebel shall be as refuse on the surface of the field, in the plot at Jezreel,' so that they shall not say, 'Here lies Jezebel.'"

This example shows that the prophecy was fulfilled in kind and extent. King Ahab did die in Samaria, but his own descendant and hence blood (the prophetic use of the same word occurs in 2 Kings 2:33), died precisely in Nabal's vineyard as stated in Elijah's prophecy. The purpose of this prophetic fulfillment was to avenge the blood of Yahweh's servants on the house of Ahab (and by implication blood of Ahab). Furthermore, the narrator indicates that Jezebel's death perfectly fulfilled one of Elijah's prophecies as well.

Even if one granted Chisholm's interpretation of many of these allegedly contingent prophecies, several of the texts Chisholm points to as alleged contingent fulfillment were written after Jonah. As such, the audience would not have been familiar with them and would more likely interpret Jonah in light of Exodus 34 and Deuteronomy 18. Also, Jonah 3 is a short-range prediction that is limited to forty days in Jonah 3:4. This would mean that even according to Chisholm's own standard, the Deuteronomic test would have to apply. Additionally, both Jonah and the Ninevites anticipate some immediate fulfillment since the Ninevites immediately repented in Jonah 3 and Jonah watched to see the outcome of his prophecy in Jonah 4. The fact that Jonah and the Ninevites anticipated the possibility of both repentance and destruction as part of the prophetic fulfillment may indicate that both possibilities are included in the prophecy itself.

Sandy and Chisholm's arguments also do not emphasize the apologetic value of prophecy enough. God's ability to make predictions and bring them to pass is one of His great attributes. Isaiah 46:9–11 in the NASB says:

> Remember the former things long past, For I am God, and there is no other; I am God, and there is no one like Me, Declaring the end from the beginning, And from ancient times things which have not been done, Saying, "My purpose will be established, And I will accomplish all My good pleasure"; Calling a bird of prey from the east, The man of My purpose from a far country. Truly I have spoken; truly I will bring it to pass. I have planned it, surely I will do it.

This passage shows that God will bring everything that He has predicted to pass. He does this by His authority, and it is not conditioned on man's response.

Once again, it is not clear why they see a few passages in narrative contexts as being sufficient to justify an argument that prophecy is usually implicitly conditional. Clearly most of the prophecies about Christ were literally fulfilled, and we still await a literal fulfillment of any messianic prophecies that have yet to be fulfilled. This literal fulfillment has great apologetic value. Additionally, there are many New and Old Testament prophecies that have yet to literally be fulfilled. Thus, Peter encourages believers in 2 Peter 3:11–16 to look for "the coming of the day of God" and to believe in a promise of a "new heavens and a new earth, in which righteousness dwells." He argues that this expectation will result in believers being "found by Him in peace, spotless and blameless." However, if most prophecy is metaphorical and conditional, one will have a difficult time applying this command. If one cannot be certain of the fulfillment of prophecy until after it is fulfilled, how can anyone truly place hope in the fulfillment of the prophecy if it often has unstated conditions?

This brief review of Chisholm and Sandy's view of implicitly conditional prophecy indicates that one cannot make sweeping statements that most prophecies had unstated conditions based on the anticipated human response. The few examples of allegedly unfulfilled prophecies do not in any way mitigate the large number of literally fulfilled prophecies. Implicitly conditional prophecies must contain either textual warrant to demonstrate their conditionality or indicate that repentance may delay the timing of the prophetic fulfillment. If anything, some of the examples that Chisholm cites point to a literal fulfillment in kind and extent.

The Use of the Term "Implicit"

Sandy and Chisholm both argue that prophecy is often implicitly conditional. However, considering their methodology, they might be better served by using the words "unstated" and "inferred." Truthfully, they are actually inferring that prophecy is conditional based on examples of how it was fulfilled rather than textually proving that the divine or human author's intent was to make the prophecy implicitly conditional. As previously mentioned, implicature is something that an author or speaker intends. Inference is something that the reader or audience deduces from what the speaker or author says. Chisholm and Sandy's view of prophecy would be better categorized as an inferred conditionality of the prophecy rather than an implicit one. In order for something to be implicit, the original author must have intended for it to be implicit. The best way to identify implicit conditionality is from textual and contextual indicators. Sandy and Chisholm reverse this process by assuming that because the fulfillment was not as originally stated by the author that the prophecy must have been implicitly conditional.

The implications of this distinction are important for this discussion. Bach states the reason as follows:

> Why is the difference important? One obvious reason is that the audience can take the speaker to be implicating

> something when in fact he isn't.... Equally obviously, a speaker can implicate something even if the audience doesn't make the intended inference. Of course, this will be a case of not *successfully* conveying the implicature but that doesn't mean that the speaker didn't implicate anything, just as a speaker can hint at something without the audience getting the hint."[84]

Whereas the conclusions of Chisholm and Sandy are theologically necessary as a result of the perceived non-fulfillment of certain passages, in order to categorize them as being implicitly conditional, they must demonstrate that the human and divine author originally intended for them to be so. The only way to do so is to exegetically demonstrate implicit conditionality from the textual and contextual evidence of the prophecy itself.

Chisholm's Terminology

Related to the use of implicitly conditional prophecy is Chisholm's distinction between announcements and decrees. Chisholm is correct that all of God's statements are not accompanied by an oath. As the previous analysis of Exodus 32:10 and 2 Samuel 12:14 showed, there are implicitly conditional statements and unconditional predictive prophecies. However, a review of the Biblical use of those terms as well as the use in systematic theology would suggest that different terminology may be needed. Chisholm might consider making the distinction between a "non-predictive warning" and predictive prophecy or foretelling. These terms are more consistent with the Biblical record and the use in systematic theology.

---

[84] Kent Bach, "The Top 10 Misconceptions About Implicature," in *Drawing the Boundaries of Meaning: Neo-Gricean Studies in Pragmatics and Semantics in Honor of Laurence R. Horn*. Ed. Betty J. Birner and Gregory Ward (Philadelphia, PA: John Benjamins Publishing Company, 2006), 23. Emphasis his.

A theological analysis of announcements and decrees in the Bible does not support Chisholm's terminology. The concept of decrees from human kings does not necessarily reflect an unconditional, unchangeable oath. For instance, Daniel 2:13 in the NASB says, "So the decree went forth that the wise men should be slain; and they looked for Daniel and his friends to kill them." This clearly was conditional since Daniel later overturned the decree (דָּת) by interpreting Nebuchadnezzar's dream. The word used for the unchanging law of the Medes and the Persians in Daniel 6:12 (אֱסָר) refers to an inter-edict and may not be a decree in the technical sense. With respect to God, Daniel 4:24 discusses a decree from the Most High upon Nebuchadnezzar in which he is going to be driven to be with the animals and act like an animal. However, Daniel's admonition to Nebuchadnezzar in Daniel 4:27 (NASB) is interesting, "Therefore, O king, may my advice be pleasing to you: break away now from your sins by *doing* righteousness and from your iniquities by showing mercy to *the* poor, in case there may be a prolonging of your prosperity." This unchanging decree still had conditions and is related to Nebuchadnezzar's response. Isaiah 10:23 speaks of a destruction that is decreed but no oath is mentioned in the passage. Zephaniah 2:1–3 (NASB) is very similar:

> Gather yourselves together, yes, gather, O nation without shame, Before the decree takes effect— The day passes like the chaff— Before the burning anger of the LORD comes upon you, Before the day of the LORD'S anger comes upon you. Seek the LORD, All you humble of the earth Who have carried out His ordinances; Seek righteousness, seek humility. Perhaps you will be hidden In the day of the LORD'S anger.

These types of decrees described in the Bible make Chisholm's distinction much less clear.

A similar challenge comes when one evaluates

announcements in the Old Testament. While Chisholm's citation of Jeremiah 26:4–6 and Genesis 12:1–2 are helpful in understanding the basis for his distinction, not all divine announcements in the Bible are consistent with his distinction. For instance, Isaiah 44:6–8 (NASB) says:

> Thus says the LORD, the King of Israel and his Redeemer, the LORD of hosts: "I am the first and I am the last, And there is no God besides Me. 'Who is like Me? Let him proclaim and declare it; Yes, let him recount it to Me in order, From the time that I established the ancient nation. And let them declare to them the things that are coming And the events that are going to take place. Do not tremble and do not be afraid; Have I not long since **announced** [emphasis mine] *it* to you and declared *it* [all italics in NASB]? And you are My witnesses. Is there any God besides Me."

In this passage, an announcement appears to be that which the sovereign God is determined to bring to pass. In fact, His ability to make this type of announcement is what distinguishes Him from the idols that are unable to announce what is coming (Isaiah 41:22). These passages use the word שָׁמַע which is often translated as "to announce" while Chisholm sites Jeremiah 26:4 which uses the word אָמַר which traditionally means "to say" or "to speak."

In the New Testament, Acts 3:18 says, "But the things which God announced beforehand by the mouth of all the prophets, that His Christ would suffer, He has thus fulfilled." The Greek word προκατήγγειλεν that is used comes from the root word προκαταγγέλλω which is defined as "to announce beforehand, foretell of prophetic utterance."[85] Christ's death on

---

[85] Frederick W. Danker and Walter Bauer, *A Greek-English Lexicon of the New Testament and Other Early Christian Literature*, 3rd ed. (Chicago, IL: University of Chicago Press, 2000), 871. Emphasis in text.

the cross should count as an eternal decree that would be part of the definitive plan of God (cf. Acts 2:23). Interestingly enough, this announcement includes a challenge in Acts 3:19–21 to "repent and return, so that your sins may be wiped away, in order that times of refreshing may come from the presence of the Lord; and that He may send Jesus, the Christ appointed for you, whom heaven must receive until the period of restoration of all things about which God spoke by the mouth of His holy prophets from ancient time." Surely Chisholm would not argue that Jesus' return is conditioned on people's repentance since it comes in an announcement form with conditions.

While Chisholm provides an insightful explanation of how God might change His mind, one must question whether his view is any less arbitrary and does not tie additional theological knots. Chisholm argues that a decree usually has a clear indication, or one could categorize it as a changing announcement. One must wonder, however, if it is not less arbitrary to state the reverse. Perhaps everything should be considered a decree unless a specific conditional statement is included in the announcement itself. For instance, should Daniel 7:23–27 be an announcement instead of a decree since there is no language of oath in the kingdom promise? Should the promise of the Holy Spirit in John 14:16–20 be an announcement instead of a decree since there is no language of an oath (in fact, one might interpret 14:15 and 14:21 as conditions of obedience in order to receive this Helper)? If an oath is required for God to not change His mind, one must wonder how many New Testament promises God will change His mind about. Identifying unmarked decrees is not any less arbitrary or theologically challenging than the anthropomorphic view. Of course, as Piper's quote in the response to the open view of God suggests, one does not even have to espouse the traditional anthropomorphic view in order to still do justice to the Biblical text.

Old Testament Scholar William D. Barrick expresses concerns about Chisholm's application of the distinction between decrees and announcements to Exodus 32:10:

> The position taken by Robert Chisholm is that God had only made an announcement, not a decree, therefore He was free to change His mind about its implementation. His position, however, has several problems. First, grammatically the distinction between decree and announcement is not sufficiently diverse. Imperative + jussive + cohortative is not exegetically distinct from *waw* + imperative + *waw* + cohortative. Second, contextually it does not take into account the direct ties to the Abrahamic Covenant (Exodus 32:10 [cf. Genesis 12:2] and Exodus 32:13) and the final declaration of unretracted judgment (32:34, 35). Exodus 32 shares elements in common with Elijah's judgment speech against Ahab in 1 Kings 21:20–24—it would still come to pass because "it was a divine decree that could not be altered."
> Third, theologically it does not make sense that Moses could "persuade Him to change His mind." Chisholm's ultimate conclusion is not consistent with the contents of the passage as a whole: "In every case where such a change is envisioned or reported, *God had not yet decreed a course of action or an outcome.* Instead, He chose to wait patiently, hoping His warnings might bring people to their senses and make judgment unnecessary." The Lord had decreed what He would do in the first half (up to the *athnach* in the Hebrew) of 32:10. The last half of the verse is obviously inconsistent with what He had decreed concerning the twelve tribes of Israel in Genesis 49. Perhaps it would be best to keep in mind Chisholm's final word (his last sentence): "At the same time such passages should not be overextended. God can and often does

decree a course of action."[86]

The labeling of such prophecies is difficult to assess. As Barrick notes, some of what Chisholm labels as an announcement is connected to decreed covenants. This makes the strict distinction between a decree and announcement hard to sustain.

Chisholm's use of the word "decree" also differs from the way the term is used in systematic theology. For instance, Ryrie says:

> The decree of God is His plan for everything. The decree contains many decrees. Decreeing and foreordaining are synonymous theological concepts, but they obviously emphasize the sovereignty facet rather than the free will aspect. The word "design" is less weighted toward sovereignty, while the word "drawing" seems almost neutral.
>
> Scripture teaches clearly that God's plan includes all things (Ephesians 1:11), but it also reveals that the degree and directness of God's relationship to specific events is varied. Sometimes He directly ordains something (Deuteronomy 32:39; Acts 5:1–11). Almost always He works through the natural laws He has ordained and does not lift them to make exceptions even for believers (Philippians 2:30). Sometimes He decides to allow people to give full expression to their sinful natures almost without restraint (Romans 1:24, 26, 28). Sometimes He expects us simply to make choices on the basis of what seems right or what we desire to do (1 Corinthians 10:27).[87]

---

[86] William D. Barrick, "The Openness of God: Does Prayer Change God?" *Master's Seminary Journal* 12, no. 2 (2001): 160. Emphasis his.
[87] Charles Caldwell Ryrie, *Basic Theology: A Popular Systematic Guide to Understanding Biblical Truth* (Chicago, IL: Moody Press, 1999), 359–60.

Chisholm's definition also differs from Chafer who says:

> "The term *Divine Decree* is an attempt to gather up in one designation that to which the Scriptures refer by various designations-the divine *purpose* (Ephesians 1:11), *determinate counsel* (Acts 2:23), *foreknowledge*, (1 Peter 1:2, cf. 1:20), *election* (1 Thessalonians 1:4), *predestination* (Romans 8:30), the divine *will* (Ephesians 1:11), and the divine *good pleasure* (Ephesians 1:9). When reference is made to divine counsels it does not suggest conference on the part of God with other beings, but that His counsels are consummately wise. In like manner, the reference to the divine will does not suggest capricious or unreasonable action. Infinite wisdom directs the divine determination. In this sense His decree is said to be the "counsel of his will." These terms certainly signify that God acts only according to an eternal purpose which incorporates all things."[88]

In Chisholm's usage, a decree is a category of God's stated plans which has an oath while Chafer and Ryrie consider a decree to encompass all of God's sovereign plans and decrees.

Dispensational systematic theologians are not the only ones who use the term "decree" this way. For instance, Grudem uses decree for more than those things that are stated with an oath, "A *decree* of God is a word of God that causes something to happen. These decrees of God include not only the events of the original creation but also the continuing existence of all things, for Hebrews 1:3 tells us that Christ is continually 'upholding the universe by his word of power.'"[89] Once again, in systematic

---

[88] Lewis Sperry Chafer, "Biblical Theism Divine Decrees," *Bibliotheca Sacra* 96, no. 147: 148. All emphasis in original text.
[89] Wayne A. Grudem, *Systematic Theology: An Introduction to Biblical Doctrine* (Grand Rapids, MI: Zondervan Publishing House, 1994), 47. Emphasis his.

theology a decree is more than that which is spoken with an oath. Thus, Chisholm's use of decree may cause unnecessary confusion.

As previously mentioned, a different choice of terms might be in order. A contrast between "a non-predictive warning"[90] and "predictive prophecy" or foretelling is recommended. Chisholm already made a very good argument for the relationship between implicit conditions and forthtelling as contrasted with foretelling. The term "warning" can avoid some of the theological difficulties of announcement. It is an ideal word to connect the covenantal aspects of God's word with forthtelling. For instance, Deuteronomy 32:46 says in the NASB, "Take to your heart all the words with which I am warning you today, which you shall command your sons to observe carefully, even all the words of this law." The idea of warning is also connected with the office of a prophet in 2 Kings 17:13, "Yet the LORD warned Israel and Judah through all His prophets and every seer, saying, 'Turn from your evil ways and keep My commandments, My statutes according to all the law which I commanded your fathers, and which I sent to you through My servants the prophets.'" Additionally Psalm 19:9-11 connects observation of the warnings of God with covenant blessing, "The fear of the LORD is clean, enduring forever; The judgments of the LORD are true; they are righteous altogether. They are more desirable than gold, yes, than much fine gold; Sweeter also than honey and the drippings of the honeycomb. Moreover, by them Your servant is warned; In keeping them there is great reward." The word "warning" is also used to indicate a conditional response upon the recipient of the warning as Ezekiel 3:18–21 shows:

When I say to the wicked, "You will surely die," and you

---

[90] In the case of something that is positively conditional, non-predictive statement would be better a better descriptor than announcement would be.

> do not warn him or speak out to warn the wicked from his wicked way that he may live, that wicked man shall die in his iniquity, but his blood I will require at your hand. Yet if you have warned the wicked and he does not turn from his wickedness or from his wicked way, he shall die in his iniquity; but you have delivered yourself. Again, when a righteous man turns away from his righteousness and commits iniquity, and I place an obstacle before him, he will die; since you have not warned him, he shall die in his sin, and his righteous deeds which he has done shall not be remembered; but his blood I will require at your hand. However, if you have warned the righteous man that the righteous should not sin and he does not sin, he shall surely live because he took warning; and you have delivered yourself.

The New Testament idea of warning also communicates the same conditional nature. Hebrews 12:25 says in the NASB, "See to it that you do not refuse Him who is speaking. For if those did not escape when they refused him who warned *them* on earth, much less *will we escape* who turn away from Him who *warns* from heaven." Thus, in the New Testament and the Old Testament, the term warning has far more connection with the prophetic office than announcement as well as a stronger specific covenantal connection.

Contrasting warnings with predictive prophecy or foretelling will also avoid some of the challenges with using a term like decree. Chisholm's use of the concept of foretelling is not at variance with the use among conservative evangelical Old Testament scholars or systematic theologians. Use of these terms can accomplish the distinction that Chisholm is trying to make without tying additional theological knots.

Sandy and Chisholm have raised some very important issues with respect to prophecy. Since this book is focused on Jonah's prophecy, one cannot address all of them. However, part of the intention of this book is to prove that Jonah's prophecy has plenty of textual indications of implicit conditionality. As a result, it is probably not best to label Jonah 3:4 as having unstated conditions or as "seemingly uncompromising."

Summary

This section has reviewed the argument for unstated conditions in prophecy. The unstated condition view argues that the prophecy is implicitly conditional based on the functional view of language. This view argues that prophecy is often implicitly conditional. As a result, authors like Chisholm and Sandy believe that the prophecy was not necessarily intended to predict the future but to elicit a response on the part of the audience. If the audience responded positively, the predicted judgment would be averted.

In contrast to this view, it should be argued that the prophecy is implicitly conditional unless there are textual markers to indicate so. Otherwise, the test of the true prophet in Deuteronomy 18 could never be enforced. In the case of Jonah 3:4, the implicit polysemantic wordplay of הָפַךְ, the forty-day period of prophecy as well as the expectations of Jonah and the Ninevites are textual indicators of the implicit conditionality of the prophecy.

THE FALSE MESSAGE TO GENERATE REPENTANCE OF THE NINEVITES

Lubeck summarizes another option as follows, "Is God more committed to the faithful fulfillment of His own uttered word or would He sacrifice His fidelity in order to forgive and save the repentant?"[91] He also gives brief variations of this view, "The biblical story is not about a prophet but about an unfulfilled prophecy. God's wonderful graciousness here explains the failure of Jonah's prediction.... Human life (and even animal

---

[91] Lubeck, "Prophetic Sabotage: A Look at Jonah 3:2–4," 40.

life) is more important to YHWH than consistently keeping to a word of judgment once spoken."[92]

Frolov argues that this view best explains Jonah's desire for death. According to Frolov, Jonah attempted to escape his prophetic calling because when "his prediction concerning the imminent overturning of Nineveh (3:4) fails to materialize" Jonah is firmly placed in "the category of false prophet."[93] As a result of this, Jonah has "nothing to live for" because his "professional career is ruined" since "no one is likely to be 'frightened' by his word, and a prophet without a scared audience is just a pitiable lunatic."[94]

Heschel also espouses this view. He argues in *The Prophets* that the "mysterious paradox of the Hebrew faith" is that the "Almighty may change a word he proclaims" and that "man has the power to modify his design."[95] He says regarding Jonah 3–4:

> God's change of mind displeased Jonah exceedingly. He had proclaimed the doom of Nineveh with a certainty, to the point of fixing a time, as an inexorable decree without qualification. But what transpired only proved the word of God was neither firm nor reliable. To a prophet who stakes his life on the reliability and infallibility of the word of God, such realization leads to despair.... God's answer to Jonah, stressing the supremacy of compassion, upsets the possibility of looking for a rational coherence of God's ways with the world. History would be more intelligible if God's word were the last word, final an

---

[92] Ibid.
[93] Serge Frolov, "Returning the Ticket: God and His Prophet in the Book of Jonah," *Journal for the Study of the Old Testament* 86 (1999): 91.
[94] Ibid.
[95] Abraham Joshua Heschel, *The Prophets*, 1st Perennial Classics ed. (New York, NY: Perennial, 2001), 367. Source originally discussed in Lubeck, "Prophetic Sabotage: A Look at Jonah 3:2–4."

unambiguous like a dogma or an unconditional decree. It would be easier if God's anger became effusive automatically; once wickedness had reached its full measure, punishment would destroy it. Yet, beyond justice and anger lies the mystery of compassion.[96]

In essence, Heschel argues that Jonah 3–4 shows that God's compassion is more important than the reliability of His prophetic word.

As previously mentioned, Jack Deere uses Jonah's prophecy as proof that modern day prophets may also have prophecies that are not fulfilled. He notes three instances when a prophecy will remain unfulfilled: (1) When the Lord did not speak the prediction; (2) The Lord may have spoken the message but the human messenger misinterpreted the message; and (3) God spoke and the messenger understood His voice accurately but a response on the part of others kept it unfulfilled.[97] This argument allows him to circumvent the Old Testament requirement that prophets be one hundred percent accurate or risk stoning as per Deuteronomy 18.

Evaluation of False Message to Generate Ninevite Repentance View

This argument appears to be a utilitarian and expedient notion of the end justifying the means. Is it okay for God to intentionally deceive the messenger in order to bring about the repentance of the Ninevites? Clearly it is not. Titus 1:2 says that God cannot lie. He would not present a case for destruction only to trick Jonah into prophesying to encourage the Ninevites to repent. Additionally, the failure of this prophecy would make Jonah a false prophet. Deuteronomy 18:22 says, "When a

---

[96] Heschel, *The Prophets*, 368.
[97] Jack Deere, *Surprised by the Voice of God: How God Speaks Today through Prophecies, Dreams, and Visions* (Grand Rapids, MI: Zondervan, 1996), 326.

prophet speaks in the name of the LORD, if the thing does not come about or come true, that is the thing which the LORD has not spoken. The prophet has spoken it presumptuously; you shall not be afraid of him." There is no exception clause for repentance of others or God's gracious elimination of predicted judgment based on revelation found in other passages (for example, Jeremiah 18:7–10).

Using Gricean theory, advocates of this view are arguing from the perspective that God and Jonah were violating the qualitative conversational maxim. Once again, this maxim deals with the truthfulness of the statement. Instead, it should be argued that the maxim of manner was what was actually violated. This would be far more consistent with the Biblical statements that God does not lie. The manner maxim says that one will speak as clearly as possible without ambiguity. However, in Jonah 3:4, the ambiguous implicit polysemantic wordplay of הָפַךְ was intended by God and Jonah in order to communicate that repentance and destruction were possible depending on how the Ninevites responded to the prophecy. The author of Jonah likely also used the polysemantic wordplay for ironic purposes.

THE LATER FULFILLMENT VIEW

This view argues that the fulfillment occurred at a later time when the Assyrian Empire was destroyed by the Babylonians. This view is held by some conservative dispensationalists as well as some early Jewish writers. While this view does take the fulfillment of the passage literally, it does not overcome the objection that the prophecy was to occur in forty days.

Walvoord argues that the prophecy was fulfilled during the fall of Nineveh in 612 BC, one-hundred and fifty years after it was actually communicated in Jonah 3:4. He argues that this judgment was deferred due to the repentance of Nineveh. In Walvoord's opinion "the narrative gave remarkable insight into

Israel's lack of ministry to the Gentile world."[98] For Walvoord, the principle prophetic significance of Jonah is the typological significance for Christ's death and resurrection.[99] As Chisholm noted, this view is typical of the methodology of some traditional dispensationalists. If they do not find immediate fulfillment, they look for fulfillment elsewhere. As previously noted, this is not uncommon since the timing of the fulfillment of some prophecies may relate to the response of the recipients of that prophecy.

The later fulfillment view is also represented in Tobit 14:4 which is translated in the King James Version of the Apocrypha:

> Go into Media my son, for I surely believe those things which Jonas the prophet spake of Nineve, that it shall be overthrown; and that for a time peace shall rather be in Media; and that our brethren shall lie scattered in the earth from that good land: and Jerusalem shall be desolate, and the house of God in it shall be burned, and shall be desolate for a time.

This early Jewish view from the second century BC argues that the fulfillment of Jonah's prophecy would be later than in the original eighth century BC timing of the message.

Lubeck correctly demonstrates that this argument would still not deal with the issue of false prophecy because the time period was clearly stated as being forty days.[100] Furthermore, the participial form of the word הָפַךְ describes something that will

---

[98] John F. Walvoord, *The Prophecy Knowledge Handbook* (Wheaton, IL: Victor Books, 1990), 298.
[99] Ibid.
[100] Lubeck, "Prophetic Sabotage: A Look at Jonah 3:2–4," 41.

happen in the immediately impending future.¹⁰¹ It also does not seem to fit into the flow and purpose of Jonah. Whereas Nahum did promise a future destruction for the Ninevites, the book of Jonah does not seem to elicit hope on a future destruction of the Ninevites. The Ninevites are portrayed as being very important to God and the objects of His mercy (Jonah 3:3, 4:11) as indicated by the phrase לאלהים which Stuart argues should be translated as "important to God."¹⁰² In fact, God used Jonah's experience with the Ninevites to show the Israelites that He would take away the curses that had been prophesied to them if they would repent.

JONAH ALTERED OR DISTORTED YAHWEH'S MESSAGE VIEW

Lubeck supports that view by saying:

In light of these contextual, grammatical, and literary considerations, we would argue that since Jonah was disobedient to Yahweh both before and after this episode, and since he nowhere in the book demonstrates repentance or a desire to please God, or willingly capitulates to Yahweh's agenda, so here also Jonah is disobedient. Jonah's message reflects his own selfish intentions — at best a half-truth intended to deceive through prophetic "disinformation."¹⁰³

However, he later clarifies his statement by saying, "we would not construe Jonah's prophecy as being false, but as a remarkable prediction which was fulfilled — in spite of his

---

[101] Hans Walter Wolff, *Obadiah and Jonah: A Commentary*, trans. Margaret Kohl (Minneapolis, MN: Augsburg Publishing House, 1986), 144.
[102] Stuart, *Hosea–Jonah*, 487.
[103] Lubeck, "Prophetic Sabotage: A Look at Jonah 3:2–4," 43–44.

sabotage and reticence."[104] In other words, Lubeck exonerates Jonah from the charge of being a false prophet by saying that despite the fact that Jonah altered the words of Yahweh, God fulfilled the prophecy in Jonah 3:4. God is exonerated from giving false information because Jonah allegedly altered the prophecy.

Cary holds a similar view. He argues that it may be possible that the Lord "fooled Jonah, giving him a message containing more good news than Jonah realizes."[105] However, he thinks that the altered message is a preferable option:

> Still, the irony of the story is even more satisfying if we suppose that Jonah himself, prophet posing as bureaucrat, supplies the evasive passive-voice term, so uncharacteristic of the Lord's very unevasive habits of speech by altering the message the LORD has given him. We can almost hear the gracious and merciful God chuckling and saying to himself, "Okay, Jonah, have it your way. You want to say Nineveh will be overturned? Well then, I will make sure Nineveh is overturned for you! I will surely turn them upside down, convert them and turn them into something altogether new."[106]

Hence, both Cary and Lubeck recognize the double entendre of הָפַךְ in Jonah 3:4, but they consider it to be an indication of Jonah's ironic word choice in his foolish attempt to alter God's message and less of God's original message.

Evaluation of the Altered or Distorted Message View

In his argumentation, Lubeck and Cary ignore an

---

[104] Ibid., 45
[105] Phillip Cary, *Jonah*, Brazos Theological Commentary on the Bible, ed. R.R. Reno (Grand Rapids, MI: Brazos Press, 2008), 109.
[106] Ibid., 109–10.

important aspect of a true prophet: Jonah was not to add to God's word or amend it. Deuteronomy 12:32 says, "Whatever I command you, you shall be careful to do; you shall not add to nor take away from it." Immediately following this verse is a test for a false prophet in Deuteronomy 13 (cf. Deuteronomy 4:2, Jeremiah 23:14–40, and Revelation 22:18–19 for similar statements). Proverbs 30:5–6 says, "Every word of God is tested; He is a shield to those who take refuge in Him. Do not add to His words Lest He reprove you, and you be proved a liar." The fact that the prophecy came true does not exonerate Jonah from the charge of being a false prophet. Deuteronomy 13:2 says that even false prophets' prophecies come true occasionally.

Lubeck also contends God was not credited with the statement when he writes:

> Lastly, conspicuous *in absentia* is the modifying phrase which accompanies the first two verbs, that he acted "according to the word of Yahweh" ([Jonah] 3:3), or mention that he did in fact speak "the proclamation which Yahweh had given him" (3:2). Either of these phrases would have verified his compliance in delivering Yahweh's message, just as his obedience to the first two verbs is confirmed; the absence of such at this critical juncture is therefore significant.[107]

However, 3:10 states that God relented from "calamity which He had declared He would bring upon them." Thus, the declaration of the prophecy is definitely attributed to God and not Jonah alone. Additionally, the phrase in Jonah 1:1 and Jonah 3:1 (וַיְהִי דְבַר־יְהוָה אֶל) that introduces the way the Word of Yahweh came to Jonah is used in the Old Testament of several true prophets of God like Samuel (1 Samuel 15:10), Nathan (2 Samuel 7:4), the

---

[107] Lubeck, "Prophetic Sabotage: A Look at Jonah 3:2–4,"43. Emphasis his.

old prophet in Bethel (1 Kings 13:20), Elijah (1 Kings 21:17 and 28), Shemiah (2 Chronicles 11:2), Isaiah (Isaiah 38:4), Jeremiah (Jeremiah 28:12, 29:30, 32:26, et al.), and Zechariah (Zechariah 7:8). This phrase is a standard way of introducing prophetic messages received from God. Hence, Trible, Lubeck, and Cary cannot attribute this statement only to Jonah.

Finally, Lubeck's arguments are primarily based on the consistent disobedience of Jonah throughout the book. He writes:

> In the first place, his thoughts and motives are left unstated, shrouded for us by our narrator. It is thus illegitimate to assume that since this *is* what Jonah said, it necessarily follows that this is what he was *supposed* to say. The narrative thus far has portrayed Jonah only as being recalcitrant and uncooperative.[108]

The fact that Jonah was not excited about the possibility of the Ninevite repentance is not disputed. However, the parallelism between Jonah 1:1–2 and 3:1–2 would cause one to lend less credence to Lubeck's notion that Jonah was consistently recalcitrant. In 1:1, Jonah is commanded to arise and cry against the great city. Jonah, however, rose and fled the presence of God. In 3:1, Jonah receives a similar command and he "arose and went to Nineveh according to the word of the LORD." If Jonah was acting according to the word of the Lord, it is hard to argue with certainty that the words he spoke were out of disobedience. This is especially true when one considers his prayer in Jonah 2 and his vow of praise and thanksgiving to God. Furthermore, 2 Kings 14:25 says, "He restored the border of Israel from the entrance of Hamath as far as the Sea of the Arabah, according to the word of the LORD, the God of Israel, which He spoke through His servant Jonah the son of Amittai, the prophet, who

---

[108] Ibid., 41. Emphasis his.

was of Gath-hepher." Jonah had a good track record of speaking the word of the Lord accurately. Furthermore, Jesus never questioned the accuracy of Jonah's preaching when he spoke about it (Matthew 12:39–41; Luke 11:29–32).

Even if the point of Jonah's disobedience were conceded, there are many examples in the Bible of prophets who were disobeying God, yet their prophecies were accurate. Balaam prophesied many clear prophecies about the future for Israel and the Messiah. When questioned about why he could not alter God's words Balaam responded in Numbers 23:26, "Did I not tell you, 'Whatever the LORD speaks, that I must do'?" John 11:51 says Caiaphas' true prophecy was not made on his own initiative. Saul was considered among the prophets (1 Samuel 10:11–12; 19:20–24). One of the amazing things about God is that His word is consistently revealed accurately despite the many prophets who disobeyed Him. Surely Jonah was not more disobedient than Balaam and Caiaphas who were not even in the covenant community! If God could use them to reveal a true prophecy accurately, it is not unreasonable to expect Him to do the same with Jonah. Thus, Lubeck's argument for Jonah's distortion of God's word based on his prior disobedience is inadequate.

The fact that Jonah desired for the Ninevites to be judged does not prove that Jonah did not desire to give a true prophecy. Jeremiah wanted judgment for his audience as well. He says in Jeremiah 12:3, "But Thou knowest me, O LORD; Thou seest me; And Thou dost examine my heart's attitude toward Thee. Drag them off like sheep for the slaughter And set them apart for a day of carnage!" In Jeremiah 20:8–9, even Jeremiah did not want to speak God's word. However, he says:

> For each time I speak, I cry aloud; I proclaim violence and destruction, Because for me the word of the LORD has resulted In reproach and derision all day long. But if I say, "I will not remember Him Or speak anymore in His name," Then in my heart it becomes like a burning fire

shut up in my bones; And I am weary of holding it in, And I cannot endure it.

As Jeremiah's example shows, even a prophet who does not want to prophesy is not inherently a false prophet.

SUGGESTED ALTERNATIVE: THE IMPLICIT POLYSEMANTIC WORDPLAY VIEW

While one cannot negate the possibility of the existence of implicitly conditional prophecies in general, Jonah 3 does not necessarily have to be taken as an unstated conditional prophecy because the context, message, and lexical features demonstrate that the message was implicitly conditional. The primary contention is that both repentance and destruction were implied by the double entendre of הָפַךְ. In this section I will discuss the implicit polysemantic wordplay view of Jonah 3.

Description of the Implicit Polysemantic Wordplay View

This view is described well by Alexander when he writes:

> The verb hāpak, "overturn", is used elsewhere to describe the destruction of Sodom and Gomorrah (Genesis 19:25; Lamentations 4:6; Amos 4:11). The basic idea underlying the verb is "to turn". On occasions it means "to overturn" (2 Kings 21:12, "to overturn a plate") However, it can also mean "to turn around", transform; (1 Kings 22:34, "to turn around a chariot"; Jeremiah 13:23, "to transform one's appearance"). With these different connotations the use of the word here is hardly accidental. Although Nineveh was not overturned, it did experience a turn around.[109]

---

[109] David W. Baker, T. Desmond Alexander, and Bruce K. Waltke, *Obadiah, Jonah, Micah*, The Tyndale Old Testament Commentaries, ed. D.J. Wiseman (Downers Grove, IL: Inter-Varsity Press, 1988) 121.

While variations of this view exist, its advocates typically argue for some form of double entendre and that this ironic polysemantic wordplay was intended by the author of Jonah.

Some variation exists among supporters of the view on whether Jonah himself recognized the wordplay. Although he argues for the polysemantic wordplay view, Lessing argues that "Jonah likely would have understood his message to be one of impending doom of the sort that befell Sodom, and the Ninevites clearly took it as a warning that they would perish."[110] Nosson and Zlotowitz agree with *Derech Hashem* that Jonah is an example of a prophet who comprehends the truth of the prophecy but does not understand all the hidden truths included in the prophecy.[111]

In contrast, it should be argued that both Jonah and the Ninevites understood the implicit opportunity for repentance or destruction in the text. Jonah seemed to believe in the possibility that God might relent from destroying the Ninevites. Jonah 4:2 says:

> He prayed to the LORD and said, "Please LORD, was not this what I said while I was still in my *own* country? Therefore, in order to forestall this, I fled to Tarshish, for I knew that You are a gracious and compassionate God, slow to anger and abundant in lovingkindness, and one who relents concerning calamity."

Jonah did not accuse God of leaving the prophecy unfulfilled. Instead, he accused God of intending to deliver the Ninevites all along. It seems that he would have gladly died in that large fish

---

[110] R. Reed Lessing, *Jonah*, Concordia Commentary (St. Louis, MO: Concordia Publishing House, 2007), 282.
[111] Meir Zlotowitz and Nosson Scherman, *Yonah = [Sefer Yonah] = Jonah: A New Translation with a Commentary Anthologized from Talmudic, Midrashic, and Rabbinic Sources*, 2nd ed., The Twelve Prophets (Brooklyn, NY: Mesorah Publications, 1980), 121.

in Tarshish if it would have saved him from delivering this message (cf. Jonah 4:8).

Jonah also recognized the possibility of destruction. In Jonah 4:5, he is sitting waiting to see what would happen to the city. If he believed that the repentance in and of itself avoided God's destruction, why would he wait? However, his reaction seems to suggest that he recognized that both the possibility of repentance and destruction were found in the prophecy. This would also be consistent with Amos 3:7 which suggests that God normally reveals even His secret counsel to the prophets first.[112]

God may have intentionally left Jonah's message ambiguous because Jonah would be less likely to give a message that did not even include the possibility of destruction. If he was preaching a message of destruction, one cannot imagine that Jonah would run from that. In fact, he might truly enjoy it. However, because the word he preached contained the possibility of repentance, he ran from God. *The NET Bible* says:

> The narrator skillfully withheld Jonah's motivations from the reader up to this point for rhetorical effect—to build suspense and to create a shocking, surprising effect. Now, for the first time, the narrator reveals why Jonah fled from the commission of God in 1:3—he had not wanted to give God the opportunity to relent from judging Nineveh! Jonah knew that if he preached in Nineveh, the people might repent and as a result, God might more than likely relent from sending judgment. Hoping to seal their fate, Jonah had originally refused to preach so that the Ninevites would not have an opportunity to repent. Apparently, Jonah hoped that God would have therefore

---

[112] While an Old Testament author did not understand all of the significance of his prophecies, he likely understood the meaning. For a defense of this position, see Walter C. Kaiser, *The Uses of the Old Testament in the New* (Chicago, IL: Moody Press, 1985), 17–23 and 61–76.

judged them without advance warning. Or perhaps he was afraid he would betray his nationalistic self-interests by functioning as the instrument through which the LORD would spare Israel's main enemy. Jonah probably wanted God to destroy Nineveh for three reasons: (1) as a loyal nationalist, he despised non-Israelites (cf. 1:9); (2) he believed that idolaters had forfeited any opportunity to be shown mercy (cf. 2:9–10); and (3) the prophets Amos and Hosea had recently announced that God would sovereignly use the Assyrians to judge unrepentant Israel (Hosea 9:3; 11:5) and take them into exile (Amos 5:27). If God destroyed Nineveh, the Assyrians would not be able to destroy Israel. The better solution would have been for Jonah to work for the repentance of Nineveh *and* Israel [emphasis in cited text].[113]

Jonah decided to avoid preaching in the hope that the Ninevites would be destroyed. However, God elected to show mercy on them instead. Thus, the potential calamity that could have resulted from this prophecy was avoided. Much to Jonah's dismay, the Ninevites' hearts were changed instead of their city destroyed.

While it is true that Jonah 3:9 shows that the king believed that destruction was actually prophesied, he also believed in the possibility of this destruction being avoided. In Jonah 3:9 he remarks that perhaps God will turn from His anger so they may not perish. The question may have been motivated by the very prophecy Jonah spoke. The message implied the possibility of destruction as the narrator states that God did not bring the calamity which He originally declared (וַיִּנָּחֶם הָאֱלֹהִים עַל־הָרָעָה אֲשֶׁר־דִּבֶּר לַעֲשׂוֹת־לָהֶם). However, if the message did not imply the possibility of repentance where would the Ninevites have gotten

---

[113] Biblical Studies Press, *The NET Bible*, first edition (Biblical Studies Press, 2005), 1737.

the idea that He might relent? Since Jonah was likely written before Jeremiah, neither the readers nor the Ninevites were familiar with the promise of God relenting from calamity in light of repentance as promised in Jeremiah 18:8 (not to mention the Ninevites were not Jews and would not have read the Hebrew Bible). The basis for their belief in the possibility of avoiding destruction is likely found in the prophecy itself. In other words, their question about whether God would relent was not a result of their hope that there was something in the prophecy that was unstated. Instead, they appear not to be certain if the repentance they showed was done quickly enough or sufficiently enough to avoid the destruction that the prophecy said was possible. Stuart writes:

> The first four words of the Hebrew of v 9 (מי־יודע ישוב ונחם "Who knows? He may change his mind") are found in the same order in Joel 2:14. This may reflect a coincidence, a dependence in either direction (Magonet [*Form and Meaning*, 77–79] argues convincingly for the priority of Jonah rather than Joel), or a mutual dependence on something in ancient Israelite liturgies or prophetic language which became popular enough to be used twice in the OT, including in a rendering of an Assyrian edict. At any rate, Joel 2:12–14 is closely related to the Jonah story through its emphasis on the possibility of repentance on the part of a truly sinful people, if the repentance is genuine, and its portrayal of God as patient and merciful (Jonah 4:2).
>
> The king's decree captures what Jonah resentfully understood all along: God can forgive anybody, even a (self-) important city famous for its wickedness, which had oppressed Jonah's own people. It was that possibility—that God would actually be true to his forgiving nature and spare Nineveh—that the Ninevites

now grasped toward.[114]

Stuart argues that both the king and Jonah recognized the opportunity for repentance in the prophecy. If one takes an early pre-exilic date of the ninth century BC for Joel there could be an allusion to Joel 2:12–14 within Jonah as well as an allusion to Exodus 34:6–7.[115] In either case, in Joel, the statement follows an explicit warning that was given in Joel 2:12 to the Israelite people. Hence, the phrase does not necessarily indicate a lack of knowledge but the necessity of a response to a condition in prophecy.

In addition to the prophecy itself, the Ninevites may have had some other reasons to respond to the prophecy. Wiseman, who adopts the implicit polysemantic wordplay view in both the Assyrian and the Hebrew, argues that the Assyrians may have responded in the way they did due to their beliefs in omens as recorded in the Enuma Anu Enlil that predicted destruction by invasion, earthquake, famine, and other supernatural events. A solar eclipse in particular would initiate a response of fasting. The king in particular was likely concerned because the Enuma Anu Enlil predicted that "the king will be deposed and killed and a worthless fellow seize the throne...there will be a famine...a deity will strike the king and fire consume the land."[116] Wiseman cites historical and archaeological evidence that a solar eclipse did occur during Jeroboam's reign and Jonah's ministry. He also points to an earthquake and a famine that occurred around the same time. In addition, there were also significant rebellions that could explain the violence described in Jonah 3:8.[117] Wiseman argues that the Assyrian word *abāku* is even used of

---

[114] Stuart, *Hosea–Jonah*, 494–95. Italics in cited text.
[115] For a defense of the early date of Joel see Hobart E. Freeman, *An Introduction to the Old Testament Prophets* (Chicago, IL: Moody Press, 1969), 147–49.
[116] D. J. Wiseman, "Jonah's Nineveh," *Tyndale Bulletin* 30 (1979): 46.
[117] Ibid., 46–50.

impending judgment on the king during a solar eclipse as well as for forgiveness of an offense.[118] All of this evidence points to a strong explanation for why the Assyrians were more receptive to Jonah's message.

Lexical Features of Jonah 3:4–10

A lexical analysis of הָפַךְ will be performed in chapter three. For now, it is important to note that certain lexical features of Jonah 3:4 also point to the possibility of repentance. Stuart notes that both the Hebrew and Aramaic contain ambiguity in the wording:

> In Assyrian the full sentence would be rendered *adi arbāt ūmē ninua innabak*, as simple and as ambiguous as the Hebrew. The ambiguities would be threefold. First, as this word was passed around among the populace, it would not automatically be clear whether Jonah had warned only the enclosed city (*ᵃˡninua*) or the entire district (*ninuaᵏⁱ*) that it would be overthrown by God. Second, the people might wonder whether the mention of "forty days" was to allow time for or simply to assure that the divine judgment repentance, was not far off. Third, by nature Heb. הפך/Assyrian *abāku* carries a certain ambiguity. The term can signify an overthrow, a judgment, a turning upside down, a reversal, a change, a deposing of royalty, or a change of heart (Wiseman, *TynB* 30 [1979] 49). In other words, Jonah's words in Assyrian, just as in Hebrew, could mean both "In forty more days Nineveh will be overthrown" and "In forty more days Nineveh will have a change of heart" (cf. Good, *Irony in the OT*, 48–49). It must be remembered that these words are not what Jonah composed, but are exactly what Yahweh told him to say

---

[118] Ibid., 49. More discussion of Wiseman's lexical evidence will occur in chapter three.

(3:2). The alert hearer/reader who would catch the ambiguity would begin to sense what 3:5 then reports.[119]

It is critical to point out that הָפַךְ can mean both repentance and destruction. A lexical study of הָפַךְ validates Stuart's claims. *Brown Driver Briggs* lists some of the following definitions for הָפַךְ: "turn oneself, turn, turn back," "to be overturned, overthrown" as well as "to change (oneself)" and to "transform oneself."[120] It is not my contention that הָפַךְ only refers to repentance. The possibility of destruction is clearly present (cf. Jonah 3:10). However, the fact that the word can also describe repentance supports the argument that the prophecy of Jonah 3:4 was implicitly conditional and 100% fulfilled within forty days when the Ninevites repented. All but one of the 33 Old Testament occurrences of הָפַךְ in the niphal it means "turned" or "changed," but never "destroyed."[121]

In that sense, Jonah could not have chosen a better Hebrew word. Nixon writes:

> There are two things to note about the word "overthrown" (הָפַךְ). First, it is indissolubly linked in the biblical tradition with the overthrow of cities of Sodom and Gomorrah described in Genesis 19:21, 25, 29. By using this particular word, the story-teller reminds the hearers of an earlier cataclysmic event. It may awaken them a sense of justice having been done: as the cities of the plain got what was coming to them, so Nineveh deserved to be overthrown for her wickedness. However, the word equally means a turning upside-down, a reversal, a change, a deposing of royalty, or a change of heart.

---

[119] Stuart, *Hosea–Jonah*, 489. All emphasis his.
[120] Francis Brown, S. R. Driver, and Charles A. Briggs, *The Brown-Driver-Briggs Hebrew and English Lexicon* (Peabody, MA: Hendrickson Publishers, 2003; reprint, Seventh), 245–46.
[121] Lubeck, "Prophetic Sabotage: A Look at Jonah 3:2–4," 44.

Deuteronomy 23:5 reads, "The LORD your God turned (הָפַךְ) the curse into a blessing for you, because the LORD your God loved you." There are other examples of the word being used in this way. The message of Jonah could therefore be understood as meaning, "In forty days Nineveh will have a change of heart." As the Jewish expositor Rashi comments, "The word 'overthrown' has two senses, good and bad. If they do not repent, they will indeed be 'overthrown', for they will have changed from evil to good."[122]

As Nixon states, there is sufficient lexical evidence to support the double entendre of הָפַךְ intended by the author in Jonah 3:4. The same word is used in 1 Samuel 10:9, "Then it happened when he turned his back to leave Samuel, God changed his heart; and all those signs came about on that day." The previously cited definitions in *Brown Driver Briggs* demonstrate the possibility of הָפַךְ meaning transforming oneself or destruction.

One other interesting point is the fact that a double entendre of הָפַךְ was likely used on more than one occasion in Hosea 11:8:

> Though angry with His disobedient people, the Lord declared that He could never totally annihilate them. Though the covenant curses warned that disobedience would bring destruction so terrible it would rival that of Sodom and Gomorrah (cf. Deuteronomy 29:23), the Lord affirmed He could never go to such extremes. The Lord's compassion was stirred, preventing Him from wiping His people from the face of the earth (Hosea 11:8–9). This emotional change from rage to compassion is highlighted by a wordplay involving the Hebrew term *hāpak*, "turn

---

[122] Rosemary A. Nixon, *The Message of Jonah: Presence in the Storm* (Leicester, England; Downers Grove, IL: InterVarsity Press, 2003), 165.

over" (translated "changed" in Hosea 11:8). This is the same word used to describe God's overthrow (lit. "turning over") of Sodom and Gomorrah (cf. Genesis 19:24–25; Deuteronomy 29:23). However, in Hosea 11:8 it is God's compassion, not His people, that is "turned over" (or "changed").[123]

It is interesting that the same word is used as a double entendre by two different prophets writing around the same time period.

What is also interesting is that other Hebrew words commonly used for repentance and destruction are used in other places in Jonah. For instance, the word שׁוּב ("to turn, repent") is used in four instances (Jonah 1:13; Jonah 3:8–10). נָחַם ("to relent, to be sorrowful, to repent") is used of God three times (3:9–10, 4:2). Similarly, the narrator used the word for destruction within the book. For instance, Lubeck notes the term אָבַד ("to destroy") in Jonah 1:6 and 1:14 connotes perishing or destruction. Forms of the root are also used in Jonah 3:9 and 4:10.[124] However, in 3:4, the author uses a completely different word that is only used this time within the entire book. Consequently, if the author intended to write a word that only meant destruction, he would have probably elected to use אָבַד as he did before.

As previously mentioned, in contrast to Lubeck's argument, God may have intentionally left Jonah's message ambiguous because Jonah would be less likely to give a message that did not even include the possibility of destruction. Jonah may have decided to preach in hopes that the Ninevites would be destroyed. However, God elected to show mercy on them instead. Stuart writes about how they beat Jonah to the punch by repenting:

---

[123] Roy B. Zuck, Eugene H. Merrill, and Darrell L. Bock, *A Biblical Theology of the Old Testament* (Chicago, IL: Moody Press, 1991), 407. All emphasis in text.

[124] Lubeck, "Prophetic Sabotage: A Look at Jonah 3:2–4," 44.

Jonah was just beginning to warm up, just starting the process, and they were already believing God *en masse* (v 5). Thus, the mention of the first day of the visit and the silence about the other days eloquently makes the narrator's point. Jonah only had to start to go (ויחל לבו) into the city with his message that first day. The Ninevites needed only that initial word, so ready were they to turn from their evil practices. Jonah's words reached eager ears right away. And the Ninevites themselves repeated the message all over the city until it touched even the king (v 6). Three days of preaching by Jonah himself would not even be needed. Like the Hebrew women who gave birth before the midwives could arrive (Exodus 1:19), the Ninevites responded to God's message almost before the preacher could finish his speech![125]

Stuart makes a good point. While the Israelites had many prophets and they refused to repent, Jonah only had to deliver God's message to see repentance in the lives of the Ninevites.

From a theological perspective, this view best reconciles the issue of how God gave Jonah a prophecy that was one hundred percent accurate and one hundred percent fulfilled. Whether he liked it or not, Jonah faithfully communicated God's word. Good translated Jonah's prophecy in Jonah 3:4 as "Forty days hence and Nineveh will be a different place."[126] Good points out that this prophecy was fulfilled in Jonah 3:5 when as he translates it "the men of Nineveh turned faithful [וְיַאֲמִנוּ] towards God."[127] This would make God completely faithful and immutable while preserving Jonah as a true prophet. God's desire was to not bring calamity on Nineveh (Jonah 4:2) and by implication Israel. The Ninevites realized that they must turn

---

[125] Stuart, *Hosea–Jonah*, 488. All emphasis his.
[126] Good, *Irony in the Old Testament*, 49.
[127] Ibid.

from their wicked ways to avoid this calamity (cf. Jonah 3:8–9) and hopefully Israel would do the same. The nature of the polysemantic wordplay in this prophecy would be the equivalent of walking into a New Testament church and saying, "In forty days, this church will be broken." Although it is unlikely that anyone has the Biblical authority to prophesy in this nature in this dispensation, this illustration shows how the word broken could either describe a destruction of the physical church building or a turning of the heart. The Aramaic and the Hebrew carry the same ambiguity in Jonah 3:4. The need for repentance of the nations to avoid destruction was revealed not only to Jonah but also to Jeremiah (cf. Jeremiah 18:7–10). Thus, God's word remains consistent throughout. Jeremiah and Jonah are not in disagreement.

Structural Analysis of Jonah 3

A structural analysis of Jonah 3 allows for the possibility of both repentance and destruction being prophesied. Contrary to Lubeck's arguments that Jonah's message was altered due to consistent disobedience, Jonah's actions in Jonah 3 are the opposite of his actions in Jonah 1. Wendland shows the following comparison:

1:1:	And it came the word of Yahweh to Jonah the son of Amittai, saying
3:1:	And it came the word of Yahweh to Jonah a second time, saying
1:2:	"Arise, go to Nineveh, the great city, and preach against it, because their evil has come up before me."
3:2:	"Arise, go to Nineveh, the great city, and preach unto it the preaching that I am giving you."
1:3:	And Jonah arose to run away to Tarshish from before Yahweh.
3:3:	And Jonah arose and went to Nineveh according to the

word of Yahweh.[128]

Furthermore, Wendland argues for a chiastic structure in Jonah 3:

> A. Story + speech: Jonah's crusade—an ambiguous synopsis of the sermon: "Nineveh will be overturned," i.e. [+] the people will "turn over" in heart/repent, or [-] the city will be completely destroyed (3:4)
> > B. Story: the Ninevites believe the message and repent with fasting and sackcloth, presumably following the king's speech of B ' (3:5)
> > > C. Story: the extreme/ultimate instance—even the king repents, wearing sackcloth and sitting in ashes (3:6)
> > B '. Speech: the royal proclamation—the motive and means of the general repentance are specified, reiterating the word "call" [qārā] of B and featuring the key word "turn"[šûb] (3:7–9)
> A '. Story: Yahweh's reaction on seeing the penitence of Nineveh—no ambiguity: [+] he has compassion on the "turned over" people, and [-] he does not "overturn" the city (3:10)[129]

Wendland's analysis indicates that the structure of Jonah 3 and the entire book necessitate the possibility of repentance and destruction in Jonah's prophecy. Repentance is both at the focus of the chiastic structure of Jonah 3 as well as the message of the book.

---

[128] Ernst R. Wendland, "Text Analysis and the Genre of Jonah (Part 2)," *The Journal of the Evangelical Theological Society* 39, no. 3 (1996): 379.
[129] Ibid., 380.

CONCLUSION

This chapter reviewed Jonah 3:4 and determined that his prophecy was one hundred percent accurate and one hundred percent fulfilled by the end of Jonah 3. All other views either diminish the immutability of God, the complete fulfillment of the prophecy in kind and extent, or the reliability of Jonah as a prophet. Additionally, the Hebrew word הָפַךְ could mean both to destroy and to change. According to Lubeck, all but one of the thirty-three instances of הָפַךְ occurring in the niphal mean change or turn.[130] Thus, it is appropriate to conclude that God intentionally used implicit polysemantic wordplay in order to communicate the blessings of repentance and the curses of disobedience. This view is not only consistent with the context but the overall purpose of the book. On this basis, advocates of the open view of God and fallible prophecy should not use this passage to defend their claims.

---

[130] Lubeck, "Prophetic Sabotage: A Look at Jonah 3:2–4," 44.

CHAPTER 3

THE POLYSEMANTIC WORDPLAY OF JONAH 3:4

This book is advocating the polysemantic wordplay of הָפַךְ in Jonah 3:4. I argue that the word הָפַךְ in Jonah 3:4 was intended by both the human and divine author to serve as an implicit polysemantic wordplay because of the fact that the word could mean both repentance and destruction in the same context. Since both repentance and destruction were possible meanings of the word, the prophecy itself was implicitly conditioned upon the Ninevites' response to the prophecy. In this chapter I will provide a lexical analysis that supports the polysemantic wordplay view of Jonah 3:4.

LEXICAL ANALYSIS OF הָפַךְ

This lexical analysis will show that הָפַךְ can mean both repentance and destruction. I do not contend that the word only means repentance. The possibility of destruction is clearly present (cf. Jonah 3:10). However, the fact that the word can also describe repentance supports the argument that the prophecy of Jonah 3:4 utilizes polysemantic wordplay. As a result, this prophecy was fulfilled within the forty-day period of time when the Ninevites repented.

Proposed Translation of Jonah 3:1–10
This proposed translation of Jonah 3:1–10 incorporates

some of the ideas discussed in this book:

> And it happened the second time the word of THE LORD *came* to Jonah saying, "Arise, go to Nineveh, the great city, and announce to her the message which I am speaking to you." And Jonah arose and went to Nineveh according to the word of THE LORD and Nineveh was a city of importance (or greatness) to God, and *it was* a visit of three days. And He caused Jonah to begin to go into the city for a one day visit and he spoke, "Yet in forty days and Nineveh will be overturned." And the people of Nineveh believed in God and they called a fast and they put on sackcloths from the greatest to the least *of them*. And the word arrived to the king of Nineveh and he stood from his throne and he removed his robe from upon himself and he really covered *himself with* a sackcloth and he sat on the ashes. And the king caused it to be proclaimed by saying, "In Nineveh, by the decree of the king and his nobles, let neither human nor animal, cattle nor sheep, taste anything; let them not eat and do not let them drink water." "And let the man and the beast cover themselves with sackcloths and let them cry mightily to God and let everyone turn from their evil ways and from their violence which is in each one's hands. Who knows if God will be moved to pity and show favor and he will turn back from his fierce burning anger and we will not perish?" And God really saw their works, namely that they repented from their evil ways, and God was moved to compassion because of the calamity which He spoke to do to them and He did not do *it*.

This translation preserves the causative nature of God's speaking through Jonah by translating the hiphil חָלַל in verse four as "and He caused Jonah to begin to go." This causative statement argues against Lubeck, Cary and Trible's contention that Jonah spoke on his own accord. It also emphasizes the translation of the passive

נִחָםas "being moved to pity or compassion" in verses 9–10.[1]

Word Study of the Use of הָפַךְ in the Niphal

As previously mentioned, Lubeck notes that in all but one of the thirty-three OT occurrences of הָפַךְ in the niphal it means "turned" or "changed," but never "destroyed."[2] An examination of the usage of הָפַךְ in the niphal validates Lubeck's claims. Since the word appears in the niphal in Jonah 3:4, this study will begin with the uses in the niphal prior to expanding the word study to include other forms of the word as well as possible derivatives. This word study of the use of הָפַךְ in the niphal will demonstrate that the primary uses describe (1) a turn or change of objects or parts of the body (2) a turning or changing of people or God (3) a change of mind (i.e. repentance) or a transformation of person.

First, the niphal of הָפַךְ often describes the turning or changing of objects. In the Exodus accounts it describes the turning of the staff to a serpent (Exodus 7:15) and the water to blood (Exodus 7:17 and 20). In Leviticus 13:16, 17 and 25 the word is used of the changing of the skin in the examination of leprosy. Joel 2:31 discusses the changing of the sun to darkness and the moon to blood. Lamentations 5:2 describes the turning over of inheritance and houses to strangers. The book of Job uses the word five times (more than any other book) and three of those uses fall into this category: the turning of food in the stomach (Job 20:14), the turning of the earth by fire (Job 28:5),[3]

---

[1] For a very helpful linguistic analysis of נחם see H. Van Dyke Parunak, "A Semantic Survey of NHM," *Biblica* 56 (1975): 512–32.

[2] R. J. Lubeck, "Prophetic Sabotage: A Look at Jonah 3:2–4," *Trinity Journal* 9:1 (1988): 44.

[3] Alden discusses the meaning of this difficult passage as follows, "While vegetation grows on the surface, below ground miners turned the earth upside down, meaning that they exposed the insides of mountains. Lacking explosives and pneumatic hammers, ancient miners would crack the rock by heating it with "fire." Two other explanations are that this line refers to a volcanic eruption or to the miners' torches." For more information see Robert L. Alden, *Job*, vol. 11, 37 vols., The New

as well as the turning of slingstones to stubble (Job 41:28). Isaiah 34:9 also describes a change of the land. Isaiah 60:5 uses this word for the turning of the sea. Proverbs 17:20 discusses a person with a perverse or turning tongue. Jeremiah 30:6 uses the word for a face that turned pale. Lamentations 1:20 describes a heart that is turned within the author. Hosea 11:8 uses a similar expression for the turning of the heart within God as his compassion is kindled. Ezekiel 4:18 refers to God's prohibition of his prophet from turning from one side to the other as part of an illustration for Israel. One instance of the niphal form of הָפַךְ in the Psalms describes the vitality of the author being turned in the heat of the summer (Psalm 32:4).

The second use of the niphal of הָפַךְ is when a person is overcome by something. 1 Samuel 4:19 describes how Phinehas' wife's pain had overcome her. Daniel 10:8 and 16 use הָפַךְ to discuss the painful effects that overcame him when he had his vision.

The third major use of הָפַךְ in the niphal describes a change of direction of people. In Joshua 8:20 הָפַךְ is used in the niphal to describe a people who fled in the wilderness only to turn back from their pursuers. Esther 9:1 describes how the enemies' plans were turned to the contrary and in Esther 9:22 and how their emotions turned from sorrow to joy. Lamentations 5:15 has a similar use with the reverse effect: their dancing is turned to mourning. The book of Job uses הָפַךְ in the context of his friends turning against him (Job 19:19) as well as persecution from God (Job 30:21).

The fourth use of הָפַךְ describes a change of mind or direction which implies positive or negative repentance. While it is a subcategory of the third use, it is highlighted here because of its relevance for this study. Psalm 78:57 and Jeremiah 2:21 describe how the rebellious Israelites turned away from God

---

American Commentary (Nashville, TN: Broadman & Holman Publishers, 1993), 272.

(Psalm 78:57). This instance is like a repentance away from God instead of towards Him. Exodus 14:15 describes the fact that Pharaoh's mind "was changed toward the people." This usage directly describes a change of mind. Another use that confirms the notion of transformation as part of the semantic range of הָפַךְ is 1 Samuel 10:6, "Then the Spirit of the LORD will come upon you mightily, and you shall prophesy with them and be changed [וְנֶהְפַּכְתָּ] into another man." This shows a prophesied transformation that would take place when the Spirit of the LORD came upon Saul.

This analysis of the use of הָפַךְ in the niphal confirms Lubeck's conclusion that the niphal never specifically means destroyed in the Old Testament. While a word study like this should not be the basis of an illegitimate totality transfer, one must note that dismissing the possibility of repentance in Jonah 3:4 would go against the majority of the uses of הָפַךְ in the niphal throughout the Hebrew Bible. In order to assert that the word only means destruction, one will need to have irrefutable lexical and contextual proof to validate that claim. The next section will expand the discussion to other aspects of הָפַךְ in order to evaluate the semantic range of the word so that the author's intended meaning can be ascertained.

Analysis of the Use of הָפַךְ as a Participle
In addition to being in the niphal form, הָפַךְ appears in Jonah 3:4 as a participle. הָפַךְ occurs several times in the Bible as a participle (cf. Genesis 3:24, Judges 7:13, Job 37:12, Psalm 114:8, Proverbs 17:20 and Amos 5:7f). In the majority of those cases, it means "to turn." Genesis 3:24 describes how the cherubim turned every way to guard the way to the tree of life. Judges 7:13 depicts a tent that turned upside down. Job 37:10 illustrates the turning of the lightning by the guidance of God. Psalm 114:8 portrays God's turning the rock into a pool of water. Amos 5:7 describes those who turn justice into wormwood. Amos 5:8 explains the change from deep darkness into morning. Proverbs 17:20 discusses an individual with a perverted (or

turned) mind. Thus, each use of הָפַךְ in the participle form points to turning or changing direction while none of them indicate destruction.

With respect to the grammatical function of the participle, Waltke and O'Connor say:

> With reference to situations which are in fact *future*, the participle may denote merely a circumstance accompanying a future event (# 31). Usually, however, it denotes the full range of ideas connoted by English 'I am going to...,' namely, certainty, often with immanency—the so-called *futurum instans* participle (## 32–37). In this function it also occurs in a main clause with some logical connection to other clauses (## 38–41) or in a temporal/conditional clause in connection with a future event (## 42–44).[4]

Hence, in the futuristic context, the participle usually indicates immediate fulfillment.[5] The use of the adversative עוֹד and the temporal indicator of forty days would also support that conclusion.[6] These indicators make the latter fulfillment view improbable. In light of this immanent expectation of future fulfillment, the only immediate action is the repentance of the

---

[4] Bruce K. Waltke and Michael Patrick O'Connor, *An Introduction to Biblical Hebrew Syntax* (Winona Lake, IN: Eisenbrauns, 1990), 627. All emphasis theirs. See also W. Dennis Tucker, *Jonah: A Handbook on the Hebrew Text*, Baylor Handbook on the Hebrew Bible Series (Waco, TX: Baylor University Press, 2006), 70–71. Tucker suggests the *futurum instans* participle may give the connotation of "I am going to."
[5] Baldwin agrees when she says, "The niphal participle of הָפַךְ (to turn, overturn) indicates the impending future, as in 3:2." See Joyce Baldwin, "Jonah," *The Minor Prophets: An Exegetical and Expository Commentary*, ed. Thomas Edward McComiskey (Grand Rapids, MI: Baker Academic, 2009), 577.
[6] Biblical Studies Press, *The NET Bible*, First Edition (Biblical Studies Press, 2005), 1735.

Ninevites in Jonah 3:5. Lessing agrees when he says:

> Participles are often used for imminent actions that will take place soon, so they can be described "as being already in progress" (Joüon, § 121e).... Since the change in Nineveh starts to take place (see 3:5–10) as soon as the words leave Jonah's lips, the best translation is "Nineveh is about to be changed." Jonah may well have hoped or expected that no change would take place in Nineveh until it would be destroyed forty days hence. However, Yahweh could foresee that the change in Nineveh (repentance) would begin immediately by the power of his preached Word, and Yahweh had instructed Jonah to use these exact words in his sermon (see 3:2).[7]

Lessing's point is helpful. The participle is used for something that is imminent and very shortly to take place (which would counteract the common argument that Jonah's prophecy is just a warning absent of any expectation of literal prophetic fulfillment[8]). Joüon cites Genesis 19:13 as an example of the future use of this participle.[9] Genesis 19:13 says in the NASB, "for we are about to destroy this place, because their outcry has become so great before the LORD that the LORD has sent us to

---

[7] R. Reed Lessing, *Jonah*, Concordia Commentary (St. Louis, MO: Concordia Publishing House, 2007), 282.

[8] See Richard D. Phillips, *Jonah & Micah*, Reformed Expository Commentary (Phillipsburg, NJ, 2010), 100. John F. Walvoord, "Millennial Series: Part 13: The Abrahamic Covenant and Premillennialism," *Bibliotheca Sacra* 109, no. 433 (1952): 42. Additionally, when Jesus mentioned this situation He pointed to Jonah as a prophet (cf. Matthew 12:39), which gives evidence to the argument that Jonah 3:4 was predictive prophecy and not simply a warning with no expected fulfillment.

[9] Paul Joüon and T. Muraoka, *A Grammar of Biblical Hebrew*, Rev. English ed., vol. 2, 2 vols. (Roma: Editrice Pontificio Istituto Biblico, 2003), 410.

destroy it." This reference is interesting because it is used of the imminent destruction of Sodom. However, here it is used of the possible destruction of Nineveh or the repentance of Nineveh. As Lessing points out, the Ninevites were already in the process of being prepared by God for this repentance. They repented within the forty-day period of time and thus fulfilled the prophecy.

Additionally, the participle also can serve as a temporal/conditional clause. Thus, the participial use can indicate an implicit condition. This is evidenced by the fact that Jonah waits in Jonah 4 in order to see whether destruction will still take place. Jonah also states that when he initially received the prophecy, he recognized that God was compassionate and that he expected for him to relent concerning the calamity. Either way, Jonah apparently expected an immediate fulfillment of the prophecy.

Analysis of the Passive Voice of הָפֻךְ

The word נֶהְפָּכֶת is in the passive voice. According to Cary, the passive voice is very significant because it does not precisely identify who will do the overturning:

> Yet even in this extraordinarily brief message there are indications that things are not what they seem. To begin with, nothing is said about who will overturn Nineveh. There is no mention of the Lord or even of some generalized concept of a wrathful deity or indeed of any agent or cause of Nineveh's overturning.... An active voice sentence would require Jonah to say *who* will overturn Nineveh. It is not characteristic of the God of the Bible to be evasive about this kind of issue.[10]

Cary suggests that Jonah intentionally left the message vague.

---

[10] Phillip Cary, *Jonah*, Brazos Theological Commentary on the Bible, ed. R. R. Reno (Grand Rapids, MI: Brazos Press, 2008), 109.

Cary's conclusion that Jonah altered the message is flawed, but the passive voice does not specifically identify who will do the overturning which adds to the ambiguity of the prophecy. The ambiguous passive voice lends credibility to the idea that the prophecy includes two options for fulfillment. The Ninevites recognized that they might be destroyed by God (Jonah 3:9). However, the possibility remained that they would be overturned and their hearts would be changed by God as Saul's was in 1 Samuel 10:26.

Word Study in Additional Forms

The Hebrew word הָפַךְ occurs over 90 times in the Hebrew Bible. The root and its derivatives occur 118 times in the Old Testament.[11] הָפַךְ occurs most often in the qal stem (55 times) and the niphal is the second most frequent usage (34). הָפַךְ occurs in the hophal and hithpael as well. This expanded word study will show that the use of הָפַךְ in the entire Old Testament leaves both the possibility of repentance and destruction.

For instance. the *Hebrew Aramaic Lexicon of the Old Testament* defines הָפַךְ as:

- Qal: 1) to turn 2) to turn upside down, overthrow 3) to turn back to the front 4) to change or to alter 5) intransitive to turn around
- Nifal: 1) to turn against 2) to be demolished, overthrown [citing Jonah 3:4] 3) to be changed, altered in heart 4) miscellaneous [for example, to come upon, to fail to function, etc.]
- Hofal: 1) to be turned upon
- Hitphael: 1) to turn round and round 2) to transform

---

[11] R. Laird Harris, Gleason Leonard Archer, and Bruce K. Waltke, *Theological Wordbook of the Old Testament* (Chicago, IL: Moody Press, 1980), 221.

oneself[12]

One will notice that the basic meaning of is הָפַךְ to turn or change but the implications of the word can focus on both repentance and/or destruction (as indicated by the verses listed in the *Hebrew Aramaic Lexicon of the Old Testament*).

The variety of meanings for הָפַךְ are reflected in several other passages. For instance, the author of Jonah is not the only author who exploits the polysemantic nature of הָפַךְ for a wordplay. הָפַךְ is used with a polysemantic wordplay in the qal form in 1 Samuel 10:9 to illustrate how God changed Saul's heart. 1 Samuel 10:9 can literally be translated as, "As Saul turned (כְּהַפְנֹתוֹ) his back to leave Samuel, God turned (וַיַּהֲפָךְ־לוֹ) his heart." Psalm 105:25 shows how God turned the Egyptians heart to hate his people. With respect to destruction, הָפַךְ is used in the qal form in Genesis 19:21 and 25 to explain God's plans to overthrow Sodom and Gomorrah. Genesis 19:29 is very interesting because it says that God destroyed Sodom and Gomorrah (בְּשַׁחֵת) and overturned it (בַּהֲפֹךְ). The author has to use בְּשַׁחֵת to clarify that בַּהֲפֹךְ means destruction. Lamentations 4:6 and Amos 4:11 also discuss the overthrow of Sodom and Gomorrah. Deuteronomy 29:23 portrays the cities of Admah, and Zeboim which God overthrew (הָפַךְ) in His wrath. Second Samuel 10:3 depicts a city that David intended to overthrow (cf. 1 Chronicles 19:3). Jeremiah 20:6 uses the word הָפַךְ while discussing the towns that the Lord overthrew without pity.

The uses of הָפַךְ for an overthrow of a city are frequent enough that a Hebrew audience would have recognized the possibility of destruction in the word. Simon writes:

> Not only does the verb *h-f-k* connote utter and complete destruction (for example,, "he *overturns* mountains by the

---

[12] Ludwig Köhler et al., *The Hebrew and Aramaic Lexicon of the Old Testament*, Study ed., vol. 1, 2 vols. (Leiden, Netherlands; Boston, MA: Brill, 2001), 253–54.

roots" [Job 28:9]; see also 2 Kings 21:13); it also particularly calls to mind the categorical punishment of Sodom and Gomorrah on account of their grave sins (cf. "just like the upheaval of Sodom and Gomorrah, Admah and Zeboiim, which the LORD *overturned* in His fierce anger" [Deuteronomy 29:22]; also Genesis 19:21 and 29; Isaiah 13:19; Jeremiah 49:18; Amos 4:11; Lamentations 4:6). In the prophet's mind (and readers' ears), this comparison of Nineveh with Sodom reinforces the earlier one, "for their wickedness has come up before Me."[13]

The fact that the same word was used of Sodom and Gomorrah provides an interesting parallel. In Genesis, Abraham prayed for the deliverance of the wicked city. Jonah hopes for the destruction of wicked Nineveh.

Word Study in Derivative Forms

There are several key derivative forms of the word הָפַךְ: הֵפֶךְ, הֲפֵכָה, הַפְכְפַּךְ, מַהְפֶּכֶת, מַהְפֵּכָה, and תַהְפֻּכָה. The derivative forms have a semantic range of a difference or turning, destruction, perversity and an exception use of stocks. The first word, הֵפֶךְ, is used twice in Ezekiel 16:34 to describe a woman who was different from most prostitutes in that she paid to be the harlot whereas most harlots are paid to be a harlot. The concept of perversity can also be found in that use. Isaiah 29:16 uses the word to describe how Israel turns or reverses things in that the clay is disputing with the potter with regard to how the nation was formed. The second word, הֲפֵכָה, clearly communicates destruction when showing how Lot was sent in the midst of the overthrow in Genesis 19:29. The same is true of מַהְפֵּכָה which consistently means to overthrow or destroy and most often refers to Sodom and Gomorrah (cf. Isaiah 13:19, Jeremiah 50:40, Amos

---

[13] Uriel Simon, *Jonah*, JPS Bible Commentary (Philadelphia, PA: Jewish Publication Society, 1999), 29. Emphasis his.

4:11, *et al.*). The next word, הַפַכְפַּךְ, is used in Proverbs 21:8 to describe a man whose way is crooked. Another word, מַהְפֶּכֶת, refers to stocks or blocks for prisoners (cf. Jeremiah 20:2–3; 29:26; 2 Chronicles 16:10). The final word, תַּהְפֻּכָה, occurs eight out of nine times in the book of Proverbs (cf. 2:12; 10:31–32; 16:30) and it primarily carries the connotation of perversity. Perhaps one of the more famous uses of this word is in Deuteronomy 32:20 which speaks of the perverse generation in whom there is no faithfulness. Thus, a summary of the related derivative words does not include the concept of repentance but primarily focuses on destruction and perversity. The most consistent cases of destruction relate to Sodom and Gomorrah.

Word Study in Other Languages

The Hebrew Aramaic Lexicon of the Old Testament lists several related words in other languages. The related Ugaritic word is *hpk*. The Arabic word *àafaka* means to distort or lie. The Akkadian word *abâku* means "to carry away." The related Akkadian word *abiktu* means to defeat.[14] The Arabic word seems to relate to the concept of perversity or distortion found in the derivative forms. The related words in the Akkadian lend themselves more to the possibility of destruction.

The Septuagint version of Jonah 3:4 uses the word καταστραφήσεται which is a form of καταστρέφω. This word is used to translate the Hebrew word הָפַךְ on several occasions (cf. Genesis 19:21, 25, 29; Deuteronomy 29:22; 2 Kings 21:13; Job 9:5; 12:15; 28:9; Amos 4:11; Jonah 3:4; Haggai 2:22; Jeremiah 20:16; Lamentations 4:6). In each of those occasions the concept of destruction is implied. This word is used several times in the Septuagint with regards to the overthrow or destruction of Sodom and Gomorrah (cf. Genesis 13:10; 19:21, 25, 29; Deuteronomy 29:22; Lamentations 4:6, *et al.*). The word is used

---

[14] Köhler et al., *The Hebrew and Aramaic Lexicon of the Old Testament*, 253.

throughout the Septuagint to describe the destruction of cities (for example, 2 Kings 21:13, Malachi 1:4, Isaiah 1:7, etc). In the New Testament, καταστρέφω is used to describe Jesus' overturning of the moneychangers' tables (Matthew 21:12 and Mark 11:15). Within the Apocrypha, the Greek word also implies destruction (cf. Sirach 10:13, 16; 27:3; 28:14, 2 Maccabees 9:28, etc). One interesting use occurs in Tobit 14:4 which is translated in the King James Version of the Apocrypha:

> Go into Media my son, for I surely believe those things which Jonas the prophet spake of Nineve, that it shall be overthrown; and that for a time peace shall rather be in Media; and that our brethren shall lie scattered in the earth from that good land: and Jerusalem shall be desolate, and the house of God in it shall be burned, and shall be desolate for a time.

In Tobit 14:4 use of the Greek word καταστρέφω in Jonah 3:4 points to destruction. Thus, the Septuagint translation of Jonah 3:4 strongly supports the meaning of destruction for הָפַךְ.

καταστρέφω is not, however, the only word used to translate הָפַךְ in the Septuagint. There are several instances when it is translated in the Septuagint by στρέφω. According to Kittel, forms of the word are used in the attic to mean "'to twist,' then 'to turn,' 'bend,' 'steer.'"[15] Plato used the word as follows, "education is called a turning (par. περιάγω) of the soul to the brightest being, the good."[16] In the Septuagint, forms of στρέφω can "refer to inner conversion through suffering or fear" and it "forms a starting-point for the concept of conversion."[17] It also

---

[15] *Theological Dictionary of the New Testament*, trans. Geoffrey William Bromiley, vol. 7, 10 vols., ed. Gerhard Kittel and Gerhard Friedrich (Grand Rapids, MI: W.B. Eerdmans, 1985), 714.
[16] Ibid.
[17] Ibid.

refers to God's turning the hearts of his people to himself.[18]

Direct translations of הָפַךְ in the Septuagint with forms of the word στρέφω do point to the possible meaning of change or repentance that Kittel proposes. 1 Samuel 10:6 describes when Saul is changed into another man. Lamentations 1:20 utilizes στρέφω for a heart that is turned within the author as he acknowledges his rebelliousness of Jerusalem. In some instances, μεταστρέφω is used in the Septuagint to translate הָפַךְ as a change of heart (cf. Exodus 14:5, 1 Samuel 10:9 and Psalm 105:25).

On other occasions, forms of the word στρέφω reflect other meanings. In Genesis 3:24, הָפַךְ is translated by στρέφω as a sword that turned in every direction. The Septuagint of Nehemiah 13:2 uses στρέφω for the turning of a curse into a blessing. Psalm 77:9 describes how the sons of Ephraim turned in the day of battle. Lamentations 5:15 describes a dance that is turned to mourning. Isaiah 63:10 describes how God turns into Israel's enemy. In Isaiah 34:9, destruction is implied. Brenton translates the Septuagint as, "And her valleys shall be turned into pitch, and her land into sulphur; and her land shall be as pitch burning night and day."[19] Job 34:25 also uses στρέφω to translate הָפַךְ in a destructive context as Brenton's translation of the Septuagint reads, "Who discovers their works, and will bring night about *upon them*, and they shall be brought low [the King James Version translates the word in this verse as destroyed]."[20] Thus, forms of the word στρέφω can be used in the Septuagint for both repentance and destruction.

Other variations of the root word στρέφω are used to translate הָפַךְ. For instance, ἀποστρέφω is used when discussing

---

[18] Ibid., 715.
[19] Lancelot Charles Lee Brenton, *The Septuagint Version of the Old Testament. With an English Translation, and with Various Readings and Critical Notes* (Grand Rapids, MI: Zondervan Pub. House, 1971), 868.
[20] Ibid., 691. Emphasis in translation.

David's men retracing their steps (cf. 1 Samuel 25:12). ἀποστρέφω is also used when the Queen of Sheba returned to her land (2 Chronicles 9:12) as well as the turning back of the Israelites (Psalm 78:57). The word ἐπιστρέφω is used when describing turning around in battle (Judges 20:41, 1 Kings 22:34, 2 Kings 9:23, 2 Chronicles 18:33, *et al.*) as well as the turning of the hand of God (Lamentations 3:3). The word διαστρέφω is used in Job 37:12 to describe a change of direction of the cloud.

In Exodus 7:20, the Greek word μεταβάλλω is used to describe the changing of the water to blood as it is in several other instances (Exodus 7:17, 20; 10:19; Leviticus 13:3f, 10, 13, 16f, 20, 25, 55; Joshua 7:8; Isaiah 60:5). For the most part, μεταβάλλω is used to translate הָפַךְ when describing the changing or transformation of objects.

There are some Greek words that only occasionally translate הָפַךְ. In Job 41:28, ἡγέομαι is used to describe the slingstones that are turned into stubble. In Proverbs 17:20, the Greek word εὐμετάβολος is used for the changing or perverse tongue.

The analysis of the various translations of הָפַךְ in the Septuagint points to an understanding of both destruction/overthrow as well as a change of heart by the Jewish translators. This helps substantiate the polysemantic wordplay view of Jonah 3:4.

One might get the impression from Tobit 14:4 that the Jewish audience would have only understood the prophecy of Jonah 3:4 as pointing to destruction. According to Wiseman, a Jewish audience would likely recognize the possibility of both repentance and destruction implied by the word הָפַךְ. He writes that this prophecy would "remind his Jewish hearers of the sudden overthrow of a city such as Sodom (Genesis 19:21,25,29; cf. Deuteronomy 29:23), or of a people (Ammon, 2 Samuel 10:3) or of the wicked in general (Amos 4:11). They would realize that the word is primarily used of a change whether of throne

(Haggai 2:27) or of attitude, heart or situation."²¹ Like Lubeck, Wiseman sees a unique way in which the niphal of is הָפַךְ used in Jonah 3:4, "Only here is the Niphal נֶהְפָּכֶת used of the overthrow of a city and its use may involve overtones or even a play of meanings with 'upheaval' and 'change of heart', of which the prophet was later to accuse Yahweh."²²

Some early Jewish works also recognize the wordplay of נֶהְפָּכֶת. An interesting statement is made in the Babylonian Talmud Sanhedrin 89B regarding Jonah's situation:

> But perhaps the decree was changed by Heaven? If it were so, all the prophets would be notified. But was not such the case with Jonah who was not notified that the decree was changed? There was the prophecy: Nineveh will be overthrown which had two meanings, to be destroyed and also to be turned over from evil to righteousness, and he did not understand the real meaning."²³

Although Tobit 14:4 points to a Jewish recognition of destruction, the Babylonian Talmud picks up on the possibility of polysemantic wordplay in Jonah 3:4. Chapter 46 verse 186 of Pseudo-Philo's *De Jonah* also states that the city was not destroyed but the hearts of the Ninevites were changed.²⁴ Additionally, Rabbi Shlomo Yitzhaki (1040-1105) acknowledges that נֶהְפָּכֶת can "be used in two different ways, bad and good. If

---

²¹ D.J. Wiseman, "Jonah's Nineveh," *Tyndale Bulletin* 30 (1979): 48–49.
²² Ibid.
²³ Michael L. Rodkinson, *The Babylonian Talmud: Tract Sanhedrin* (Whitefish, MT: Kessinger Publishing, 2004), 255.
²⁴ Beate Ego, "The Repentance of Nineveh in the Story of Jonah and Nahum's Prophecy of the City's Destruction – A Coherent Reading of the Book of the Twelve as Reflected in the Aggada," in *Thematic Threads in the Book of the Twelve*, ed. Paul L. Redditt and Aaron Schart (Berlin, Germany; New York, NY: Walter de Gruyter, 2003), 158.

they do not repent, Nineveh will be 'overturned.' If they do repent, then that which was proclaimed concerning the people will be 'overturned.'"²⁵ Isaac Abarbanel (1437-1508) alludes to the multiple meanings of הָפַךְ in Lamentations 1:20 and Genesis 19:29 to prove that the term can refer to "destruction like the destruction of Sodom and Gomorrah...since the word *nehepachet* includes both meanings, overturned and destroyed."²⁶ If Jewish commentators understood the double entendre, one should not be surprised that the original audience would have understood it.

Not only would the Hebrew audience have understood the polysemantic wordplay, but Wiseman argues that the Assyrians would have as well. He writes:

> An Assyrian hearer would also interpret Jonah's prophecy or omen (adi arbât ūmē ᵃˡninuaᵏⁱ innabak) in a similar ambivalent way. Abāku was used for both "to overthrow, bring judgment, take away (of men and animals)" and "to turn upside down"; in the Niph'al "to be reversed, change of behaviour and judgment on sin." It is so used in an apodosis relating to a solar eclipse ("the king will be driven from the throne") and in the latter sense "I forgave (changed, reversed) his countless sins and disregarded his offence." Such a double meaning or word play on "overturn" and "change of heart" of which that prophet was to accuse Yahweh (ch. 4) would also be in the minds of the Assyrian wise men. This old view has much to commend it and it is not for us today to think it

---

²⁵ Steven Bob, *Go to Nineveh: Medieval Jewish Commentaries on the Book of Jonah* (Eugene, Oregon: Pickwick Publications, 2013) 14. Emphasis in original text. Bolded words represent translation of original words. Text that is not bolded represents comments by author Steven Bob.
²⁶ Ibid., 98. Emphasis in original text. See footnote 264 for explanation.

"oversubtle."[27]

This insight (which was also mentioned by Stuart) makes the irony of the situation even more likely. Not only could the Hebrew author have recorded the polysemantic wordplay but the original audience of the prophecy as well as the Hebrew audience of the book would have perfectly understood it.

Alternate Words Used in Jonah

It should be argued that the word that Jonah used in Jonah 3:4 (הָפַךְ) left the possibility for repentance or destruction. The use in the niphal throughout the Old Testament points to transformation or change. The other uses of the word as well as the derivative forms and the other languages indicate destruction. This book also investigates the other words used throughout Jonah that directly mean repentance or destruction. If the author of Jonah solely intended to imply either meaning, he could have used other words that previously occur in the book.

It is important to note that both of the Hebrew words commonly used for "repent" are used in other places within Jonah. For instance, the word שׁוּב is used in four instances (Jonah 1:13; Jonah 3:8–10). נָחַם is used of God three times (3:9–10, 4:2) with the idea of relenting. There is a very interesting wordplay that makes up Jonah 3:8–4:2. In Jonah 3:8, the Ninevite king gives a proclamation that everyone should turn (שׁוּב) from his wicked and violent ways. His hope is that God will turn (שׁוּב) and relent (נָחַם) from His anger so they do not perish (אָבַד). God sees the Ninevites' repentance from their actions (שׁוּב) and he relents (נָחַם) from the disaster (רָעָה) that He said would come upon them. In Jonah 4, he gets angry at God for being so compassionate and relenting (נחם) from disaster.

Similarly, the narrator uses the word for destruction

---

[27] Wiseman, "Jonah's Nineveh," 49.

within the book. For instance, Jonah uses the term אָבַד in Jonah 1:6 and 1:14 in the dialogue that the sailors have of their hope to receive God's deliverance from perishing. In Jonah 3:9, the Ninevites express their hope that perhaps God will also deliver them from perishing in response to their perishing. In Jonah 4:10, Yahweh describes how Jonah expressed pity for the plant which perished in the night. However, in 3:4, he uses a completely different word that is only used this time within the entire book. Consequently, if the narrator intended to write a word that only meant destruction, he would have probably elected to use אָבַד as he did before.

SUMMARY

This chapter provided a word study of the Hebrew word הָפַךְ in the same form throughout the Bible (niphal), multiple forms, derivative forms, other languages, and contrasted it with words that were used in the book. The basic conclusion is that the word הָפַךְ can mean either repentance or destruction. The most common use in the niphal is to turn, change or transform. The concept of repentance occurs in select circumstances. Aside from the consideration of Jonah 3:4, הָפַךְ never means destroy in an exclusive sense in the niphal form. In other forms, the semantic range goes from repentance, transformation, or change, to destruction. The word basically connotes the idea of turning. In derivative forms the concept of destruction is emphasized more. In the Septuagint, the translations of הָפַךְ indicate a turning of heart, people or objects as well as destruction. According to Stuart and Wiseman, the original Assyrian word abāku would have implied both repentance and destruction. In light of the other Hebrew words within Jonah that mean repent or destroy, this word which was only used one time was likely selected for its ability to serve as an ironic polysemantic wordplay. Therefore, based on the lexical meaning, the possibility of a polysemantic wordplay in Jonah 3:4 is strong. The next chapter will evaluate whether the immediate and larger context will allow for this possibility.

CHAPTER 4

CONTEXT AS EVIDENCE FOR IMPLICIT CONDITIONALITY

The third chapter analyzed the lexical context of הָפַךְ in order to assess the potential for implicit polysemantic wordplay. Of course, a word study alone will not settle the matter. One must also be able to prove contextually that a polysemantic wordplay of הָפַךְ was intended by the original author. Walvoord's methodology for interpreting prophecy as well as Grice's category of occasional meaning require an exploration of the immediate and larger context. This chapter will explore the immediate context of Jonah as well as the larger context of the historical background of Jonah, the purpose of Jonah, the message of Jonah and the genre of Jonah in order to establish an implicit polysemantic wordplay of הָפַךְ in Jonah 3:4.

THE IMMEDIATE CONTEXT

Jonah contains several indicators that demonstrate the implicit conditionality of Jonah 3:4. While an implicit polysemantic wordplay of נֶהְפָּכֶת is one indicator, other contextual clues exist that point to the implicit conditionality of Jonah 3:4. One would likely be able to prove textual indicators for implicit conditionality of Jonah 3:4 with or without the polysemantic wordplay of הָפַךְ. However the polysemantic wordplay does strengthen the case for the implicit conditionality of Jonah 3:4 and the fulfillment of the prophecy in Jonah 3:4. This chapter explores those clues by exploring the immediate context of Jonah 3. The narrator, the Ninevites, Jonah, and Yahweh all give indications of the conditionality of Jonah 3:4.

The Word of the Lord Given to Jonah

Unlike the other views cited in chapter two, a contextual and lexical analysis points to an accurate prophecy that was fulfilled by the end of Jonah 3. In order to uncover the exact message that God gave to Jonah, one must understand how the narrator of Jonah describes the prophecy. In the New American Standard Version, the phrase the "word of the Lord" is used three times (Jonah 1:1; 3:1, 3). The word of the Lord is most likely a subjective genitive that could literally be translated as "the Lord said." Against Trible and Lubeck's assertion that Jonah did not proclaim the word of the Lord is the representation of the Aramaic Targum of this prophecy, "There was a word of prophecy from the Lord" (cf. Hosea 1:1)."[1] The word that was given in Jonah 1:1 and 3:1 was extremely similar as noted by Stuart:

> Where בן אמתי "son of Amittai" stood in 1:1, שנית "a second time" stands in 3:1. Otherwise the verses are identical. If one has listened or read carefully, there can be no doubt that the story is, as it were, starting over. Once again Jonah has heard the word of Yahweh. Jonah is back where it all started. His attempted flight had no effect.[2]

This shows that despite Jonah's reluctance to preach God's word, God's desire to use Jonah as his spokesman had not changed. In 1:2, the word of the Lord is for Jonah to "Arise, go to Nineveh the great city, and cry against it, for their wickedness has come up before Me." In Jonah 3:2, God says, "Arise, go to

---

[1] Biblical Studies Press, *The NET Bible*, First Edition (Biblical Studies Press, 2005), 1728.
[2] Douglas K. Stuart, *Hosea–Jonah*, vol. 31, 52 vols., Word Biblical Commentary (Waco, TX: Word Books, 1987), 482.

Nineveh the great city and proclaim to it the proclamation which I am going to tell you." In English, as well as the Hebrew, the cautious reader can note that while the same verb "proclaim" is used (קְרָא), there is a shift from the proclamation again in 1:2 (וּקְרָא עָלֶיהָ) to proclaim to (וּקְרָא אֵלֶיהָ).[3] This shift from the adversative phrase to a more positive position demonstrates God's intentions to forgive the Ninevites if they were willing to repent.[4] Also the wickedness of Nineveh is not emphasized in Jonah 3:2 as it was in Jonah 1:2. Instead, the narrator focuses on the fact that Jonah was told this a second time (3:1) and that He is to proclaim the proclamation God gave him. Stuart analyzes these differences as follows:

> Nothing essential has changed in the divine command except that the mention of Nineveh's trouble in 1:2 is now no longer necessary, and more attention is paid to the fact that Jonah must obediently preach exactly what he is given to say. If anything, this new injunction ("speak to it the speech which I will say to you") reminds Jonah that he has no option but to obey. The style of the command is terse *figura etymologica* (like that of וייראו יראה "and they feared a fear" in 1:10, 16, etc.; cf. Jepsen, *Wort-Gebot-Glaube*, 298). Jonah has already learned that he cannot escape Yahweh's call to Nineveh. Now he is reminded that he cannot hope to influence or adjust the message Yahweh will give him. He must resign himself to the fact that Yahweh is concerned for Nineveh.[5]

As Stuart mentions, Jonah learned the hard way that he cannot escape God's sovereign command.[6] Not even his attempts to run

---

[3] Biblical Studies Press, *The NET Bible*, 1735.
[4] Ibid.
[5] Stuart, *Hosea–Jonah*, 482. Emphasis his.
[6] God's sovereignty is demonstrated throughout the book of Jonah. This would also argue against the open view of God. God sovereignly controls

away and die allow him to avoid this call. Instead, he is resigned to proclaim the proclamation that God called him to proclaim. God gives him a second chance and emphasizes the importance of obeying this time.

Not only that, but the word הַקְּרִיאָה is a fairly neutral term that does not necessarily imply destruction. Lessing writes:

> This noun is only used here in the OT. It is a neutral term in that it does not indicate whether the content of the message is judgment or salvation. If a judgment oracle were intended here, one might have expected a term such as מַשָּׂא, "oracle," which is often used to introduce judgment oracles to Gentile nations (see, for example, Isaiah 13:1; 15:1; 17:1; 19:1; 21:1), including an oracle against Nineveh (Nahum 1:1). Therefore, like the change from עַל to אֶל... the use of this term too may subtly prepare us for the unexpected salvation of Nineveh.[7]

Stuart agrees:

> It is important to note that he still does not know for sure whether or not God will spare the city. Concern does not equal a guarantee of grace. The same technical ambiguity found in 1:2 prevails here also. The content of the speech (קְרִיאָה) itself is left unspecified. Neither Jonah nor the hearer/reader knows yet—regardless of how strong their suspicions may be—if the city will actually be punished or destroyed. We find out in 3:4 that the speech he must give is indeed richly ambiguous, requiring a precise

---

the circumstances throughout the book in order to ensure that His message will be preached by Jonah (for example, through the large fish, etc.). It is hard to imagine that a God who is that sovereign would be waiting for humans to determine how they will respond to Him.

[7] R. Reed Lessing, *Jonah*, Concordia Commentary (St. Louis, MO: Concordia Pub. House, 2007), 271.

wording. Jonah, in other words, is here commanded to say *exactly* and *only* what Yahweh will tell him to say. He is held to a tight leash in terms of his verbal freedom.⁸

At this point, by the author's design, the reader is uncertain what the message of Jonah's prophecy will be. However, there are clear indications that Jonah will obey this time.

After hearing God's word in 3:2, the narrator says that Jonah "arose and went according to the word of the Lord" (Jonah 3:2). The words "arose and went" correspond in Hebrew as well as English with the command to arise and go in Jonah 1:2 and Jonah 3:2. Jonah's obedience could not be described more clearly. Lessing also mentions that the word דְּבַר is in the construct form with the Tetragrammaton with the preposition כְּ which would emphasize Jonah's conformity to Yahweh's standard.⁹ Lessing refers to several instances in the Old Testament when this phrase describes "how believers faithfully carry out a divine mandate."¹⁰ Jonah 4:2 also gives an indication of what God asked Jonah to do even though it does not specifically use the phrase "the word of the Lord." Jonah 4:2 says:

> And he prayed to the LORD and said, "Please LORD, was not this what I said while I was still in my own country? Therefore, in order to forestall this I fled to Tarshish, for I knew that Thou art a gracious and compassionate God, slow to anger and abundant in lovingkindness, and one who relents concerning calamity."

Jonah 1:1 demonstrates that God had told Jonah to cry against Nineveh because of their great wickedness. When Jonah

---

⁸ Douglas Stuart, *Hosea–Jonah*, 482. Emphasis his.
⁹ R. Reed Lessing, *Jonah*, 272.
¹⁰ Ibid.

received this word, he fled because he wanted to forestall God's gracious act of mercy on the Ninevites. Jonah 4:2 refers to what Jonah said while he was in his own country. Fruchtenbaum provides an interesting explanation of why Jonah initially fled Yahweh's call:

> In the Hebrew text, the emphasis is on the words *my country*. Unfortunately, Jonah is often interpreted to be an anti-Gentile bigot, but this is not the problem. If he were, he would not have wanted to go to Tarshish either, since Tarshish was also a Gentile city. The problem was not that he was anti-Gentile, but rather, that he was pro-Israel, a nationalist. This is seen from his statement, *my country*.
>
> From the preaching of Amos, Jonah already knew that Assyria had been chosen by God to destroy Israel. If Nineveh was spared destruction, that would signal the certainty of the coming destruction of Israel. What Jonah did not want to be was the instrument that God would use to bring Nineveh to repentance, and therefore, be spared. Furthermore, he knew that if he were the instrument of Nineveh's coming to repentance, he would also be an instrument, albeit in an indirect or secondary way, of Israel's destruction.[11]

Jonah was aware of God's compassion because it was revealed in Exodus 34:6–7. He initially believed that if the Ninevites did not have the opportunity to repent, they would be considered guilty and punished. Perhaps if they were punished, God could not use them as an instrument to punish Israel. Youngblood writes, "Though Jonah readily acknowledged God's sovereignty over all the earth (1:9), he struggled with the equally universal

---

[11] Arnold G. Fruchtenbaum, *The Messianic Bible Study Collection* (Tustin, CA: Ariel Ministries, 1983), 79:16. All emphasis his.

scope of God's mercy, once he realized that not even Assyria, Israel's dreaded enemy, was excluded."[12]

Three important observations can be made from this analysis. First, Jonah 1:1 demonstrates that a rebuke of the Ninevites' wickedness was part of this message. Jonah 3:8 shows that the Ninevites certainly got the message that they should turn from their wicked ways. Second, the possibility of mercy in light of repentance must have been a condition of the word of the Lord because Jonah fled. Jonah would not flee from announcing irrevocable destruction. His poor track record of obedience would also not have caused him to run from changing God's word. As previously mentioned, he probably would have been rather excited to deliver such a message. However, a message that offered a hint of a possible merciful response on the part of God would be unattractive to Jonah. Third, the exact message would be given to Jonah after 3:1. Contrary to Trible, Cary and Lubeck's arguments, there is no passage in the rest of Jonah that indicates that Jonah preached any message other than the one God gave him. The narrator never casts poor light on Jonah's words but he does say in Jonah 3:3 that Jonah acted according to the word of the Lord. Despite his opposition to God's word, like Balaam and Jeremiah, Jonah may have been unable to preach anything else.

Furthermore, Jonah's experience of grace may have made Jonah willing to deliver the word God gave him. Jonah 2:8–9 says in the NASB, "Those who regard vain idols Forsake their faithfulness, But I will sacrifice to You With the voice of thanksgiving. That which I have vowed I will pay. Salvation is from the LORD." Possibly, while in the belly of the fish and under the influence of grace, Jonah vowed to take the salvation of Yahweh to the Ninevites. In Jonah 1:16 the sailors vowed to fear Yahweh as a result of God's deliverance from the storm and

---

[12] Kevin J. Youngblood, *Jonah: God's Scandalous Mercy*, ed. Daniel Block (Grand Rapids, MI: Zondervan, 2013), 132.

now Jonah, the reluctant prophet, vows to do the same. Spender writes:

> Jonah knew that there was no strength or hope in the gods of the foreign nations. He gave similar testimony to the sailors who threw him overboard. Jonah further realized that as long as people held ("clung," NIV) to their empty idols they were forsaking any potential of grace from God. The very fact of holding tightly to a system that opposes God or attempts to replace God negates one's ability to see Him. Idolaters are resolutely looking away from God. In the final analysis Jonah lifted his voice in thanksgiving and confessed that salvation was from the Lord. He, like the sailors, made vows to the Lord. For his deliverance he praised God and affirmed his willingness to fulfill what he vowed (2:9).[13]

The Hebrew word נָדַר is often used of a vow to fear or serve God in response to His deliverance (cf. Genesis 28:20–22, Numbers 21:2, 1 Samuel 1:11, 1 Kings 1:29–30, Psalm 22:25, Psalm 50:14, Psalm 56:12, Psalm 61:5, Psalm 116:14, *et al*). However, even a rash vow would still be required of the person making it. Deuteronomy 23:21 says, "When you make a vow to the LORD your God, you shall not delay to pay it, for it would be sin in you, and the LORD your God will surely require it of you" (cf. also Ecclesiastes 5:4–5). By making such a vow, Jonah shows he intends to obey God's original command. However, his statement may indicate a reason for this willingness: his belief that the idolatrous Ninevites may have forsaken the grace that could be theirs. Jonah proclaims that those who regard worthless idols forsake their faithfulness (חַסְדָּם). The only other use of the word in the book of Jonah is in Jonah 4:2 where Jonah is saying that

---

[13] Robert Spender, "Reading Jonah Again for the First Time," *Emmaus Journal* 10 (2001): 82.

he recognizes that God is abundant in lovingkindness. Perhaps part of Jonah's expectation, hope and motivation is that his prophecy would serve as a basis for the destruction of the Ninevites rather than their repentance. While he is doing this, the sailors are giving legitimate sacrifices and vows to Yahweh and thus showing that God shows grace to repentant idolaters.

Dorsey also recognizes the contrast between the Gentile sailors and Jonah:

> Like the preceding episode about Jonah and the sailors, this prayer features a highlighted final unit that also speaks of vows and sacrifices to Yahweh (2:9 [2:10])—which of course invites the audience to compare the two passages. The ironic contrast between the two is unmistakable. In the latter, Jonah boasts: "Those who serve empty idols forfeit (your kindness); but I, on the other hand, will offer you sacrifice with thanksgiving. I will pay my vows!" (2:8–9 [2:9–10]). Ironically, while the rebellious prophet is making these self-righteous boasts and promises from the fish's belly, the praiseworthy pagan sailors are up above, happy recipients of Yahweh's kindness, doing precisely what Jonah can only promise to do (and what he assumes nobody except faithful Israelites like himself do): they are sacrificing to Yahweh and making vows to him (1:16)! By this structuring strategy the author helps the audience understand how Jonah's pious prayer is to be heard—as hypocritical![14]

Dorsey's point shows the interesting relationship in the contrast between Jonah in Jonah 2 and the sailors in Jonah 1. It will also set up an interesting contrast with the Ninevites in Jonah 3 and his other prayer in Jonah 4.

---

[14] David A. Dorsey, *The Literary Structure of the Old Testament: A Commentary on Genesis–Malachi* (Grand Rapids, MI: Baker Books, 1999), 293–94.

Not only this, but when Jonah gives his prophecy of the overturning of Nineveh in Jonah 3:4, the Ninevites also react by offering the sacrifices that Jonah originally promised to offer. They express hope in Jonah 3:9 that God will not destroy them as a result of their turning from their violence in Jonah 3:8. In this sense, their hope is that somehow they had not forsaken God's compassion but instead hoped to benefit from it by repenting.

Jonah's prayer in the belly of the fish sets up the context of Jonah 3. When he gives his prophecy of the overturning of Nineveh in Jonah 3:4, the Ninevites react by offering the sacrifices that Jonah promised to offer. They express hope in Jonah 3:9 that God will not destroy them as a result of their turning from their violence in Jonah 3:8. Their hope is that they had not forsaken God's compassion but instead hoped to benefit from it by repenting.

Jonah 2 also provides an interesting comparison between Jonah and the other Gentiles in Jonah. John Hannah notes some remarkable similarities between Jonah's prayer and the situation in the first chapter:[15]

Ch. 1: The Sailors		Ch. 2: The Prophet	
1:4	Crisis on the sea	2:3–6a	Crisis in the sea
1:14	Prayer to Yahweh	2:2, 7	Prayer to Yahweh
1:15b	Deliverance from the storm	2:6b	Deliverance from drowning
1:16	Sacrifice and vows offered to God	2:9	Sacrifice and vows offered to God

The Gentiles throughout the book present an interesting contrast to Jonah. He repeatedly descends to the bottom (even as far as the bottom of the boat and the bottom of the belly of the fish). As previously mentioned, the sailors ask Jonah to cry out

---

[15] John D. Hannah, "Jonah," *The Bible Knowledge Commentary: An Exposition of the Scriptures*, ed. John F. Walvoord and Roy B. Zuck (Wheaton, IL: Victor Books, 1985), 1467.

to his God and the sailors cry out to God. Jonah goes through the same basic process in Jonah 3. Rather than being at the bottom of a boat sleeping, he is in the belly of a fish praying. Perhaps, his own perspective in 2:8 might have given him hope that the idolatrous Ninevites may have forsaken their faithfulness and as a result God would inevitably destroy them.

One other comparison is between the prayer in Jonah 2 and the one in Jonah 4:2–3. A comparison of the two prayers yields some interesting similarities and differences. Allen argues that the first prayer was one of thanksgiving while the second is one of complaint.[16] Dorsey argues that each prayer is in response to Yahweh's sparing a guilty party (Jonah and the Ninevites), both have a similar introduction of Jonah praying (וַיִּתְפַּלֵּל) to Yahweh (אֶל־יְהוָה), and both have the same keywords of love (חֶסֶד), life (חַי) and soul (נֶפֶשׁ).[17]

Dorsey also identifies some key differences between the two prayers:

> What is striking, however, is their differences. The first, Jonah's prayer of thanksgiving to Yahweh for sparing him, is beautiful, almost serene. It is steeped in piety and rich theology. In contrast, the second prayer, in which Jonah reacts angrily to Yahweh's sparing pagan Nineveh, is no beautiful, serene, pious, or theologically rich. Rather it is an indignant outburst, petty, small, mean-spirited. In the first prayer Jonah celebrates Yahweh's kindness (ḥesed), which pagans forfeit (2:8 [2:9]); in the second Jonah complains that Yahweh's ḥesed has been extended to pagans—as Jonah feared it would (4:2). In the first prayer Jonah is grateful that his "life" (ḥayyay) and "soul" (napšî). In the first prayer, Jonah praises Yahweh for sparing him—one person—from the punishment he

---

[16] Allen, *The Books of Joel, Obadiah, Jonah and Micah*, 228.
[17] Dorsey, *The Literary Structure of the Old Testament: A Commentary on Genesis–Malachi*, 291.

deserved (although he apparently has not repented of his disobedience!); whereas in the second prayer Jonah is angry that Yahweh has spared many thousands of *innocent* [emphasis his] children; as well as people who *have* [emphasis his] sincerely repented.

That the pious prayer of chapter 2 is matched by the mean-spirited prayer of chapter 4 helps the reader, in retrospect, to see the first prayer as the author intended: self-righteous, hypocritical and selfish.[18]

Thus, the prayer of thanksgiving in Jonah 2 of Jonah is critical for the contrast with the prayer in Jonah 4. The author designed them both as a contrast to each other in order to make ironic distinctions between the two. The prayer in Jonah 4 demonstrates Jonah's true attitude towards God and the Gentiles despite his feigned piety earlier in the book.

The Importance of Nineveh

One interesting indicator of God's intention for Nineveh is provided by the narrator of Jonah when he writes the mysterious phrase "וְנִינְוֵה הָיְתָה עִיר־גְּדוֹלָה לֵאלֹהִים." This phrase has been variously translated. Some commentators argue that the phrase refers to the large size of Nineveh.[19] Others argue that it means that the city belonged to God.[20] Lessing says that the view that Nineveh belongs to God is consistent with Jonah's proclamation of God's authority over creation in Jonah 1:9 and his own statements regarding his creation of Nineveh in Jonah

---

[18] Ibid.
[19] For an example of this view, see Brynmor F. Price and Eugene Albert Nida, *A Translators' Handbook on the Book of Jonah* (Stuttgart: United Bible Societies, 1978), 90.
[20] Jack M. Sasson, *Jonah: A New Translation with Introduction, Commentary, and Interpretation*, 1st ed. (New York, NY: Doubleday, 1990), 229.

4:10–11.[21]

However, Stuart proposes an alternate translation that the city was important to God. He gives the following justification for this view:

> From Joshua 10:2 ("Gibeon was an *important* city like one of the royal cities" [NIV]) it is evident that (ה)גדול could be used in connection with a city to indicate significance rather than size. Gibeon was in fact physically rather small, being less than two and one-half acres in extent (see Pritchard, *Gibeon*, 10), a size that is surely not "great" as compared to other ancient Canaanite/Israelite dries. In light of the usage already established in 1:2, גדול can certainly connote importance as well as physical size, yet we must not too readily assume that גדול, used in two different ways in the book (see *Introduction*) should mean "important" *here*. It could as well mean "large," and in that sense relate to the emphasis placed upon its population in 4:11. But population also correlates with importance just as well as with size. And the emphasis of the book is upon Nineveh's relationship to God.... Here, as long as גדולה is understood to mean "important" rather than simply "large," לאלהים may best be translated simply "to God." Alternatively, translate "extraordinarily important," but not "extraordinarily large."
>
> The point is that Nineveh was a city God was concerned for, one that was by no means insignificant to him. Nineveh's physical size may have figured prominently in its importance, as may have its population, but there is no ground for assuming that size per se is the issue in 3:3b.[22]

---

[21] R. Reed Lessing, *Jonah*, Concordia Commentary (St. Louis, MO: Concordia Pub. House, 2007), 279–280.
[22] Douglas K. Stuart, *Hosea–Jonah*, vol. 31, 52 vols., Word Biblical Commentary (Waco, TX: Word Books, 1987), 486–87. Emphasis his.

Of the two options, the argument for the city being important to God fits the immediate context and the overall purpose of Jonah. However, even if the correct translation is that it is a city belonging to God, either translation would point to the implicit possibility of repentance more than destruction. This statement, as well as God's statement in Jonah 4:11, show God's overall concern as a reason for His willingness to show compassion on Jonah and offer them the opportunity of repentance. This overall concern is part of the reason for sending Jonah in the first place. As Fruchtenbaum has mentioned:

> Judgment was not unavoidable, otherwise, there would be no need for the warning. God did not send prophets to Sodom and Gomorrah to warn them of the coming destruction. The fact that God would send a prophet to Nineveh to warn them that they had forty days before destruction showed this was a conditional prophecy.[23]

In agreement with Fruchtenbaum, the fact that God sent a prophet at all seems to indicate his compassionate intentions.

Forty Days

Another line of evidence for the implicit polysemantic wordplay view is the significance of the forty-day period in Jonah 3. Youngblood sees a connection between the forty days to be an allusion to the flood and Moses' intercession for Israel. As a result, he argues that both allusions would convey two different fates for Israel, "On the one hand, in the event that they fail to heed God's warning and continue in their great wickedness, the forty day period would symbolize doom as in the flood. On the other, hand, in the event they respond to God's warning with repentance, the forty days would symbolize the possibility of rescinding of annihilation as in the case of Moses' intercession

---

[23] Fruchtenbaum, *The Messianic Bible Study Collection*, 79:15.

of Israel at Sinai."[24]

Wolff also notes that the forty days can symbolize repentance:

> Forty days are a long time. It is the time conceded for a comprehensive world judgment (Genesis 7:4, 12); it is the time Yahweh needs to instruct Moses fully (Exodus 24:18; 34:28; Deuteronomy 9:9) and the time required for Moses' great vicarious repentance, which he took on himself in order to turn away Yahweh's wrath from his people (Deuteronomy 9:18). These forty days are granted to Nineveh. According to the narrator's intention, the time is required, first, so that the message may reach all the inhabitants of the huge city; also, and especially, that it may be brought to the notice of the king and his great men, and may bring out the necessary decisions (v. 6f); and finally, to make possible the ritual of repentance and a new way of life for every individual in the metropolis (vv. 8, 10).[25]

Wolff provides an exceptional explanation for the forty-day period: to afford the opportunity for repentance. If God's original intent was to destroy people, why would he offer so much time for the message to reach them and why would they repent? Since forty days often connoted the opportunity for repentance it appears that part of God's intent in giving the prophecy was to provide an opportunity for repentance.

Stuart also discusses the relationship between repentance and forty in Jonah 3:4:

> Jonah's message mentioned "forty days." In spite of its potential ambiguity, this must have seemed to many

---

[24] Youngblood, *Jonah: God's Scandalous Mercy*, 134.
[25] Hans Walter Wolff, *Obadiah and Jonah: A Commentary*, trans. Margaret Kohl (Minneapolis, MN: Augsburg Pub. House, 1986), 149–150.

Ninevites to be an invitation to repentance, giving hope that they and their city or land might not be destroyed. "Forty" (אַרְבָּעִים) is a term which is often used in the sense of "a good many" or "dozens." It does not necessarily connote a literal forty, i.e., one more than thirty-nine (cf. Numbers 13:25; Joshua 4:13; Judges 3:11; 5:8; 13:1; etc.). Its association with time for purging, in the OT at least (for example,, the wandering in the wilderness for forty years which eliminated the unfaithful; the forty days of rain which began the flood and thus eliminated the wicked; the forty years of Egypt's desolation prior to its restoration, in Ezekiel 29:11–16, etc.), and at least once with fasting (Deuteronomy 9:18, 25; cf. Matthew 4:2) might reflect a similar association elsewhere in the ancient Near East (cf. also 1 Kings 19:8; Exodus 24:18; Numbers 13:25). To the original Israelite/Judean audience the multiple implications of "forty" would be heard; to Jonah they would be evident, and apparently the point was not lost on the Ninevites, either.[26]

Stuart effectively argues the use of forty would have brought to mind a message of repentance in the minds of the Ninevites as well as the original Jewish audience of Jonah. Since one of the purposes of the book was to demonstrate that Jews also could avoid destruction if only they would repent, the literary implications of the use of forty would be apparent to the audience. This is especially true when one considers Loken's argument that Israel may have been destroyed forty years after Jonah's ministry. Israel was destroyed in 722 BC and Jonah ministered between 793 and 755 BC. Thus, Jonah could have been written in 762 BC, which would have been forty years before the destruction of Israel.[27]

---

[26] Stuart, *Hosea–Jonah*, 489.
[27] Israel Loken, *The Old Prophets: An Introduction*, forthcoming.

The Response of the Ninevites

The Ninevites also provide indications that they considered the prophecy to be implicitly conditional. First, they responded by believing in God. As Lessing notes, the combination of אָמַן and בְּ should be rendered to "have faith in."[28] This is the same construction for the faith of Abraham in Genesis 15:6 and the faith of the Israelites after salvation in the Red Sea in Exodus 14:31.[29] Some commentators question whether the belief and repentance was genuine. However, Luke 11:32 indicates that the Ninevites will rise up against the unrighteous generation of Jews and judge them. One must assume that the fact that these men are resurrected and in a position of judgment that they were in fact redeemed.

However, what is more important for the sake of this book is what did the Ninevites believe in? As Stuart previously stated Jonah was commanded to proclaim the proclamation Yahweh gave him—no more or no less. The only basis for belief is in the prophecy. Hence, the Ninevite reaction must have been to the prophecy and the God of the prophecy. Laetsch argues that the Hiphil of אָמַן with בְּ "denotes saying yeah and Amen to God's Word as it is revealed to them by the prophet."[30] Alexander argues that the Hebrew phrase means more than believing in what a person says but trusting in a person. He says that it is the type of response God expected of the Israelites (cf. 2 Chronicles 20:20) but he did not receive (cf. Numbers 14:11, 20:12; Deuteronomy 1:32, 2 Kings 17:14, Psalms 78:22).[31]

---

[28] Lessing, *Jonah*, 283.
[29] Ibid.
[30] Theodore Ferdinand Karl Laetsch, *Bible Commentary: The Minor Prophets* (Saint Louis: Concordia Pub. House, 1956), 235. Originally cited in Lessing, *Jonah*, 284.
[31] David W. Baker, T. Desmond Alexander, and Bruce K. Waltke, *Obadiah, Jonah, Micah*, The Tyndale Old Testament Commentaries, ed. D. J. Wiseman (Leicester, England; Downers Grove, IL: Inter-Varsity Press, 1988) 121. Originally cited in Lessing, *Jonah*, 284.

Clearly the Ninevites recognized the possibility of destruction (Jonah 3:9–10) but they also recognized the possibility of repentance.

The Ninevites all demonstrated their repentance by wearing sackcloth. This response was something that God desired of his people (cf. Joel 1:13–14, Amos 8:10, etc.).[32] According to Stuart, this event represents "a rather logical and therefore commonly attested order in the OT in which (a) a threat of harm is followed by (b) repentance, and then (c) by God's decision not to bring about the harm after all (cf. 1 Samuel 7:3–14; Ezra 8:21–23; Jeremiah 36:3; Joel 2:11–29)."[33] The fact that this model is so frequent throughout the Old Testament increases the probability of implicit conditionality in Jonah 3:4.

The king also arose (וַיָּקָם) from his throne and issued a proclamation for all of the animals and beasts to wear sackcloth. He called (וַיִּקְרָאוּ) upon everyone to turn (וְיָשֻׁבוּ) from their wicked (הָרָעָה) way. The Ninevite king agreed with God's assessment of the Ninevites in Jonah 1:2 and they repented. This parallels Joel 2:12 in which the Israelites are commanded by God to return to Him with fasting, weeping and mourning. The basis for this command is on the character of God as expressed in Joel 2:13 (which is very similar to Jonah 4:2). In exchange, perhaps God will turn and relent and leave a blessing behind him. Whereas Yahweh had overturned (כְּמַהְפֵּכַת) Israel (Amos 4:11) as Sodom and Gomorrah, they had refused to turn (שַׁבְתֶּם) to Him. The contrast is very clear. As Lessing points out, the Ninevite repentance "exceeds any recorded in Israel."[34] However, the Jews refused to repent despite the messages of greater prophets like Hosea, Amos and eventually Jesus.

The Ninevite king asks the question "Who knows" (מִי־יוֹדֵעַ) whether God will turn and relent so they will not perish. A

---

[32] Baker, Alexander, and Waltke, *Obadiah, Jonah, Micah*, 122.
[33] Stuart, *Hosea–Jonah*, 489.
[34] Lessing, *Jonah*, 285.

similar phrase is found in Joel 2:14. In this passage, the question does not reflect a lack of knowledge of stated possibility of God's conditional intention because Joel 2:13 already says that God relents of evil. Instead, it reflects a hope that God's mercy will be shown to Israel if they respond to the prophecy with sincere repentance. David hoped for a similar result when he used the expression in fasting for his child (2 Samuel 12:22). In fact, when this phrase is used, it often describes that which God only ultimately knows (cf. Proverbs 24:22, Ecclesiastes 3:21 and 6:12). Sometimes this phrase is used of desired deliverance (Joel 2:14 and 2 Samuel 12:22) and other times it is used of imminent destruction (Proverbs 24:22) and the anger of God (Psalms 90:11). When the king said this he realized that both destruction and compassion were a possibility.

As previously mentioned in chapter one, the decree of the king and the nobles in Jonah 3:9 is very similar to Moses' plea in Exodus 32:12b when he asks God in the NASB to "turn from Your burning anger and change Your mind about doing harm to Your people."[35] When God saw that the Ninevites had turned from their wicked way, he relented concerning the calamity that He had declared through Jonah would come upon them. As Lessing points out, the statement "God saw" is indicative of more than physical observance but it often points to God's compassion as in Exodus 2:25.[36] This concept of God relenting from calamity occurs frequently in the Old Testament (Exodus 32:12, 14; 2 Samuel 24:16; 1 Chronicles 21:15; 42:11; Jeremiah 18:8, 10; 26:3, 13, 19; 42:10; Ezekiel 14:22; Joel 2:13; Jonah 3:10; 4:2). In fact, Jonah 3:10 is almost an exact quote of Exodus 32:14 which the NASB translates as, "So the LORD changed His mind about the harm which He said He would do to His people."[37] To a certain degree, Jonah is the opposite of Moses in this passage. Whereas

---

[35] Ibid., 368.
[36] Ibid., 293.
[37] Ibid., 368.

Moses intercedes for a nation, Jonah requests the destruction of Nineveh. Both Moses and Jonah recognize God's compassionate character. However, the person who is most like Moses is the Gentile king. Like Moses, he expresses hope that God will turn from his anger (Exodus 32:12 and Jonah 3:9). Whereas Moses hoped in the unconditional promise of God to the Israelite people (as previously mentioned, the promise of Exodus 32:13 was given to Moses in Exodus 6:8[38]), the Ninevite king placed his hope on the implicitly conditional promise of Jonah. It is important to note that neither Moses nor the Ninevite king were expressing hope that was contrary to the message they had been given; they were expressing hope for deliverance because of the message they had been given.

Jonah's Response to Ninevite Repentance

Jonah's response to the Ninevite repentance also provides clues of the implicit conditionality of his prophecy. If the book strictly dealt with God's response to the Ninevite repentance, one would think it would have ended after the third chapter. Under this scenario, Jonah's prophecy would have been successful, his obedience to the call would have been demonstrated, the Ninevites would have been spared and Yahweh would have been worshiped. Instead, the narrator has been building towards this important climax. There are still some lingering questions that he wants to answer such as Jonah's motivation for leaving. These questions could have easily been answered in Jonah 1 or 3 but the narrator has postponed the answer until now for dramatic effect. Lessing writes:

> Throughout chapter 1, the prophet maintained icy silence toward Yahweh, but with the first verse of chapter 4, this

---

[38] Jonathan Master, "Exodus 32 as an Argument for Traditional Theism," *Journal of the Evangelical Theological Society* 45, no. 4 (2002): 587.

> conflict erupts in Jonah's open hostility toward Yahweh, bringing confusion and surprise upon us readers.... Herman Gunkel observed that the OT seldom probes the psychology of its characters.... The fact that the narrator supplies Jonah's inward feelings moves us as close as possible to a full definition of this prophet's character. Reading up to 3:10, we have been led to conclude that all is well regarding the Ninevites—and that is true about their relationship to God. But now Jonah's anger over the salvation of the Ninevites calls for us to reevaluate Jonah.[39]

As Lessing points out, Jonah 4 gives the reader the opportunity to evaluate Jonah's character (and by implication the Israelites' character whom Jonah represents). In terms of the success of his prophecy, Jonah was one of the most successful prophets in the Old Testament. The response to his prophecy far exceeded Elijah's or Amos'. However, the key question at this point is regarding his character as well as his view of Yahweh. His knowledge level of theology is fine, but his practical application of his theology is wanting.

Jonah 4 begins with Jonah's assessment of the Ninevite response to his prophecy. In Jonah 3, the Ninevites rightly agreed with God's assessment that they were wicked (cf. Jonah 1:2 and Jonah 3:8) and they responded by repenting. Jonah, on the other hand, still considers the Ninevites to be wicked and he does not rightly assess himself. In fact, he questions whether God's actions towards the Ninevites are right. Of course, this type of dialogue with God is common in the Old Testament. Two notable examples are Moses and Elijah. Master describes the dialogue between Moses and Yahweh in Exodus:

> As the chapters progress, the reader sees Moses' own

---

[39] Lessing, *Jonah*, 357–358.

imperfection as he resists the Lord's call and fails to circumcise even his own son. Moses as the human mediator between God and the people is not portrayed as an individual without fear or faults. Yet, even so, he is the one chosen by God. A God looking for a willing and able deliverer would have rejected Moses immediately. A God prone to frequently change his mind would soon have seen Moses' inadequacy. Instead, from the outset, Exodus presents a God who is *not* [emphasis his] thwarted by man and who is unswerving in his commitment, first to bless and redeem Israel, and then to use Moses as the mediator of that redemption and blessing. Moses' role as mediator, especially as it relates to the argument of the book, will take on increasing significance as the story progresses. For now, it is enough to note two things: that God is Creator and not thwarted in his plans, and that Moses is his chosen mediator. These two facts, so clearly in evidence within this section, provide the backdrop for Exodus 32. In fact, they provide the basis for Moses' own theology. As he later dialogues with a God, he knows him to be the Creator and is convinced that his plans for redemption are unassailable.... Two things must be noted from this introductory dialogue pattern. First, it is within the context of dialogue (with its apparent give-and-take) that God reveals himself and his nature. Understanding the function of dialogue within Exodus in this way is critical. Second, there is no implication that Pharaoh can disappoint or thwart the plans of God. In fact, even Pharaoh's rejection of both Moses and Aaron is in keeping with God's plan. Pharaoh's rejection cannot even be said to be an evidence of his free will; it is God who hardens him, and God who prophetically speaks of Pharaoh's future action. Although Moses is introduced as the conduit of God's redemption and the messenger of his promised release, it is God himself who is the main character of the story. His work in redemption cannot be thwarted. Even the resistance to his plans was both foreknown and under his control. Hence the reader can see both a pattern of revelation (dialogue), which comes at key points in the story, and a theological foundation, which affirms God as unassailable Redeemer.[40]

One can note several similarities between the two situations. First, the dialogue in Jonah 4 reveals the theology and character of God and Jonah. Second, the dialogue in Jonah 4 reveals God's sovereign right to redeem (in this case the Ninevites) as well as His sovereign control over creation. Third, the dialogue reveals God's compassion toward Jonah (and by implication Israel). God compassionately corrects Jonah's evil attitudes as opposed to meeting his request for death by instantly destroying him. Fourth, the dialogue shows God's sovereign will. As Master noted regarding Moses, if God were fickle and did not know the future so He regularly changed his mind, one might expect Him to be unable to make such bold predictions (regarding Israel and Nineveh) and simply dismiss Moses and/or Jonah upon learning of their deficiencies.

Of course, the careful reader may note some interesting distinctions. While Moses pleaded for compassion for Israel, Jonah resented God for showing compassion to Nineveh. While Moses intercedes with God on the basis of His word, Jonah appeals on the basis of his word (דְבָרִי) instead of God's. Whereas Moses appealed to Yahweh's character as a reason to beg God to relent concerning the threatened calamity towards Israel (Exodus 32:12), Jonah resents God's compassionate character (Jonah 4:2). Moses requested to die (Numbers 11:15) because of the lack of repentance of the Israelites. Jonah requested to die because the Ninevites repented (Jonah 4:3). Jonah requested death because he preferred death over repentance (cf. Amos

---

[40] Jonathan Master, "Exodus 32 as an Argument for Traditional Theism," 587–588.

5:14–15) in both his request to be thrown overboard in Jonah 1:12 as well as in his requests in Jonah 4:3 and 4:8–9.[41] As Amos 5:14–15 (NASB) says, the Israelites of Jonah's time were commanded "seek good and not evil" and to "establish justice in the gate" in order for God to "be gracious to the remnant of Joseph." Instead, the Israelites were seeking the day of the Lord because they assumed they were righteous and God would judge their enemies. However, as Jonah illustrates, he prefers to label the work of God and the Ninevites as evil. Jonah 4:1 could literally be translated as "However, it was evil to Jonah—a great evil—so it inflamed him."[42] As Lessing rightly argues, the antecedent to Jonah 4:1 likely refers to all that happened in Jonah 3:5–10: the Ninevites' belief in God, the acts of repentance and God's relenting concerning the destruction.[43] Jonah does not love God's good character and decision—he actually has come to the point of being angered by it! As a result, he prefers death to the life God gives through repentance and faith. As Amos 6:3 (NASB) says, Jonah was literally trying to put off the day of calamity by disobeying God. Smith describes the significance of Amos 6:3 as follows:

> The term translated "put off" occurs elsewhere only in Isaiah 66:5, where it means to "exclude" or "reject." Here it means they rejected the idea of "the evil day." They were confident such a day was reserved for God's enemies. What they failed to see was that *they* [emphasis his] might be God's enemies. Any thought of a day of disaster for Israel was put off to the distant future.[44]

---

[41] Loken, *The Old Prophets: An Introduction*, forthcoming.
[42] Translation taken from Lessing, *Jonah*, 350.
[43] Ibid., 351.
[44] Billy K. Smith and Frank S. Page, *Amos, Obadiah, Jonah*, vol. 19B, 37 vols., New American Commentary (Nashville, TN: Broadman & Holman, 1995), 118.

Whereas in Jonah 3:8 the Ninevites had turned from their evil (הָרָעָה) and calamity (הֶחָמָס), the Israelites were trying to put off the day of calamity (רָע) and bring violence (חָמָס) on themselves. Whereas the sailors and the Ninevites pray to God so they will not perish, Jonah tells God he wishes he would die. Jonah demonstrates the attitude Amos speaks of in Amos 6:3 in Jonah 4. He considers the actions of God and the Ninevites to be evil while he justifies his own acts before God. God deals with his evil by sending the *qiqayon* plant and removing it from him. Rather than repenting, Jonah justifies his anger at God and requests death. Both the possibility of repentance and destruction exist for Jonah and Israel (as it had for Nineveh in Jonah 3:4). Unfortunately, both Israel and Jonah eventually choose death over repentance.

The comparison with Elijah also has some interesting contrasts as well. Jonah and Elijah prophesied around the same period. The Word of Yahweh also came to Elijah (1 Kings 21:17). Elijah is commanded to arise and go (קוּם לֵךְ) to Zarephath in a similar way as Jonah was to Nineveh. Unlike Jonah's first response, Elijah arose and went (וַיָּקָם וַיֵּלֶךְ).[45] Like Moses, Elijah requested death as a result of the lack of repentance of the Israelite people (1 Kings 19:4). Like Moses and unlike Jonah, their reason for the request to die differed even though Jonah made his request under his *qiqayon* plant and Elijah made his under a broom tree.[46] Like Moses and Jonah, God used dialogue to address Elijah's concern. Like Jonah, God also used nature to illustrate the point of his teaching to Elijah.

These comparisons might help the reader better understand Jonah 4. As previously mentioned, Jonah reacts to Jonah 3:5–10 by declaring all of it to be exceedingly evil. Of course, the fact that the prophet is even making this assessment causes the reader to question Jonah's character. Lessing writes:

---

[45] Lessing, *Jonah*, 51.
[46] Ibid.

> The irony is that the Ninevites turn away from their "evil" (רָעָה in 3:8, 4:1), which in turn prompts Yahweh to change his verdict about the "evil" (destruction) he had threatened (רָעָה in 3:10b), whereupon double "evil" (both the verb and the noun) immediately comes upon Jonah! In the Hebrew word order, this "evil" literally encloses the prophet: his name "Jonah," is sandwiched between the preceding verb and the following noun (וַיֵּרַע אֶל־יוֹנָה רָעָה). What Nineveh and God have turned from in 3:8–10 now inflames Jonah, and in his anger, he surrounds himself with "evil."[47]

The author builds up to this conclusion throughout the narrative. In a similar approach to Amos, the author initially assesses the evil of a Gentile nation (which the readers would have agreed on) and then turns the tables to show that the Jews were also evil and deserved the same judgment as the nations. The greatest evil (the only one using the phrase רָעָה גְדוֹלָה) is Jonah's! Lessing discusses how the author sets the stage for this conclusion:

> "Evil" frames the entire narrative. The book begins with the "evil" perpetrated by the Ninevites (1:2). "Evil" affects the sailors in the form of a storm sent by Yahweh (1:7–8). Then the focus returns to the Ninevites as they repent and turn away from their "evil way" (3:10a). Thereupon God changes his verdict and does not carry out the "evil" destruction of the city (3:10b); Yahweh characteristically changes his verdict about "evil" (4:2). Finally, "great evil" comes to Jonah (4:1), from which God seeks to save him (4:6).[48]

---

[47] Ibid., 359.
[48] Ibid.

The narrative builds to a chilling conclusion for the original audience: the prideful Israelites are evil and are subject to the same judgment that was originally given to the Ninevites.

Of course, Jonah does not see this. He prays to the Lord (which ironically uses the same Hebrew word וַיִּתְפַּלֵּל that is used in Jonah 2:2). Whereas the prayer of Jonah 2 praises God for his deliverance from death, Jonah requests death in his prayer in Jonah 4. The narrator skillfully uses gaps in the narrative to climactically provide an explanation for why Jonah did not go to Nineveh as called in the first chapter. Lessing writes:

> It is even possible that we might have correctly inferred that Jonah fled toward Tarshish precisely because of a mean spirit toward Nineveh: he did not want to preach to it because he did not want it to be saved. But we could not be absolutely sure that was the reason until Jonah speaks his mind in 4:2.
>
> So the narrator keeps us guessing almost to the end of the book. The reversal in 3:10–4:3 (when Nineveh is spared, Jonah changes from the prophet who faithfully spoke Yahweh's word in 3:2–4 to an angry antagonist who opposes Yahweh in 4:2–3) shatters any benign view of Jonah and changes our entire view of the narrative. Ironically, the same kind of change or overturning that was promised in 3:4 also happens to us as we read the narrative! By means of this gap that is now filled, we become more intimately involved.[49]

As Lessing points out, the overturning of Jonah 3:4 is true of the audience's perception of Jonah's character in Jonah 4.

In words echoing the grumbling Israelites' complaint in Exodus 14:12,[50] Jonah questions why he left his own country.

---

[49] Ibid., 363.
[50] Lessing, *Jonah*, 352.

The Israelites asked why Moses took them out of Egypt only to die in the wilderness and Jonah requests death in the wilderness. He says that he anticipated that this deliverance would happen. The Hebrew word means to "anticipate or forestall."⁵¹ The Greek word in the Septuagint, προφθάνω, essentially means the same thing. The Septuagint version of Jonah 4:2 can be translated as "I anticipated this and so I fled."⁵² This verse gives every indication that Jonah knew God would relent concerning the calamity (which supports the likelihood of polysemantic wordplay of נֶהְפָּכֶת in Jonah 3:4). Neither Jonah nor God were surprised by the repentance of the Ninevites (it seems somewhat unusual that advocates of the open view of God argue that God could not know that which Jonah already stated he anticipated). Both were aware of the possibility of repentance contained in the original prophecy. Instead, Jonah attempted to flee from God's sovereign plan. Jonah's attitude is reminiscent of Amos 9:10, "All the sinners of My people will die by the sword, Those who say, 'The calamity will not overtake or confront (וְתַקְדִּים) us.'"

Jonah hoped to keep Yahweh from sparing the nation that was prophesied to judge Israel. Stuart says, "Jonah did not want Yahweh to do what was right and proper according to his merciful nature. Instead of showing to Assyria the kind of undeserving favor he had granted to Israel, he should punish the Assyrians without giving them any chance to repent."⁵³ To a certain degree, Jonah was hoping that by fleeing Nineveh, he would prevent God from relenting concerning calamity towards Nineveh which was consistent with Yahweh's character. Stuart writes:

---

⁵¹ Francis Brown, S. R. Driver, and Charles A. Briggs, *The Brown-Driver-Briggs Hebrew and English Lexicon* (Peabody: Hendrickson Publishers, 2003; reprint, Seventh), 245–46.
⁵² Lessing, *Jonah*, 353.
⁵³ Stuart, *Hosea–Jonah*, 502.

At any rate, by citing this ancient formulation, Jonah confesses eloquently that hoping to see Nineveh destroyed even after he has preached there (4:5) he was actually expecting God to suppress his own natural inclination to show mercy wherever possible. It was not simply the case that Jonah could not bring himself to appreciate Nineveh. Rather, to a shocking extent, he could not stand God![54]

Ironically, the one thing that allowed Jonah to prophesy (that he might not have anticipated) was God's mercy and compassion on him! Perhaps Jonah thought that by running from God, he disqualified himself from giving the message. Of course, his compassionate and sovereign God gave him a second chance to deliver the message (Jonah 3:1).

In Jonah 2, he thanks God (2:9 NASB) while he criticizes him in 4:2. In Jonah 2:9, he recognizes that all salvation is from Yahweh. Youngblood notes the irony that Jonah 2 is a thanksgiving psalm in contrast to the prayer in Jonah 4 which is a complaint against the mercy he praises in Jonah 2.[55] In Jonah 4, Jonah questions the way God administers his salvation. As Lessing has effectively argued, Jonah 2 and 4 do not present two different Jonahs. Jonah 2 seems to be an expanded version of the type of rejoicing that occurred in Jonah 4:6 over the *qiqayon* plant.[56] In both situations, Yahweh appointed something to deliver Jonah from his difficult situation. In both prayers, there is no admission of guilt or promises of repentance that one might find in a penitential psalm (which would be most appropriate considering Jonah's sins).[57] However, Jonah's evil is exposed in Jonah 4 when the

---

[54] Ibid., 503.
[55] Kevin J. Youngblood, *Jonah: God's Scandalous Mercy*, ed. Daniel Block (Grand Rapids, MI: Zondervan, 2013), 102.
[56] Lessing, *Jonah*, 364.
[57] Ibid.

plant is taken from him. Page writes:

> One irony of this segment is that although destruction is a recurring theme of the book, the only destruction that occurs in the Book of Jonah is that of this vine. So destruction came not upon Nineveh but upon something that had become very important to Jonah, something that had brought him great joy.[58]

Thus, destruction is not the primary aspect of Jonah's prophecy as it relates to the Ninevites. However, destruction plays a key role as one assesses the future state of the Israelites.

This raises the lesson God gives with Jonah and the *qiqayon* plant. While Jonah is waiting to see what happens to the Ninevites, God teaches him an important lesson. In Jonah 4, an unrepentant Jonah is shown mercy when God allows a plant to grow over Jonah. Once his comfort is taken away from him, Jonah demonstrates great anger and requests death. Whereas Yahweh's anger subsides in light of the Ninevite repentance, Jonah's gets heated up. Jonah's anger (חָרָה) parallels the type of anger demonstrated by Cain in Genesis 4:5–6. Cain also becomes angry (וַיִּחַר לְקַיִן מְאֹד). God asks him why he is angry. He tells him that if he does well (תֵּיטִיב) his offering will be accepted. However, if he does not do well (תֵיטִיב), sin will overcome him. God asks Jonah if he does well (הַהֵיטֵב) to be angry. Jonah does not respond the first time (perhaps he is waiting to see what will happen to Nineveh before he decides to respond) but the second time he responds by saying that it is right for him to be angry even to the point of death (הֵיטֵב חָרָה־לִי עַד־מָוֶת). Jonah does not respond to God's questions with recognition or confession of his sin. Instead, he brazenly asserts his righteousness in Jonah 4:9 (in Jonah 2 he contrasts himself with those who regard vain idols). This response is quite unfortunate when compared to

---

[58] Smith and Page, *Amos, Obadiah, Jonah*, 279.

Hosea 6:1 in the NASB, "Come, let us return to the LORD. For He has torn us, but He will heal us; He has wounded us, but He will bandage us."

God's Response to Jonah

The end of Jonah is perhaps the biggest gap in the book. As Lessing states, "Jonah ends with such a permanent gap because we are never told how Jonah responds to Yahweh's formal question (4:11)."[59] The gap is intentional. The original audience was left to evaluate to what extent they were like Jonah. Hosea 7:10–16 in the NASB says:

> Though the pride of Israel testifies against him, Yet they have not returned to the LORD their God, Nor have they sought Him, for all this. So Ephraim has become like a silly dove, without sense; They call to Egypt, they go to Assyria. When they go, I will spread My net over them; I will bring them down like the birds of the sky. I will chastise them in accordance with the proclamation to their assembly. Woe to them, for they have strayed from Me! Destruction is theirs, for they have rebelled against Me! I would redeem them, but they speak lies against Me. And they do not cry to Me from their heart When they wail on their beds; For the sake of grain and new wine they assemble themselves, They turn away from Me. Although I trained and strengthened their arms, Yet they devise evil against Me. They turn, but not upward, They are like a deceitful bow; Their princes will fall by the sword Because of the insolence of their tongue. This will be their derision in the land of Egypt.

Although Hosea 7:11 is usually translated that "Ephraim has become like a silly dove," a literal rendering of it could be

---

[59] Lessing, *Jonah*, 363.

"Ephraim has become like Jonah." In Jonah's pride he tried to escape the presence of God. God spread his net and provided a fish to capture him. He chastised Jonah for straying from Him. Jonah had an insolent tongue.

In Jonah 4:10–11, Yahweh compassionately addresses Jonah. This rebellious prophet could not cause the plant he rejoiced over to grow but he felt he had the right to be angry over the plant. However, the sovereign God had a right to show compassion for the Ninevites, who had less discernment than Jonah and repented at his prophecy.

Yahweh now argues that just as he had compassion on Jonah, now he has compassion on the Ninevites. Even though this horrifies Jonah because he knows Assyria will attack Israel, these Ninevites are recipients of God's compassion. If the Israelites who know the law and the righteous requirements of God were shown compassion, how much more should the Ninevites who lack spiritual discernment receive compassion from Yahweh? Even the animals repented and they will receive mercy. Even though Habakkuk occurs later than Jonah, it seems like they are both struggling with the same issue. How can a righteous God use unrighteous people (in the case of Habakkuk the Chaldeans and in Jonah's case the Assyrians) to judge his chosen people? The answer goes back to Exodus 34:6–7. The same merciful God who spares the repentant judges the unrepentant (Exodus 34:7) and Israel was due for judgment. The Ninevites repented and were spared by God. Eventually they will be used as tools to judge the Northern Kingdom. Of course, as Nahum later states, they too would be judged for their disobedience to God.

Summary

This section reviewed the immediate context of Jonah 3 in order to evaluate the contextual clues for the implicit polysemantic wordplay view of Jonah's prophecy in Jonah 3:4. Initially, Jonah was commanded to proclaim the proclamation that God had given Him. The shift from the adversative וּקְרָא עָלֶיהָ

to the more positive וּקְרָא אֵלֶיהָ indicates a gracious intention of Yahweh towards the Ninevites. The fact that the more positive הַקְּרִיאָה is used instead of מַשָּׂא points to a greater possibility of mercy. Furthermore, Nineveh is described as a city that is important to God. This would hardly describe a place He is intent on destroying. Even the fact that God sent a prophet like Jonah to warn them and give them forty days to repent (a long time by most standards) points to a compassionate act on Yahweh's part that would point to gracious intentions. If God desired to simply destroy them, he would not likely need to send a prophet to do so (especially a reluctant one like Jonah). Upon hearing Jonah's prophecy, they believed in God. Everyone from the king, to the nobles, to the least significant members of society (not to mention even the animals) repented and cried out to God. The Ninevite king's statement in Jonah 3:9 was reminiscent of Joel 2:14 and Exodus 32:12. God's response to their works in Jonah 3:10 was similar to Exodus 32:14. All of these indicators point to the possibility of repentance in the initial prophecy.

If the book of Jonah was a record of how the Ninevites averted judgment, the book of Jonah could have easily ended after the third chapter. However, the author of Jonah had greater intentions. He wanted to expose the character flaws of Jonah and by implication Israel. Whereas the Ninevites rightly recognized their evil and repented of it, Jonah looked upon God's mercy to the Ninevite and angrily considered it to be evil. He told Yahweh that he anticipated that his prophecy would result in the Ninevite repentance, so he fled. Jonah protested God's compassionate nature. God, in turn, gave Jonah an illustration that involved mercy and destruction. He first mercifully gave him a *qiqayon* plant to help him with his discomfort and evil. He then destroyed the plant and the sun beat on his head. Once again, Jonah requested death over repentance due to his own self-righteousness. God, in turn, reminded Jonah of His sovereign control over nature and His sovereign right to show mercy. The audience was then left without knowing what Jonah will ultimately decide to do.

HISTORICAL CONTEXT OF JONAH

In this section, I will assess the historical background of Jonah to defend the implicit conditionality of Jonah 3:4. As Walvoord's method for interpreting prophecy from chapter one indicates, each prophecy should be interpreted in its historical and cultural context. This book assumes the eighth century BC date of Jonah.[60] The historical events in the eighth century BC point to an implicitly conditional prophecy in Jonah 3:4.

The Historical Background of Jonah

The key historical marker is found in Jonah 1:1 which says in the NASB, "The word of the LORD came to Jonah the son of Amittai saying." From this description of the prophet a connection can be made with 2 Kings 14:23–25, which says in the NASB:

> In the fifteenth year of Amaziah the son of Joash king of Judah, Jeroboam the son of Joash king of Israel became king in Samaria and reigned forty-one years. He did evil in the sight of the LORD; he did not depart from all the sins of Jeroboam the son of Nebat, which he made Israel sin. He restored the border of Israel from the entrance of Hamath as far as the Sea of the Arabah, according to the word of the LORD, the God of Israel, which He spoke through His servant Jonah the son of Amittai, the prophet, who was of Gath-hepher.

This quotation tells the reader that Jonah was the son of Amittai. Little is known about his father. Jonah's small town is

---

[60] A response to common critical arguments for the late date of Jonah are found in Appendix C.

about five kilometers northeast of Nazareth. Jonah lived during the reign of Jeroboam which began in the fifteenth year of Amaziah. Jeroboam reigned for a total of forty-one years. He was an evil king, but God blessed Him by restoring the territory of Israel according to the word of Yahweh through Jonah.

Merrill says this was an exceptional time in the history of Israel:

> The account of Jeroboam's reign is sparse indeed in historical texts, but, as we shall see, the prophets of the period have much to say about the conditions which existed during his rule. The judgment is that he was evil in the same way as was his namesake, Jeroboam ben Nebat. What he lacked in godliness, however, he made up for in sheer political leadership. Following in the footsteps of his father Jehoash, whom he presumably aided in his military campaigns, Jeroboam was able not only to recover the territories of Israel proper which had fallen over the years to Damascus, but to bring all of the south of Aram and Transjordan back under Israelite hegemony (2 Kings 14:25–28). Not since the days of Solomon had Israel dominated such a vast area.[61]

Someone in an Old Testament mindset based on Deuteronomy 28–30 might conclude that Yahweh blessed Jeroboam for his personal obedience to Yahweh. However, this was not the case. 2 Kings 14:24 says in the NASB, "He did evil in the sight of the LORD; he did not depart from all the sins of Jeroboam the son of Nebat, which he made Israel sin." Yahweh blessed the nation of Israel during this time because of His grace and mercy. Merrill says:

---

[61] Eugene H. Merrill, *Kingdom of Priests: A History of Old Testament Israel* (Grand Rapids, MI: Baker Book House, 1987), 374.

> But all this came to pass not because of Jeroboam's piety; to the contrary, it was despite his wickedness. For, as Jonah the prophet proclaimed, the reason for Israel's deliverance was that Yahweh had mercy on his people and remembered his pledge not to destroy them from under heaven (2 Kings 14:25–27). The day of Israel's judgment would surely come, but this was not the time. This, rather, was a time for reprieve and even favor. Perhaps the recovery of the kingdom would move the nation to a recovery of covenant obedience.[62]

As Merrill points out, God's gracious favor allowed for this time of blessing in the land despite the disobedience of the people. He refers to 2 Kings 14:23–25, which describes how Jeroboam, an evil Israelite king, benefits from the mercy of God by receiving deliverance despite his willful disobedience. 2 Kings 14:26–27 (NASB) clarifies why, "For the LORD saw the affliction of Israel, which was very bitter; for there was neither bond nor free, nor was there any helper for Israel. The LORD did not say that He would blot out the name of Israel from under heaven, but He saved them by the hand of Jeroboam the son of Joash." God utilized a disobedient king to save a disobedient nation because of His great mercy. One can instantly see the parallel between a disobedient prophet (i.e. Jonah) that God used to deliver a message to a disobedient king in order to repent so that God would not punish his disobedient nation (i.e. Nineveh) because of His mercy.

However, as Merrill writes, judgment was forthcoming. As a result, Jeroboam heard prophecies of blessing and judgment in his lifetime. Hosea and Amos prophesied judgment. One significant prophecy of judgment to Jeroboam is Amos 7:7–17:

---

[62] Ibid.

Thus He showed me: Behold, the Lord stood on a wall made with a plumb line, with a plumb line in His hand. And the Lord said to me, "Amos, what do you see?" And I said, "A plumb line." Then the Lord said: "Behold, I am setting a plumb line In the midst of My people Israel; I will not pass by them anymore. The high places of Isaac shall be desolate, And the sanctuaries of Israel shall be laid waste. I will rise with the sword against the house of Jeroboam." Then Amaziah the priest of Bethel sent to Jeroboam king of Israel, saying, "Amos has conspired against you in the midst of the house of Israel. The land is not able to bear all his words. For thus Amos has said: 'Jeroboam shall die by the sword, And Israel shall surely be led away captive From their own land.'" Then Amaziah said to Amos: "Go, you seer! Flee to the land of Judah. There eat bread, And there prophesy. But never again prophesy at Bethel, For it is the king's sanctuary, And it is the royal residence." Then Amos answered, and said to Amaziah: "I was no prophet, Nor was I a son of a prophet, But I was a sheepbreeder And a tender of sycamore fruit. Then the Lord took me as I followed the flock, And the Lord said to me, 'Go, prophesy to My people Israel.' Now therefore, hear the word of the Lord: You say, 'Do not prophesy against Israel, And do not spout against the house of Isaac.' Therefore thus says the Lord: 'Your wife shall be a harlot in the city; Your sons and daughters shall fall by the sword; Your land shall be divided by survey line; You shall die in a defiled land; And Israel shall surely be led away captive From his own land.'"

Thus, if Jeroboam did not repent of the evil that he and the nation of Israel were doing, God would not relent in judging them. While Amos's prophecy involved Jeroboam's house, the message was clear. Jeroboam and the nation of Israel were given the same message and opportunity that the Ninevites were. Both repentance and destruction were possible. The only problem was that they had two different responses. Whereas the Ninevite king repented, Jeroboam and his line after them refused to repent. Consequently, destruction was assured.

Cole says that this military success was accompanied by economic success. As a result of their military victories, Israel was able to control many of the important trade routes. They were also able to become much wealthier due to increased tribute from their vassal areas.[63] Consequently, this time was so economically successful that the rich were able to live in homes of hewn stone and ivory (cf. Amos 5:11). It was one of the greatest financial times in the memory of any living Israelite. According to Cole, "from a financial perspective, things could not have been better for the Northern Kingdom."[64]

Because of their pride due to their wealth, the people began to oppress the poor.[65] Amos rebukes the nation of Israel for this oppression by calling them cows of Bashan and threatening that God will eventually judge them by taking them away with meat hooks (i.e. destruction). Apparently, they also charged a heavy rent to the farmer and exacted tribute from their grain (Amos 5:11). Even worse, they denied justice to the poor at the gate (Amos 5:12). According to Hosea 12:7–8, the merchants had false balances, and they loved to oppress. Despite all of this, they said, "Surely I have become rich, I have found wealth for myself; In all my labors they will find in me No iniquity, which would be sin." They apparently believed that they were blessed by God and without sin.

This period of time also brought about a great deal of spiritual complacency. They became prideful in the midst of their blessing. The Israelites of Jonah's day consistently considered themselves to be better than the other nations because they were chosen and they believed that calamity would

---

[63] Alan D. Cole, "The Purpose of the Book of Jonah" (Th.M. Thesis, Detroit Baptist Theological Seminary, May 1989), 24.
[64] Ibid., 25.
[65] For an extended discussion on this see Ibid., 25–27.

not befall them (Amos 9:10). Hosea told them that pride was one of their chief downfalls (Hosea 5:5). The Israelites were selected among many throughout the earth for God's specific purposes but were not in agreement with God's plans (Amos 3:2–3). They were very religious and brought their tithes and sacrifices as Jonah did in Jonah 2 (Amos 4:5–6). They called out to Yahweh, but they did not exalt Him (Hosea 11:7). The Israelites of Jonah's day received many blessings, but they were not willing to return to Yahweh (Amos 4:8). For this reason, God prophesied destruction on them (Amos 3:14). Some of them pridefully longed for the day of the LORD without realizing that their disobedience merited destruction (Amos 5:18). Others were consulting wooden idols as spiritual harlots who had departed from God (4:12). Excavations in Samaria Ostraca have yielded as many shrines with local names compounded with Baal as the name Yahweh.[66] As a result, God promised to leave them alone and cut them off (Hosea 8:4).

Ultimately Yahweh says in Amos 6:8, "I abhor the pride of Jacob and detest his fortresses; I will deliver up the city and everything in it." With respect to this charge, Smith writes, "Most interpreters take 'the pride of Jacob' to be an attribute of the people, their arrogant nationalistic and military self-confidence, or their overconfidence in the mountain of Samaria."[67] Despite all of this, repentance was still part of God's plan as it was for the Ninevites (Hosea 6:1, Amos 9:10–15). Repentance is an essential aspect of Jonah's prophetic message to the Ninevites and by implication the Israelites.

One of the greatest arguments for the historicity of Jonah and the early date of Jonah is the situation described in eighth century BC. The historical milieu fits right into the intended message of the book of Jonah. The book was written to a group

---

[66] John Bright, *A History of Israel*, 4th ed. (Louisville, KY: Westminster J. Knox Press, 2000), 260.
[67] Smith and Page, *Amos, Obadiah, Jonah*, 121.

of Israelites who were in need of the same repentance that the Ninevites demonstrated. They were also threatened to be destroyed in the same manner that Jonah had said that the Ninevites could be destroyed.

The positive circumstances for Israel during Jeroboam's reign occurred because Assyria was extremely weak at the time. Merrill writes:

> Jeroboam's exploits were possible first of all because of Assyria's inability to intervene. The mighty empire was at such a nadir that it was totally immobilized as far as foreign affairs were concerned. As for Ben-Hadad II of Damascus, he had suffered a crushing blow at the hands of Zakir of Hmath in about 773. Indeed, he may have died in that battle. Having previously lost a number of cities to Jehoash of Israel, he left Damascus in a greatly weakened condition at his death.[68]

In contrast to Israel, Assyria had been significantly weakened. Some thought they were experiencing the judgment of the gods. As previously mentioned, Wiseman argues that the omens recorded in the Enuma Anu Enlil that predicted destruction by invasion, earthquake, famine and other supernatural events probably contributed to the Ninevite repentance.[69]

Thus, the historical period is critical for interpretation. Fruchtenbaum argues that Jonah prophesied during Jeroboam's reign at some point between 824–783 BC.[70] He says that it was a time of material prosperity. The borders had been expanded to the extent of the borders during the time of David and Solomon. However, Fruchtenbaum describes this period as a time of

---

[68] Merrill, *Kingdom of Priests: A History of Old Testament Israel*, 374–75.
[69] D. J. Wiseman, "Jonah's Nineveh," *Tyndale Bulletin* 30 (1979): 45–51.
[70] Arnold G. Fruchtenbaum, *The Messianic Bible Study Collection* (Tustin, CA: Ariel Ministries, 1983), 79:4.

inward spiritual corruption. As previously mentioned, Fruchtenbaum considers it to be significant that Amos had preceded Jonah in informing the Northern kingdom of its immanent destruction by the Assyrian empire. Jonah's message was a follow up to Amos' preaching to demonstrate God's immediate plan for both Assyria and Israel.

This is one of the rare times in history when Israel was powerful and independent while Assyria was weak. However, this arrangement would not last for long. One can see a very strong parallel between the nation of Israel during Jeroboam's reign and Jonah. They were prideful and hypocritical in their worship. They willingly accepted the unmerited blessing of God, but they chose not to extend it for others. They had little compassion for the needy among them. This is exactly how Jonah is portrayed in the book. The message is clear. If the Israelites repent, God will relent. If they do not, they will be destroyed.

The precise date of the prophecy is affected by which of Jonah's prophecies came first. Fruchtenbaum argues that Jonah gave the prophecy described in 2 Kings 14:25 first and then gave the one in Jonah 3:4 second. Merrill places the prophecy in 2 Kings 14:25 at a few years earlier than 773 BC[71] and he suggests that Jonah's prophecy occurred during the reign of Ashur-dan III which he dates between 773–755.[72] Faulstich argues that Jonah's prophecy to Nineveh occurred on June 15, 763 BC and that Jonah reported the change of heart of the Ninevites to the Israelites afterwards in order for them to recover the territories which they had lost to Assyria and Judah.[73] Of these options, Merrill and Fruchtenbaum are most likely to be correct. First, Jonah's disobedience in Jonah 1 makes him an unlikely

---

[71] Merrill, *Kingdom of Priests: A History of Old Testament Israel*, 387.
[72] Eugene H. Merrill, "The Sign of Jonah," *Journal of the Evangelical Theological Society* 23, no. 1 (March 1980): 26.
[73] E.W. Faulstich, "Jonah: The Sign for Israel," (Spencer, IA: Chronology Books, 1989), 7.

candidate to deliver a prophecy to Jeroboam II after this experience. Despite the disobedience of the Israelites at this time, it is unlikely that they would attack a nation because they had repented of their sin. Furthermore, it seems less likely that Yahweh would order them to do so under these conditions. Instead, it would seem to be a better contrast to view Jonah as willing to give a good message to a rebellious Israelite king but unwilling to deliver the message to a rebellious Ninevite king. If he had delivered the message to Jeroboam II first, the portrayal of him as being an uncompassionate and prideful prophet would be further strengthened.

Summary

This section provided a basic historical background of Jonah's prophecy as part of the process of establishing the historical context of the prophecy for interpretation. As Walvoord argued, the historical context is critical for prophetic interpretation. In this case, the historical background gives additional evidence to the argument for implicit conditionality in Jonah 3:4. Jonah prophesied during the reign of Jeroboam II which has been dated anywhere from 824–753 BC. The internal evidence suggests an early date because of the overall correspondence with the historical situation happening in both Israel and Assyria during that period of time. Furthermore, the historical situation suggests that both repentance and destruction were critical to Jonah's message and his prophecy.

THE PURPOSE OF JONAH

As Walvoord and Master demonstrated in chapter one, the larger context of the purpose of Jonah should be considered when interpreting Jonah 3:4. While the book of Jonah is often used as a demonstration of why Christians should evangelize,[74] interpreters must remember that the book was written to Israel for Israel. However, even if there is agreement on that premise, there is often disagreement on what the purpose of writing and the ultimate message to Israel would be. The purpose of the book should uncover why it was written. The message should help determine what the book was written about. Cole lists the following popular options on the purpose of the book of Jonah: the universal-missionary purpose, typological purpose, God's sovereign will, God's mercy, and the repentance of Israel.[75]

The Proposed Purposes of the Book of Jonah
As previously mentioned, Cole lists five categories of purposes of the book of Jonah: the universal-missionary purpose, typological purpose, God's sovereign will, God's mercy, and the repentance of Israel.[76] This section of the chapter will evaluate each of these views in order to assess the implicit conditionality of Jonah 3:4. Ultimately, I will conclude that the repentance of Israel view best addresses the purpose of the book.

The first view is the universal missionary purpose. Cole argues that the universal-missionary purpose describes the intent of the book as an attempt to help Jonah (and by implication Israel) overcome his biased attitude so that both Israel and Jonah would fulfill their responsibilities as missionaries. Feinberg argues that Jonah is "the greatest mission book in the Old Testament, if not in the whole Bible. It is written to reveal the heart of a servant of God whose heart was not touched with the passion of God in missions."[77] Additionally, one commentary suggests that the author of Jonah

---

[74] See Charles Elliott, "Jonah," *The Old and New Testament Student* 10, no. 3: 139–40.
[75] Cole, "The Purpose of the Book of Jonah", 90–111.
[76] Ibid.
[77] Charles Lee Feinberg, *The Minor Prophets*, Combined ed. (Chicago: Moody Press, 1976), 151–52.

was sent to communicate "the ideal of Israel's mediatory service for mankind in bringing the knowledge of the true religion to the ends of the earth."[78] This view primarily focuses on the universality of God's love for the world and the Israelite's mission in expressing that love to others.

According to Cole, this view does not adequately address the fact that Jonah's message is primarily one of doom and judgment instead of the gospel. Furthermore, the concept of a missionary is primarily a New Testament concept and not an Old Testament one. While Israel was called to be a light to the nations, they primarily were supposed to live in such a way that foreigners would come to Israel in order to worship in their temple (which Jonah himself said he would do in Jonah 2:4). This can even be seen in Jesus and the Apostles' mission in which they primarily started with the Jewish groups and then extended their ministry to the Gentiles.

The second view that Cole addresses is the typological purpose. According to Cole, this view espouses Jonah as a type, primarily of Christ but also of Israel. Perhaps one of the greatest proponents of this view is Stanton in his article entitled "The Prophet Jonah and His Message: Part 1."[79] In this article, Stanton makes an argument for Jonah as an Old Testament type for Christ. In his second article, "The Prophet Jonah and His Message: Part 2," Stanton argues that Jonah is a type for Israel.[80]

Stanton makes a connection between the description of the sign of Jonah and the use of types as follows, "The use of types was sanctioned by Christ, as is clearly illustrated by His

---

[78] Hinckley G. T. Mitchell, J. M. Powis Smith, and Julius A. Bewer, *A Critical and Exegetical Commentary on Haggai, Zechariah, Malachi and Jonah* (Edinburgh, T. & T. Clark, 1971), 8.
[79] Gerald B. Stanton, "The Prophet Jonah and His Message Part 1," *Bibliotheca Sacra* 108, no. 430 (1951): 244–49.
[80] Gerald B. Stanton, "The Prophet Jonah and His Message Part 2," *Bibliotheca Sacra* 108, no. 431 (1951): 373–76.

use of Jonah in the twelfth chapter of Matthew concerning the time of His resurrection. 'As Jonah was…so shall the Son of man be.'"[81] Stanton defines a type as a symbol and representation while he considers the antitype to be the doctrine and reality. He encourages the exercise of caution in handling typology since every detail does not necessarily fit the type and since he believes that many different types clearly portray the character of Christ or the work of redemption. However, he identifies several types in Jonah. He believes "the book assumes a greater present meaning when this is clearly seen."[82] He states the value of studying types as follows:

> Many a minister would have been saved from an acceptance of the documentary hypothesis and from liberalism if he had realized the typical significance of the Scriptures. For 'the typology of the Old Testament is the very alphabet or the language in which the doctrine of the New Testament is written.' Types are the Old Testament foundations under New Testament doctrine, but with this restriction—the doctrine is not derived from the type, although it is illustrated and amplified by it; the type is interpreted by the doctrine.[83]

Stanton sees typological significance with Christ in Jonah's childhood, message, preaching, and experience in the fish. For instance, Stanton detects typology in some aspects of their childhood. He argues for a typology of Jesus in Jonah's name which means dove because the dove symbolizes peace. He connects this Old Testament typology with Christ who is the Prince of Peace and made peace by the death of His cross. Stanton cites Isaiah 9:6, Luke 2:14 and John 14:27 to defend his

---

[81] Stanton, "The Prophet Jonah and His Message Part 1," 245.
[82] Ibid.
[83] Ibid., 245–246.

claim. Stanton also argues for typology in Jonah's hometown which was Gath-Hepher since it was only four miles from the childhood home of Jesus in Nazareth. He then argues that both were Galilean prophets, and little is known of their childhood. These arguments are a significant stretch to prove exegetically. There are many prophets of whom there is little information about their childhood given.

The greatest likelihood of a typology is in what happened after Jonah was thrown out of the boat. According to Stanton, the Lord prepared a great fish to swallow Jonah, and for His Son there was a prepared tomb (Matthew 27:60). Jonah was taken to the bottom of the ocean while Christ was swallowed by death and the grave. Jonah lived in the valley of the shadow of death for "three days and three nights." Before Christ died, He prophesied clearly "and the third day he shall rise again" (Matthew 20:19). Stanton also says, "Jonah is not primarily a type of the Lord Jesus in His death, for Jonah did not die. Jonah is primarily a type of Christ in His resurrection from the dead, and was the important sign used of Christ before an unbelieving generation that He would rise from the grave (Matthew 12:3–41)."[84] Of all the options Stanton cites, this one is the most likely to prove to be a typology because Jesus makes the direct comparison between Himself and Jonah in Matthew 12:39–40.

Stanton argues for a contrast between the preaching of Christ and Jonah:

> Christ preached to the Gentiles and through His death we are no longer severally either Jew or Gentile, but one new man in Christ Jesus. But Christ never failed in His mission. He never fled and needed a second call. He set His face toward the cross, using Jonah as the sign of His impending death and subsequent resurrection. In His death and in the grave, and in that victory over death, He

---

[84] Ibid., 247–248.

manifested to all the truth of His own words: 'Behold, a greater than Jonas is here!' (Matthew 12:41).[85]

It is possible on the basis of Matthew 12:41 to argue that the preaching of Jonah was typological of Christ. Both preached repentance to the Gentiles as well as the possibility of destruction. Both were an object lesson to the nation of Israel for their disobedience. Both saw many Gentiles repent while the nation of Israel remained fairly unchanged.

With respect to Israel, Stanton argues for several typological similarities between Israel and Jonah. He argues that they were both: called, disobedient, in trouble, identified, cast overboard, contributors to Gentile salvation, preserved, never digested, and recommissioned.[86] While Jonah is symbolic of Israel in this book, it is doubtful that the original human or divine author intended all of these types. The original audience would have seen parallels between their disobedience to his calling as well as the possibility of their recommission based on repentance. However, it is doubtful that either they or future audiences would have viewed themselves as having been never digested for example.

While Stanton is correct that typology is important in the Old Testament, his claims are overexaggerated. From a scriptural point of view, the New Testament primarily points to Jonah's preaching and his experience in the fish as typological for Christ. Cole rightly questions whether typological significance was the primary purpose of the author, "The book of Jonah has a type in it, but it is not a book of types. The incident of the fish does not embrace the whole book nor does the typological view explain the interpretation of the work within its own historical context. In light of these points, the position

---

[85] Ibid., 249.
[86] Stanton, "The Prophet Jonah and His Message Part 2," 363–65.

should be set aside."[87]

The third view that Cole addresses is that of the purpose of describing God's sovereign will. He cites Bullock[88] and Ellison[89] as supporters of this view. According to this view, the purpose of Jonah is to affirm God's irresistible will in the world. While Cole correctly acknowledges God's sovereignty in the book, he rightly points out that it is not likely the primary purpose. Several Old Testament authors wrote about the theme of God's sovereignty but what seems unique in this book is God's sovereign response to repentance.

The fourth view discussed by Cole is that Jonah is primarily a book that intends to describe God's mercy. One commentary suggests this purpose:

> So here among the "Minor Prophets" is a book about a prophet and his reaction to those who listened to him. It differs from all the other books in this section of the Old Testament, which contain God's word to Israel and the nations through his prophets. Instead, this book contains God's word to a prophet through other people, all of whom are non-Israelites, but who are able to teach him something which he did not fully appreciate before about the God of Israel, who is "a loving and merciful God, always patient, always kind," even to those least deserving of his grace and even to a stubborn prophet.[90]

---

[87] Cole, "The Purpose of the Book of Jonah", 100.
[88] C. Hassell Bullock, *An Introduction to the Old Testament Prophetic Books* (Chicago: Moody Press, 1986), 51.
[89] H.L. Ellison, "Jonah" in *The Expositor's Bible Commentary: With the New International Version of the Holy Bible: Daniel – Minor Prophets*, ed. Frankank Ely Gaebelein and Dick Polcyn (Grand Rapids, MI: Zondervan Pub. House, 1985), 363.
[90] Brynmor F. Price and Eugene Albert Nida, *A Translators' Handbook on the Book of Jonah* (Stuttgart, Germany: United Bible Societies, 1978), 45.

Wolff also argues that one of the narrator's guiding concerns is that the same mercy that is promised to Israel applies to strangers as well.[91] Cole states the position as follows, "The basic teaching of this position reflects on the conflict between Israel's unwillingness to accept the extension of God's mercy to nations outside her borders."[92]

Cole also considers God's mercy to be an important theme to this book. However, Cole rightly argues that the primary condition for mercy is repentance.[93] The book was not necessarily written as an instruction on divine mercy, but to encourage the Israelites (like the Ninevites) to repent in order to avoid the imminent destruction that awaited them.

The final purpose that Cole evaluates is repentance for Israel. Advocates of this purpose argue that the author of Jonah writes to utilize Jonah's example to Israel as their need to repent in order to avoid the impending judgment on the nation. Cole espouses this position and it is the best of the five options. Cole prefers this position for several reasons. First, he argues that this purpose fits best with the historical situation in Jonah's day. Second, he believes that this purpose is most consistent with the genre of the book. Third, he argues that that this position carries the message of Jonah to the fullest conclusion.[94] Cole makes very strong arguments for the purpose of the book. This view also best addresses the prophetic intent of Jonah to spur the nation to repentance as many other prophets had done before him. It best fits the historical background discussed earlier in the chapter.

THE MESSAGE OF THE BOOK OF JONAH

The purpose of Jonah helps determine why the book was

---

[91] Hans Walter Wolff, *Obadiah and Jonah: A Commentary*, trans. Margaret Kohl (Minneapolis, MN: Augsburg Pub. House, 1986), 87.
[92] Cole, "The Purpose of the Book of Jonah", 105.
[93] Ibid., 107.
[94] Ibid., 110.

written. The previous section established that the purpose of Jonah was to motivate the nation of Israel to repent. The message of the book evaluates what the book is about. Two views are examined here. (1) Critical scholars, who espouse a late date for Jonah, often argue that Jonah is primarily a book about love that was intended to encourage the nation of Israel to overcome their anti-Gentile prejudice that began in the Ezra-Nehemiah era. Adherents of the second view argue that (2) Jonah serves as a negative example for Israel of their pride as God's covenant nation and their expectation that they did not need to repent in order to continue to receive God's blessing. The key message is that they too could receive deliverance from the impending judgment of Yahweh if they would repent. This author argues in favor of the second view.

The Critical View

R. B. Y. Scott espouses a late date for Jonah and argues for this message of the book:

> Thus, when we find evidence that there developed in Judaism at the time a tendency toward rigidity in belief and religious exclusiveness, with a new note of bitterness toward non-Jews, the setting of such a book as Jonah and the need for it become apparent....The stringent measures taken by Nehemiah to prevent the total disappearance of the Jewish people through assimilation (Nehemiah 13:23–25) may have been totally politically necessary, but they bore bitter fruit. The figure of Jonah is thus a portrait, exaggerated doubtless for emphasis, of those among the writer's co-religionists who have given way to bitterness and unrighteous anger because of all they had suffered at the hands of their enemies.[95]

---

[95] R. B. Y. Scott, "The Sign of Jonah," *Interpretation* (1965): 25.

In addition to this original message, he makes this application to the church:

> But the church as a whole does not take risks with its institutional existence by venturing far off from familiar paths into the heart of pagan Nineveh. Too many of us would watch with equanimity the destruction of what we personally detest by providing we can stay in shelter, comforting ourselves with the thought that our enemies are, after all, God's enemies.... But God said to Jonah, 'And I, should I not be sorry for that great city?' For God so loved the world.[96]

However, not all critical scholars consider this position to be plausible. R. E. Clements, in his article "The Purpose of the Book of Jonah," questions the traditional critical view.[97] Although he dates the book in the sixth century BC, he questions the traditional universal approach to the book based on the lack of acceptance of non-Jews in the book. Furthermore, he believes that the entire story does not have a single example of the issues that affected Jews and non-Jews during the time of Ezra-Nehemiah (for example, mixed language, mixed marriages and pagan uncleanliness).[98] Clements writes:

> If the intention of the book of Jonah is to encourage Jews to display to the heathen a charity and love comparable to that which God displays to the Ninevites, then it does nothing to show how this should be done, and what actions are required to express it. These considerations become all the stronger once we reflect upon the fact that the so-called separatism of Nehemiah and Ezra was not

---

[96] Ibid.
[97] R.E. Clements, "The Purpose of the Book of Jonah," *Supplement to the Vetus Testamentum* 28 (1974): 16–28.
[98] Ibid., 19.

> so much concerned with making a distinction between Jew and Gentile, a distinction which had existed in Israel for centuries, but with a division between Jews and those who laid claim to being Jews. The issues which reveal themselves in the Chronicler's history are primarily those of a growing separation between communities living in the territories of Judah and Samaria regarding the status and obligations of those who claimed to be heirs of the promises given to Israel. It is not clear that the book of Jonah has anything to say to such factions, except that the worst may be accepted by God if they repent.[99]

Clements' point is a good one. Ezra and Nehemiah do not present these alleged differences between Jews and Samaritans as something that God was trying to fix via universalism. The fact that Jonah says nothing of this conflict is a strong argument against the traditional critical view of the message of Jonah.

In light of these objections, Clements ultimately summarizes the purpose of Jonah as:

> The purpose of the book is to demonstrate the nature of God's dealings with men, particularly in regard to the bearing this has upon prophecy. When God passes a sentence of death upon a people, as he does upon the Ninevites, he leaves a way of salvation open to them in the possibility of repentance, As far as the intention of the author is concerned it seems primarily to have been his purpose to show that such a way of salvation was a possibility for Israel.[100]

In a general sense, this purpose statement addresses more of the concerns of the book. Clements' work tends to focus too much on

---

[99] Ibid.
[100] Ibid., 22.

God changing His prophecy and not on the implicitly conditional nature of the prophecy. Furthermore, while he attempts to connect this purpose with both the historical situation in Jonah's lifetime and the situation in the sixth century, he does so under the assumption that the author studied the situation in Jonah's life and tailored the story in such a way to address his current audience. A more plausible explanation would be that the author lived in the eighth century BC and he addressed the circumstances of that era. However, Clements has at least addressed many of the problems with the traditional critical view of the purpose of Jonah.

Regarding the message of Jonah espoused by many critical scholars, Stuart writes:

> At one time it was popular to assume that Jonah was written as a kind of universalistic treatise against the rigid, narrow reformist views of Ezra and Nehemiah. This view rightly lost favor on two accounts. First, the book is hardly universalistic. The fact that God should be concerned for Assyrians and be moved by their repentance is not the equivalent of saying that all people are God's chosen people or that the fate of all nations will ultimately be the same—i.e., salvation. The book nowhere implies that the Ninevites somehow became, as it were, God's chosen nation by reason of their occasion of repentance at Jonah's preaching. Second, the predominant concerns of Ezra and Nehemiah were the restoration of pentateuchal ritual practices, the security of Jerusalem, the elimination of foreign influences, and the prevention of mixed marriages. The fact that Jonah addresses none of these topics, even indirectly, means that it probably would never have occurred to the ancient Jews of the mid-fifth century BC that Jonah somehow was an attack on Ezra and Nehemiah. If this then was the purpose of the book, the author has kept that purpose

so well hidden that it is undiscoverable.[101]

Stuart's points are well taken. There is not a universalistic theme in Jonah. While the Ninevites and the Gentile sailors repented of their actions, there is no real proof that they followed Yahweh. The consummation of the future destruction prophesied by Nahum shows that they did not escape judgment based on God's love because they continued in disobedience. Thus, the book was written to a group of Israelites who were in need of the same repentance that the Ninevites demonstrated because they were just as likely to be destroyed in the same potential manner that the Ninevites were almost destroyed.

A Conservative Alternative View

In light of the historical situation, the eighth century BC northern tribes of Israel most likely received this prophetic message. Klingler writes:

> Given the fact that Jonah was from a member of the northern tribes who prophesied to Jeroboam II (cf. II Kings 14:25) and that the story of Jonah concerns Nineveh, the very capital of the nation which would eventually conquer Israel, the message of the Book of Jonah was most likely directed to the ten tribes which made up the northern kingdom. During the time of Jonah's ministry, his contemporaries (Amos, Hosea, Isaiah, and Micah) were preaching the message of repentance. The book of Jonah was written to a disobedient northern kingdom for the purpose of sending the warning, "Don't be like Jonah."[102]

---

[101] Douglas K. Stuart, *Hosea–Jonah*, vol. 31, 52 vols., Word Biblical Commentary (Waco, TX: Word Books, 1987), 434–435.
[102] David Klingler, "Jonah: A Call for Repentance" (Th.M. Thesis, Dallas Theological Seminary, 2004), 14.

Thus, Jonah represents the prideful disobedience of the Israelite nation during the eighth century BC. Jonah, like the Israelites, accepted the blessings of God's favor but did not repent in order to avoid His judgment. While the love of God for all people is a theme of the book, it is not the overriding message. Neither is sharing the gospel in a missionary sense. At best that is an application of the book, but most critical scholars have the overall message wrong. As mentioned earlier in this chapter, one of the strongest arguments for an early date of Jonah is the precise historical situation the book was written to address.

The Gentiles serve as a foil to Jonah (and by implication the Israelites). Jonah is contrasted to every character in the book.[103] Whereas the sailors cry out to Yahweh and offer vows, Saldivar argues that Jonah is full of religious talk but empty of practice. Whereas the Ninevites repent from the smallest to greatest of them, Jonah is stubborn and unrepentant.[104]

This is not only true in the story but in a historical sense as well. In fact, this may be the key lesson of the book:

> The lesson that he [Jonah] had to learn was that, while God had repeatedly appealed to Israel, his own people had not mourned or cried unto the Most High; and yet here was Nineveh, which he despised, fasting and wearing sackcloth at the preaching of a strange prophet. And the question which is put to Jonah is: Inasmuch as these two, Israel and Nineveh, are in the balances, upon whom shall God have mercy, and to whom shall he give the victory and the world power? Shall he destroy a city in which there are thousands who do not know their right hand from their left and spare Israel, exalting Israel to such greatness as the ambition of Jeroboam desired,

---

[103] Samuel Saldivar, "A Literary, Theological and Canonical Analysis of the Book of Jonah" (Ph.D. Dissertation, Bob Jones University, May 2006), 72.
[104] Ibid., 73.

when Israel had full knowledge of God and yet was wicked and stubborn?[105]

Spender also agrees with the role of contrast for understanding the message of Jonah:

> The message for Israel was an indicting one. If a foreign Gentile people like the Assyrians could repent and seek God why couldn't Israel? If God had compassion on Nineveh would He not have compassion on His own people? The answer to that question is of course "yes" but the condition of repentance remains. Israel needed to turn and repent but in the eighth century BC they were still running away from God. For years, the recipients of His grace, they had turned their backs on Him and fled to idols. Jonah's realization that "those who cling to worthless idols forsake the grace that could be theirs," (2:8, NIV) was equally meant for Israel.[106]

This message would have been a great indictment for Israel since they did not have the same willingness to repent that the Ninevites demonstrated. Stuart says:

> Jeremiah 36:9–31 makes clear that Jehoiakim of Jerusalem was notably unmoved by Jeremiah's words and therefore was denounced for his obstinance. But his pagan predecessor, the king of Nineveh, acted quite differently. Though as the despot of a vast empire he might be expected, of all people, to remain aloof from the vicissitudes of popular religious trends, in this case "even" (נגע אל) he was affected. And even he donned

---

[105] Arthur W. Ackerman, "The Purpose of Jonah's Mission to Nineveh," *Biblical World* 12 (September 1898): 194.
[106] Robert Spender, "Reading Jonah Again for the First Time," *Emmaus Journal* 10 (2001): 90.

sackcloth and left the throne to sit humbly in ashes in the Semitic posture of mourning and penitence. The emperor of the Assyrian empire abjectly appealed for mercy from the God on whose authority a vassal Israelite prophet had preached![107]

Thus, the key theme of Jonah is repentance. The book of Jonah basically encourages the Israelites to avoid acting like Jonah. To some degree, like Jonah, they became prideful in their position as God's chosen people and embraced Yahweh's compassion when it was shown to them but rejected His compassion when it was shown to others. In this book, God flips the tables to show that, like the Ninevites, the Israelites have acted in such a way that they deserve destruction. However, he also provides the opportunity for deliverance from this destruction if they are willing to repent. Thus, the ultimate contrast in the book is between Jonah (and by implication the nation of Israel) and the Ninevites. According to Saldivar, in contrast to Yahweh, Jonah "appears vindictive, self-righteous, powerless and bigoted."[108]

In light of this, the purpose and message of the book of Jonah can be summarized as follows, "The book of Jonah was written to Israel in order to describe Yahweh's compassion to Nineveh in response to their repentance in order to demonstrate to the nation of Israel, which was symbolized by the prideful and disobedient prophet Jonah, that they too could enjoy the same deliverance if they would repent." This statement describes the Israel focused message for the eighth century BC and emphasizes the key concept of repentance.

In relation to this book, the proposed purpose and message of the book supports the case for implicit conditionality in Jonah 3:4. If the purpose of the book was to motivate Israel to

---

[107] Stuart, *Hosea–Jonah*, 490.
[108] Saldivar, "A Literary, Theological and Canonical Analysis of the Book of Jonah", 74.

repent, then it only stands to reason that the condition of repentance would be found in Jonah's prophecy to the Ninevites. Repentance is critical to both the purpose and message of the book of Jonah. The implicit polysemantic wordplay view provides a textual indicator that would have helped the audience recognize this purpose and message.

GENRE OF JONAH

Since Walvoord's methodology incorporates the cultural context, the genre of Jonah should be evaluated. One of the greatest debates regarding the book of Jonah is the genre. In his article entitled "Jonah and Genre," Alexander gives a partial list of some of the proposals for the genre of Jonah: allegory, midrash, parable, prophetic parable, legend, prophetic legend, novella, satire, didactic fiction, satirical, and didactic short story.[109] This section of the book will explore several of the proposals for the genre and give a recommendation.

The critical views of Jonah vary considerably. Trible writes:

> If it can be demonstrated that this little book exhibits the characteristics of Jewish Literature in a post-exilic era, then this fact would support a late dating. One must show caution in limiting a given <u>Gattung</u> to certain areas; yet in relationship to the category of midrash the argument here is not without force."[110]

Allen says midrash is unlikely because the midrashic method is not as old as Jonah appears to be and it is difficult to pinpoint the text that the midrash of Jonah would be based on. Budde has

---

[109] T. Desmond Alexander, "Jonah and Genre," *Tyndale Bulletin* 36 (1984): 37.
[110] Phyllis Trible, "Studies in the Book of Jonah" (Ph.D. Dissertation, Columbia University, 1963), 115–16.

proposed 2 Kings 14:25 while Brockington proposed Jeremiah 18:8 and Trible argued for Exodus 34:6. Knight argued that Jonah was the second half of Isaiah.[111] Allen concludes:

> It is best to confine the definition of the literary form of the book to that of a parable with certain allegorical features. Rabbinic parables sought not only to interpret OT texts but to explore God's dealings with man, and in this second regard the little book of Jonah stands out as an illustrious ancestor.[112]

Wolff does not consider Jonah to be either a legend or a midrash but labels it as a novella.[113]

In light of the diverse opinions among critical scholars regarding the genre of Jonah, one must question why they would argue for a late date based on the genre. Stuart rightly identifies the main problem that critical scholars have with identifying the genre: their assumptions. They come to the text with an anti-supernatural bias:

> Miraculous events are chronicled in various places throughout the Bible. One can reject these on the basis of a systematic anti-supernaturalist bias, but one cannot single out Jonah in this regard. The argument that 'miracles can't happen, therefore they don't' is a subjective, not an objective, basis for discounting the factuality of the miracle narratives in Jonah.[114]

One of the more popular arguments of the genre of Jonah is that the book is parabolic. A parable is a literary story with a

---

[111] Allen, *The Books of Joel, Obadiah, Jonah and Micah*, 180.
[112] Ibid., 181.
[113] Wolff, *Obadiah and Jonah: A Commentary*, 80–85.
[114] Stuart, *Hosea–Jonah*, 440.

moral behind it.[115] Allen advocates this view by arguing that Jonah is a rabbinic parable. The greatest challenge with this view is that parables did not often involve true historical people. Even critical scholars believe that the Jonah of 2 Kings 14:25 was an actual historical person. Jesus Christ affirmed that Jonah was an actual person. As previously mentioned, Jesus compared Jonah's experience in the large fish to his death, burial and resurrection in Matthew 12:39–41. Jesus not only affirmed the historical validity of the event itself but also the response of the Ninevites. Jesus argued that the Ninevites repented at hearing his preaching and responded to his sign. Even if one could argue that Jesus was referring to a legendary story of Jonah's experience in a fish, how could Jesus argue that the Israelites should repent because one greater than Jonah was present if the Ninevites never repented and Jonah never went to them?

Second, most Old Testament parables are specifically introduced as such (for example, Ezekiel 17:2 and 24:3). Stuart provides strong arguments for why the book of Jonah is not parabolic:

> As sensational, didactic, prophetic narrative, the book shares features with those genres of literature known as parable and allegory, but it is not correct to identify it with either of these. 'Parable' is variously defined; but strictly speaking, a parable is invariably brief (not four chapters in length, in other words) normally having: a single scene but at most two or three (as in the parable of the lost son in Luke 15); elements of comparison to people or things outside the story who are the *real* focus; and some sort of a 'shock' or punch line which draws the hearer up short as it teaches a lesson, the reader seeing

---

[115] Andrew E. Hill and John H. Walton, *A Survey of the Old Testament*, 2nd ed. (Grand Rapids, MI: Zondervan Publishing House, 2000), 495.

himself or herself in the story. Moreover, true parables also have anonymous figures as their characters. The book of Jonah borders on some of these characteristics of parable, but actually manifests none of them exactly. And most significantly, parables are obviously *fictional*. Though the reader or hearer may choose to conclude upon reflection that the book of Jonah is fictional, the story is by no means *obviously* fictional. Indeed, it is our position, in concert with the traditional view, that the book is not fictional at all.[116]

Stuart rightly distinguishes the book of Jonah from a parable. Those qualities which are often considered to be parabolic are simply aspects of prophetic narrative.

The next possibility that is popular among critical scholars is the allegorical view. An allegory is a literary story in which the characters and events are symbolic.[117] Since they deny the historicity of Jonah, they prefer to allegorize not only the story but the sign that accompanies it. Trible rightly questions this view when she writes:

> An allegorical interpretation of <u>Jonah</u> is primarily derived from and dependent upon many other parts of Scripture. To deduce literary <u>form</u> and meaning of one passage from the <u>contents</u> of other scattered passages is a highly dubious methodology. It certainly provides an opportunity for one to read into the passage ideas which are not really there, even though they sound plausible."[118]

Stuart similarly argues against allegory for the following reasons:

---

[116] Stuart, *Hosea–Jonah*, 436. Emphasis his.
[117] Hill and Walton, *A Survey of the Old Testament*, 495.
[118] Trible, "Studies in the Book of Jonah", 158. Emphasis hers.

> An allegory is a kind of extended analogy, sometimes including extended metaphors, in which the meaning of the story is not to be found in the concepts and actions presented, but in concepts and actions outside the story, to which the story points analogically. It would be an unusual allegory indeed that waited to the end (the fourth chapter in the case of Jonah) to reveal the point of its hero's actions. Allegories are distinctly constructed so as to point beyond themselves at each stage. The figures in an allegory are patently symbolic and fictional, and the audience must realize this at once if the allegory is to be effective. Jonah does not fit this pattern, either.[119]

Trible and Stuart's arguments cast doubt on whether Jonah is an allegory.

Some like Trible label Jonah as a midrash. A midrash is "a story which is intended to convey a religious truth by elaborating and embellishing an event in a historical setting."[120] Stuart rightly criticizes this option:

> Jonah is also not midrash. Midrashic literature functions as commentary upon particular biblical texts and may include illustration as well as propositional explanation. Midrash is patently didactic, but by no means is all didactic literature, including narrative, to be identified as midrashic. The Bible contains two references to midrashim, both in 2 Chronicles. Mention is made in 2 Chronicles 13:22 of "the Midrash of the Prophet Iddo" and in 2 Chronicles 24:27 "the Midrash of the Book of Kings." Both of these must have contained stories, but it is an unwarranted conclusion to assume that they were composed of nothing but stories. Probably they included commentary and other

---

[119] Stuart, *Hosea–Jonah*, 436.
[120] Hill and Walton, *A Survey of the Old Testament*, 496.

expansions upon the historical narratives they reproduced, though little can be known for certain about their content. For Jonah to be convincingly identified as a midrash, it would need to be demonstrated that the story was composed to serve as an illustrative explanation of something taught elsewhere in the OT. Not only can this never be done convincingly in light of the lack of data relevant to the task. It would be virtually the reverse of a typical biblical period midrash. The early midrashim we do know about are characterized by analytical discussion of stories, laws, or other "primary" material. By its nature Jonah appears far more likely to be not the midrash but the primary material, so that any midrash would be secondary, i.e., a discussion of the truth contained in Jonah. Attempts to relate Jonah in a midrashic manner to Joel 2:13, 14 or to Amos (Coote, *Amos Among the Prophets*) have therefore remained speculative.[121]

Stuart shows the speculation required for midrash since Jonah describes historical events.

Another popular view is that the book of Jonah is a satire or a parody.[122] This view basically argues that the narrative takes a stock character prophet and introduces situations that are consistent with the prophetic genre with an exaggerated twist that will be interpreted with humor by the audience.[123] For instance, whereas some prophets like Moses or Jeremiah were reluctant to serve in a prophetic role, Jonah goes as far away as possible. Whereas other kings responded to the prophetic message, the Ninevites go to such an extent that they even cause

---

[121] Stuart, *Hosea–Jonah*, 436. Emphasis his.
[122] John A. Miles, Jr., "Laughing at the Bible: Jonah as Parody," *Jewish Quarterly Review* 65, no. 3: 168–81.
[123] For a critique of this view of Jonah see Adele Berlin, "A Rejoinder to John A. Miles, Jr., with Some Observations on the Nature of Prophecy," The *Jewish Quarterly Review* 66 (April 1976) 227–235.

their animals to bear sackcloth and ashes. While there is a great deal of irony in the book, the historical nature of the book does not lend itself to the genre of satire. In Matthew 12 and Luke 11, Jesus uses the example of Jonah as a case for repentance on the part of his hearers, not as a funny story to illustrate a point. He treats Jonah and the Ninevites as actual historical people and encourages the Jewish listeners to repent like the Ninevites repented. Thus, the irony of the book may be a result of the didactic nature of teaching from the least to the greatest. If the worst nation, who was addressed by the worst prophet (who ran from his calling) with a short sermon, repented, how much more should the Israelite nation who had the revelation of God and many prophets repent in light of their impending destruction?

Conservative scholars also have a variety of opinions on the subgenre of Jonah. Most conservative scholars rightly agree that Jonah is some form of historical narrative. The author of Jonah presents the book as though it is a historical document. The main character, Jonah, is identified along with his father. Jonah contains all of the elements necessary for identifying a historical narrative: setting, characterization, plot, point of view and style.[124] In fact, Loken lists word play as a key indicator of style often found in historical narrative.[125] As the section on the historicity of Jonah pointed out, the supernatural events in Jonah should not cause scholars to discount the historical nature of the book. Furthermore, the traditional interpretation of Jonah from Tobit to Jesus to Josephus to Justin the Martyr to Calvin was to interpret the book as a historical document.

What form of historical narrative is it? The challenge with identifying the subgenre is incorporating the poetic aspects with the prose, prophetic, comic and tragic/dramatic portions of

---

[124] These elements were taken from Israel Loken, *The Old Testament Historical Books: An Introduction* (Longwood, FL: Xulon Press, 2008), xii.
[125] Ibid., xiii.

the story. Some suggest that Jonah is a prophetic biography[126] while others consider it to be a prophetic narrative.[127] Both of these subgenres are preferable to the aforementioned critical ones because they recognize the historicity of the book. However, they do not really address the prophetic aspects of the text as well as the ironic aspects of it. The text itself has a great deal of irony and in many ways Jonah himself represents a warning message to Israel.

Branson L. Woodard addresses the tragic aspects of the book when he writes:

> Throughout the book, then, Jonah demonstrates the downward movement typical of tragedy, in which a privileged protagonist falls from a position of honor and respect, here the ministry of a prophet, to one of rebuke and death. The narrator, in fact, makes this movement clear through repetition: His special standing is established by the phrase "son of Amittai," i.e., truth, and by the call to ministry itself (1:1). Without further delay, however, the narrator explains Jonah's fall, particularly through repetition. He "went down" to Joppa (1:3); aboard the ship in a storm, he had "gone below" (v 5). Later he descended "into the deep" (2:3) and "sank down" (2:6). This entire scene is filled with images of death. And the narrative concludes with Jonah's two death wishes (4:3, 8) and the death of the plant (4:7). His shame is complete, and the irony most strong, as the book ends; the "son of truth" who well knows Yahweh's grace must hear a plea from Yahweh to believe it. This low point is probably the

---

[126] Robert B. Chisholm Jr., *Handbook on the Prophets: Isaiah, Jeremiah, Lamentations, Ezekiel, Daniel, Minor Prophets* (Grand Rapids, MI: Baker Academic, 2002), 406–07.
[127] Stuart, *Hosea–Jonah*, 435.

most degrading one in the book.[128]

Woodard defends his position by giving examples of ironic and tragic aspects of the book. For instance, he characterizes Jonah's tragic attempt to run from the calling of God that was ultimately rooted in his pride. This pride results in Jonah serving as a tragic figure:

> What could gratify a believer any more than that? Not Jonah, though; he grows angry at Yahweh's grace. Moreover, he asks to die (4:3), as Elijah had requested for himself (1 Kings 19:4). These two details, in addition to other images of death in chapter 4 (and throughout the book), present Jonah less as a satirized prophet and more a tragic figure. Some humor may arise from the narrative, but the laughter turns to mourning as the intended Hebrew audience considers the Abrahamic Covenant (Genesis 12:3). How utterly disgraceful for the melancholic evangelist to seek death for himself and destruction for the Ninevites, rather than further Yahweh's plan to make of Abraham a great nation and through his progeny to evangelize the Gentiles. That blessing, in Jonah anyway, has turned into a curse, though never apart from divine superintendence.[129]

Woodard then solidifies the evidence for his position by comparing Jonah's story to other tragic stories in the Bible like Samson as well as Adam and Eve.

Some aspects of the story that some might identify as satirical, Woodard considers to be essential to the purpose. For example, he writes:

---

[128] Branson L. Woodard, "Death in Life: The Book of Jonah and Biblical Tragedy," *Grace Theological Journal* 11, no. 1 (1990): 12.
[129] Ibid., 11.

DID GOD CHANGE HIS MIND? 223

> Sincere doubts about the inclusion of the animals have prompted some commentators to interpret this scene as grotesque and, literally, fantastic. But the narrator may have a different (nonsatiric) intention, to dramatize the depth of God's concern for the Ninevites and even for their animals, a compassion expressed also in the conclusion of the book."[130]

His point is a good one. Yahweh's compassion for the animals is a reflection of His care for the least of all creation and His response to all forms of repentance—even animals.[131]

Woodard's argument for tragedy explains many of the ironic aspects as well as the historical message of Jonah. However, Wendland's tragicomedy view better incorporates the irony of the parody with the historicity of the prophetic narrative as well as the tragic aspects of the story. Wendland writes:

> In any case, Jonah presents us with a problem because our evaluation will depend upon what we see as being the book's central theme and purpose: Does this involve the pagan cast, the sailors and residents of Nineveh, in which case we are clearly dealing with comedy, or is the main spotlight upon the prophet's experience, in which case tragedy would appear to be a more accurate description? Perhaps in this instance (as in many other aspects of this brief but complex composition) it is better to allow for both possibilities—that

---

[130] Ibid., 10.
[131] Woodard says, "That animals are described as sharing human experiences is not limited to Jonah 3:7–8 anyway. The prophecy of Joel refers to beasts engaged in moaning and suffering (1:18), 'panting for' God (1:20), and being instructed not to fear past devastation of crops (2:20). Although the uncertain dating of Joel's prophecy (from the ninth century to a post-exilic period) makes any further connection between the two books mere conjecture, the similarity of the two descriptions of animals warrants further study" (Ibid).

is, tragicomedy. The dominant emphasis does seem to be on Jonah, the central (human) character. But his pathetic case, which really comes to the fore only in the climactic fourth chapter through dialogue with the Lord, is made to stand out more sharply by being juxtaposed with the two comic conversion accounts (chapters 1, 3).[132]

Wendland's point is an interesting one. From the perspective of Jonah, the book is a tragedy. However, the Gentiles appear within the text having characteristics that would be typical of a comedy.[133] Unlike the American genre of a comedy, the Hebrew comedy often involves an exalted or redeemed hero that comes from a low status (or a satirized noble person) that enjoys a blessed ending thanks to the sovereign involvement of God when the crisis or conflict is overcome.[134] The Gentiles seem to perfectly fit this description. They often serve as a foil of faith to Jonah who ran from Yahweh. In fact, the one thing they all have in common is that they were saved by the grace of God. Therefore, it seems hard to imagine that God's original intent would be to destroy the very group of people that He is intending to use as an object lesson for Jonah and the rest of the Hebrews.

However, since Jonah is the main character of the book,

---

[132] Ernst R. Wendland, "Text Analysis and the Genre of Jonah (Part 1)," *The Journal of the Evangelical Theological Society* 39, no. 2 (1996): 194–95.

[133] Wendland classifies Jonah "not in terms of a single genre but in compound fashion as a dramatic (due to its clear-cut scenic structure and large proportion of dialogue), didactic, typological, tragicomic narrative. In other words, for various reasons (to be discussed more fully below) I consider it to be essentially an historical (factive), plot-oriented text, but one that is artistically patterned both to maintain interest and also to highlight or reinforce key aspects of the hortatory message. It is a prophetic 'word of the Lord' to his people, then and now. Furthermore, the discourse is rhetorically shaped by means of a heavy overlay of irony that borders on the satiric in order to teach a lesson."

[134] Ibid, 194.

the tragic aspects are more pronounced. In a sense, Woodard's explanation for tragedy emphasizes how Jonah's attitude is intended to be a lesson to the Ninevites. Wendland's explanation for tragicomedy does provide the added benefit of incorporating the tragedy but also explaining the comedic and ironic aspects of Jonah's foils.

Wendland's conclusion that Jonah is a tragicomedy supports the argument for implicit conditionality in Jonah 3:4. With respect to the Ninevites who enjoy the comedic aspects of the book, the prophecy provides the opportunity for repentance. However, with respect to Jonah and Israel who he symbolizes, the prophecy is a tragic sign of the impending destruction that awaits them if they do not repent. Both themes of repentance and destruction/judgment contribute to the tragicomedy genre of Jonah.

SUMMARY

This chapter explored the immediate context as well as the larger context of the historical context, purpose, message, and genre of Jonah. Similar to Master's approach to Exodus 32:10 and the methodology espoused in chapter one, arguments for implicit conditionality should be consistent with the immediate context as well as the purpose and message of Jonah. The immediate context strongly points to the implicit conditionality of Jonah's prophecy to the Ninevites. The narrator presents strong evidence that Jonah's prophecy did come directly from Yahweh. The switch from the adversative (וּקְרָא עָלֶיהָ) to the more positive phrase (וּקְרָא אֵלֶיהָ) increases the probability of implicit conditionality. Nineveh is described as a city that is important to Yahweh which reveals his compassionate intentions. Perhaps this is why Yahweh gives the Ninevites forty days to repent. The Ninevites indicate hope that God will relent. In Jonah 4, Jonah accuses God of wanting to relent from punishment all along. However, he sits east of the city the waiting to see if God will judge them or deliver them. This strongly indicates that Jonah recognized that destruction and repentance were possible results of his prophecy.

Walvoord argues in his method for interpreting prophecy that the historical context should be explored as well. The eighth century BC historical context strongly points to implicit conditionality. Similar to the Ninevites, the Israelites had an evil king (Jeroboam) who needed to repent so that his nation would not be destroyed. However, unlike the king of Nineveh, Jeroboam refused to repent despite hearing several prophecies and consequently Israel was due for judgment. Jonah is written in order to encourage the Israelite audience to repent or risk judgment.

Walvoord's emphasis on the cultural context requires the examination of the purpose, message and genre of Jonah. Hence, this book incorporated a holistic view that assesses the larger literary context of Jonah in order to demonstrate that the implicit conditionality espoused by the implicit polysemantic wordplay view is completely consistent with the purpose, message and genre of Jonah. The purpose and message of the book of Jonah were summarized as follows, "The book of Jonah was written to Israel in order to describe Yahweh's compassion to Nineveh in response to their repentance in order to demonstrate to the nation of Israel, which was symbolized by the prideful and disobedient prophet Jonah, that they too could enjoy the same deliverance if they would repent." Since repentance is critical to both the purpose and message of the book, it was likely implicit in the prophecy in Jonah 3:4. The implicit polysemantic wordplay gives the best way for textually indicating this implicit condition. Furthermore, the book was labeled as a historical narrative with a subgenre of tragicomedy. The tragicomedy subgenre points to the possibility of both repentance and destruction since both the Ninevites (comedy) and Jonah (tragedy) play important roles in the book of Jonah.

CHAPTER 5

THEOLOGICAL ANALYSIS: JESUS'S REFERENCES TO JONAH

Jonah's prophecy to the Ninevites is not mentioned in the Old Testament outside of the book of Jonah. For a canonical context on the prophecy, one will have to go to the preaching of Jesus on Jonah in the New Testament. This chapter is intended to demonstrate that Jesus used Jonah as a sign of repentance for the Ninevites but destruction for the generation of Israelites present at His first coming. Jesus Himself confirms that the sign of Jonah involves both repentance and destruction as the message and purpose of Jonah suggest.

THE BIBLICAL TEXTS

Jonah is mentioned directly in three New Testament passages (Matthew 12:39–41, 16:4, and Luke 11:29). In both cases in Matthew, Jonah was discussed after a request for a sign by some of the religious leaders in Israel. In Luke's account, Jesus follows His discussion of the blasphemy of the Holy Spirit with two discussions addressed to the crowd. His first address in Luke 11:27–28 (NASB) is to a woman who proclaims, "Blessed is the womb that bore You and the breasts at which You nursed." Jesus responds by focusing on practical obedience, "On the contrary, blessed are those who hear the word of God and observe it."

The first discussion of Jonah is in Matthew 12:39–41 (NASB) where Jesus makes the following statement in response to the Pharisees' request for a sign:

> But He answered and said to them, "An evil and adulterous generation craves for a sign; and *yet* no sign will be given to it but the sign of Jonah the prophet; for just as JONAH WAS THREE DAYS AND THREE NIGHTS IN THE BELLY OF THE SEA MONSTER, so will the Son of Man be three days and three nights in the heart of the earth. The men of Nineveh will stand up with this generation at the judgment and will condemn it because they repented at the preaching of Jonah and behold, something greater than Jonah is here."

Christ is critical of the religious leaders' desire for a sign. He states that the specific sign He will give is the sign of Jonah. His critique of them being an evil and perverse generation is probably an allusion to Deuteronomy 32:1–20. In this Song of Moses, Moses refers to the characteristics of an evil and perverse generation twice (32:5, 20). In this passage, Moses asks the heaven and earth to listen to his teaching because he proclaims the name of Yahweh, the perfect and faithful Rock. Despite Yahweh's faithfulness to them, the Israelites committed the following sins in verses 5–6: "They have acted corruptly toward Him, They are not His children, because of their defect; But are a perverse and crooked generation. Do you thus repay the LORD, O foolish and unwise people? Is not He your Father who has bought you? He has made you and established you." The people are foolish because they have dealt corruptly with Yahweh. In 32:16–17, Moses says that they "made Him jealous with strange gods" and "provoked Him to anger." They did so by sacrificing "to demons who were not God." They neglected the Rock and forgot about Him (32:18). As a result, in Deuteronomy 32:19–20 Yahweh "saw this" and "spurned them because of the provocation of His sons and daughters." He then said, "I will hide

My face from them, I will see what their end shall be; For they are a perverse generation, Sons in whom is no faithfulness." Therefore, according to Deuteronomy 32:21–23, Yahweh will "make them jealous with those who are not a people" and bring many misfortunes (including famine and death) upon them.

Despite Christ's righteousness, the religious leaders were acting corruptly toward the Messiah by requesting a sign. Their foolishness indicates that they are not His children. They are a generation which does not demonstrate faithfulness. All they had to do was recognize they were under Gentile control in the land to realize they were under a curse by God for their unfaithfulness (cf. Deuteronomy 28:31–33). However, the religious leaders are persecuting the Messiah who could set them free. As a result, they are heading for judgment according to Deuteronomy 32:31–33.

Consequently, Jesus said in Matthew 12:39–40 that as Jonah was in the belly of the sea monster for three days and three nights, so will the Son of Man be three days and three nights in the heart of the earth.[1] This statement points to the death, burial, and resurrection of Christ being the sign of Jonah.[2] Thus, Jesus' resurrection was the ultimate confirmation of His identity as Messiah. However, like all the other signs, most Jews would not believe. They had already attributed the lesser sign of demonic exorcism to Beelzebul (Matthew 12:24),

---

[1] This book will not address the issues associated with how the three days and nights are accounted for. While this is a topic that is worthy of consideration, it falls out of the scope of this work. For more information on how the days would be reckoned for Christ's crucifixion and resurrection, see Harold W. Hoehner, *Chronological Aspects of the Life of Christ* (Grand Rapids, MI: Zondervan Publishing House, 1977), 65–74.

[2] There is some debate among commentators about whether Jonah's cry from Sheol in Jonah 2:2 indicates he died or if this was hyperbolic. Even if it was hyperbolic, he was at the point of death (Jonah 2:5) in the depths of the pit (Jonah 2:6). Typology typically includes escalation in the New Testament so one should not be surprised to see Jesus die and be buried without Jonah having the same precise experience.

and they refused to believe in the greater sign of Christ's resurrection (Luke 16:31).

It is important to note that Christ also said that the men of Nineveh repented at the preaching of Jonah (which did include his prophecy). Therefore, there is a direct correlation with Jonah's sign, which validated his preaching and led to the repentance of the Ninevites. Additionally, Jesus used a common rabbinical approach called a *qal wahomer* which is to argue from the light to the heavy (or the lesser to the greater).

This chart best summarizes the comparison of the Ninevites to the religious leaders that Jesus addressed:

To the Scribes and Their Followers:	To the Ninevites
It is the Son of God himself who addresses them again and again, and bids them to repent (Matthew 4:17; 11:28–30; 23:37).	It was a minor prophet who preached to them.
This Christ is completely sinless (12:17–21; John 8:46), filled with wisdom and compassion (Matthew 11:27–30; 15:32; 1 Corinthians 1:24).	This prophet was a sinful, foolish, and rebellious person (Jonah 1:3; 4:1–3, 9b).
He presents the message of grace and pardon, of salvation full and free (Matthew 9:2; 11:28–30; Luke 19:10; John 7:37).	His message was one of doom. Though a call to repentance was certainly implied, the emphasis was on "Yet forty days, and Nineveh shall be overthrown" (Jonah 3:4).
This message is being fortified by miracles in which prophecy is being fulfilled (Matthew 11:5; Luke 4:16–21; cf. Isaiah 35:5, 6; 61:1–3; John 13:37).	There were no miracles or other authenticating signs to confirm Jonah's message.
It is being brought to a people who have enjoyed ever so many spiritual advantages (Deuteronomy 4, 7, 8; 19:4; Psalm 147:19, 20; Isaiah 5:1–4; Amos 3:2a; Romans 3:1, 2; 9:4, 5).	Jonah's message was addressed to a people with none of the advantages that scribes, Pharisees, and their followers had enjoyed.[3]

---

[3] William Hendriksen and Simon J. Kistemaker, *Exposition of the Gospel According to Matthew*, vol. 9, New Testament Commentary (Grand Rapids, MI: Baker Book House, 1953–2001), 535.

The preaching and person of Christ was superior to that of Jonah. Furthermore, the Israelites had far more access to revelation than the Ninevites. Jesus is arguing that if the (lesser) wicked Ninevites repented at the preaching of the inferior prophet Jonah (lesser), the Jews of His day (greater) should repent at the coming of the Messiah (greater). This is consistent with the message and purpose of the book of Jonah. Jesus is recognizing the possibilities of repentance or destruction in Jonah's prophecy, and He is applying the same options of repentance or destruction to His Jewish audience that the original author of Jonah presented to the Ninevites.

Matthew 16:4 is the shortest of the three references to the sign. In this passage Jesus is responding to the request of the Pharisees and Sadducees who are testing Him by asking for a sign from heaven. Jesus responds by saying:

> When it is evening, you say, "It will be fair weather, for the sky is red." And in the morning, "There will be a storm today, for the sky is red and threatening." Do you know how to discern the appearance of the sky, but cannot discern the signs of the times? An evil and adulterous generation seeks after a sign; and a sign will not be given it, except the sign of Jonah.

Once again, Jesus criticizes the religious leaders for seeking a sign. He makes another *qal wahomer* argument that if they are able to discern the signs of the sky, why are they not able to understand the signs of the time. He reiterates the promise of the sign of Jonah.

Luke 11:29–30 is the other notable passage where the sign of Jonah is directly mentioned. The passage says, "As the crowds were increasing, He began to say, 'This generation is a wicked generation; it seeks for a sign, and yet no sign will be given to it but the sign of Jonah. For just as Jonah became a sign to the Ninevites, so will the Son of Man be to this generation.'" As previously mentioned, this rebuke is not only given to the religious leaders but also is a caution given to the crowd regarding the consequences of rejecting Christ. While there are many additional differences between Luke's portrayal and Matthew's, one is focused on here. The chief difference is the fact that Jonah himself is declared to be a sign to the Ninevites.

Whereas in Matthew Jesus described the sign of Jonah, Luke points out that Jonah himself *was* a sign. Merrill is correct in arguing that the name Jonah should probably be taken as a genitive of apposition with sēmeion so that he himself is the sign.[4] Not only this, but Luke specifies what Matthew implies by saying that Jonah was a sign to the Ninevites. Merrill elaborates on the implications of this key textual difference as follows:

> On the basis of the Matthean account most interpreters of this phrase correctly see that Jesus is making an analogy between Jonah's three days and three nights of incarceration in the belly of the fish and Jesus' confinement to Sheol. Equally correctly, many go on to suggest that Jonah's miraculous experience is a prophetic type of the death, burial, and resurrection of Christ. But this type is of necessity limited as a sign by its application to the scribes and Pharisees and other post-resurrection witnesses, including this present generation. Matthew, however, proposes a correspondence between the experience and the preaching of Jonah on the one hand and the subsequent repentance of Nineveh on the other. More pointedly, Luke states that Jonah was a sign "to the Ninevites" (Luke 11:30). Most scholars are satisfied to see Matthew's version as an embellishment of Luke's, but the phrase "to the Ninevites" is in fact an addition not found in Matthew in so many words—though, as we have suggested, it is implicit in Matthew. The point that Luke,

---

[4] Eugene H. Merrill, "The Sign of Jonah," *Journal of the Evangelical Theological Society* 23, no. 1 (March 1980), 25.

especially, is making is that Jonah was in some way such a powerful sign to the people of Nineveh that they repented at his preaching.[5]

Merrill's point is well made. There must be a sense in which Jonah himself was such a sign that the Ninevites would repent at his preaching. Thus, the sign should relate to both Jonah's deliverance from the fish and the response to his preaching.[6]

It is critical to note that Jesus refers to Jonah as a sign that was intended to induce repentance and not necessarily destruction only. This is especially true in light of the repentance of the Ninevites that resulted from Jonah's preaching and his presence in the belly of the sea monster for three days and three nights. However, Jesus also demonstrates that the sign of Jonah was a sign of judgment (and ultimately destruction) to the unbelieving Jews because they did not respond to Him in the same way that the Ninevites did to Jonah. Ironically the repentant Gentile Ninevites themselves would rise in judgment against the unbelieving Jews who did not repent at the preaching of Jesus, the greater Jonah (cf. Matthew 12:41 and Luke 11:32). Michael Ben Zehabe further notes that Jesus preached for approximately three years, and approximately forty years later Jerusalem was destroyed (which corresponds interestingly to Jonah's three days in the belly of a fish and the forty days that the Ninevites had to repent).[7] Thus, the sign of Jonah is a sign of repentance to the Ninevites but destruction to the Jews which is consistent with the implicit polysemantic wordplay view.

---

[5] Ibid.

[6] This section of the book will not address different interpretations of the sign of Jonah. Alternative views to Merrill's will be briefly described and evaluated in Appendix D.

[7] Michael Ben Zehabe, *A Commentary on Jonah: Accidental Hebrew for Christians* (Los Angeles, CA: Shema Publishing Company, 2011), 62.

JONAH AS SIGN TO THE NINEVITES BECAUSE OF THEIR GOD

Eugene Merrill is not the originator of this position, but he has probably articulated it better than anyone else. In 1892, H. Clay Trumball argued for a similar position based on archaeological evidence.[8] While the New Testament does not change the meaning of the text in the Old Testament, it can at least inform the church on how it was interpreted, especially when Jesus did the interpreting. Essentially, Merrill argues that Jonah's survival in the belly of the fish was interpreted by the Ninevites as confirmation that Jonah was a messenger from the gods because of their belief in a fish-man-god. This explains the prompt and even extreme reaction of the Ninevites to his prophecy.

Summary of Merrill's View

Some of Merrill's background research is helpful for establishing the implicit conditionality of Jonah 3:4. According to Merrill, the sign of Jonah relates to Christ's death, burial, and resurrection:

> Jonah, having been thrown overboard by the Phoenician sailors, found himself swallowed up by the great fish in whose belly he remained for three days and three nights. Whether he died or not during that time and was then resuscitated is incidental both to Jesus' use of the story as an analogy to his death, burial and resurrection and to Jonah's being a sign to the Ninevites. The thrust of Jesus' remarks was that he, like Jonah, would be confined for three days and three nights."[9]

---

[8] For more information on Trumball's arguments see H. Clay Trumbull, "Jonah in Nineveh," *Journal of Biblical Literature* XI, no. Part I (1892): 53–60.

[9] Merrill, "The Sign of Jonah," 28.

Merrill considers the main thrust of Jesus' argument to be that Jesus would be in the tomb for three days and three nights before rising again. He does not consider the question of whether Jonah died in the fish to be essential to the debate.

Merrill's view does not discount the identification of the sign of Jonah with the resurrection of Jesus; it simply adds a greater understanding of the significance of the sign of Jonah in its time as well as the sign of Jesus in His time. Essential to Merrill's view is his definition of what a sign is. Merrill defines σημεῖον as "a miraculous act produced to authenticate its agent and to induce faith in God on the part of the observer."[10] As previously mentioned, Merrill discusses some important distinctions between Matthew's and Luke's accounts. Whereas Matthew focuses on Jonah's experience in the fish and his preaching, Luke also notes that Jonah himself "became a sign to the Ninevites" (Luke 11:30).[11] Therefore, Merrill concludes, "The point that Luke, especially, is making is that Jonah was in some way such a powerful sign to the people of Nineveh that they repented at his preaching."[12]

How was Jonah a sign to the Ninevites? Merrill makes some interesting observations. He points out that Nineveh's name "was formed of the composite Sumerian logogram NINUA, the interior sign of which is KU_6 or, in Akkadian, nūnu, 'fish'" and that "a town of identical name (Nina) near Lagash worshipped the fish-goddess Nanshe, so it is suggested that she was also the chief deity of early Nineveh."[13] He also elaborates on an Assyrian tradition that "Assyria's arts and sciences were brought from the Persian Gulf by a half-fish, half-man deity called in the Greek Oannes."[14] Merrill notes that all these facts give further insight into Jesus' statement that Jonah himself

---

[10] Ibid., 23.
[11] Ibid., 24.
[12] Ibid.
[13] Ibid., 26.
[14] Ibid.

was a sign to the Ninevites. If Jonah had survived in the belly of a large fish and had come to pronounce a message of potential judgment and deliverance, this would have captivated their attention. In fact, Merrill says this is one of the reasons Jonah received such a captive audience in such a short period of time:

> In Matthew, attention is drawn to Jonah's having been in the belly of the fish for three days and three nights, but since Luke specifies that Jonah was a sign to Nineveh that experience in the fish must have been communicated to the Assyrian capital and have become to the Ninevites a sign that Jonah was a divine messenger. Such a sign would be particularly convincing to a people whose aetiology taught them that their city had been founded by a fish-god. The spectacular and timely arrival of Jonah among them created a curiosity and receptivity to his message that would have been possible in no other way. When the truth of the message of Yahweh was then proclaimed, the response was the repentance and faith.[15]

Merrill's point is an interesting one. Jonah came in a way that would generate interest in Jonah as a divine messenger. This allowed for greater attention to his message and validated for the Ninevites that God was sending this message. This enhanced the possibility of destruction (since it was a true message from God) as well as repentance on the part of the Ninevites (since the true God was warning them).

Archaeological Evidence to Support Merrill's Claim

As previously mentioned, Merrill is not the first to explore this possibility. One of the oldest advocates of this view is H. Clay Trumbull in his article "Jonah in Nineveh," which was written in the *Journal of Biblical Literature* in 1892. Many of

---

[15] Ibid., 29–30.

Trumbull's archaeological arguments support Merrill's position.

For instance, Trumbull says that the ancient Assyrians worshipped Dagan who was part man and part fish. He cites images from Layard's *Nineveh and its Remains* of the fish-god that was guarding the palace and temples of Nineveh as well as images on some of the ancient Babylonian seals. Apparently Dagan's body was similar to a fish and under his fish head there was a man's head and under his tail he had man's feet.[16] In order to demonstrate that this god had a long history of being worshipped in the time of Jonah, he cites evidence from Tiglath-Pileser II who refers to an ancient ruler of Assyria named Ishme Dagan from 1840 BC.[17]

The legends of Assyria recorded that Dagan was very articulate and would often converse with men. He would normally provide insight into letters, sciences, mathematics, and the arts.[18] What is most interesting is Trumbull suggests the reference is to a legend from the third century Chaldean historian and priest Berosus:

> Berosus also records that from time to time, ages apart, other beings of like nature with this first great teacher came up out of the sea with fresh instructions for mankind; and that each of these avatars, or incarnations, marked a new epic, and the supernatural messenger bore a new name. So it would seem to be clear that, in all those days of Israel's history within which the book of Jonah can be assigned, the people of Nineveh were believers in a divinity who from time to time sent messages to them by a personage who rose out of the sea, as part fish and part man.[19]

---

[16] Ibid., 55.
[17] Ibid.
[18] Ibid., 56
[19] Ibid.

Based on this information, one can see why the Ninevites responded so quickly to a person who came out of the sea with a direct message from God for them. Trumball continues:

> What better heralding, as a divinely sent messenger to Nineveh, could Jonah have had, than to be thrown up out of the mouth of a great fish, in the presence of witnesses, say, on the coast of Phoenicia, where the fish-god was a favorite object of worship? Such an incident would have inevitably aroused the mercurial nature of Oriental observers, so that a multitude would be ready to follow the seemingly new avatar fish-god, proclaiming the story of his uprising from the sea, as he went on his mission to the city where the fish-god had its very centre of worship.[20]

Consequently, God sovereignly chose for Jonah to be a sign that would elicit repentance from the Ninevites because of His compassion for the people. Trumbull says:

> In short, if the book of Jonah is to be looked upon as veritable history, it is clear, in the light of Assyrian records and Assyrian traditions, that there was a sound reason for having Jonah swallowed by a fish in order to his coming up out of a fish; and that the recorded sudden and profound alarm of the people of an entire city at his warning was most natural, as a result of the coincidence of this miracle with their religious beliefs and expectations. Hence the two stock arguments against the historicity of the book of Jonah no longer have the force they have seemed to possess.[21]

---

[20] Ibid.
[21] Ibid., 57

As Trumbull so eloquently states, this understanding of Assyrian history not only proves the historicity of Jonah, but it also explains an objection that is often raised by critical scholars.

It is also important to note that God does work through these types of means to accomplish His sovereign purposes. Trumbull writes:

> It would certainly seem to be true that, if God desired to impress upon all the people of Nineveh the authenticity of a message from himself, while leaving to themselves the responsibility of a personal choice as to obeying or disregarding his message, he could not have employed a fitter method than by sending that message to them in a way calculated to meet their most reverent and profound conceptions of a divinely authorized messenger. And this divine concession—as it might be called—to the needs and aspirations of a people of limited religious training, would be in accordance with all that we know of God's way of working among men; as shown, for example, in his meeting of Joseph in Egypt through the divining cup, and of the Chaldeans through their searching of the stars.[22]

God often chooses to communicate in a way in which the people can relate. Whether it is using Moses to give signs that serve as an apologetic to the Egyptian gods or Paul preaching about the Unknown God in Mars Hill, God's purposes are always served.

In addition to Trumbull's arguments, Theophilus G. Pinches provides some archaeological evidence that would substantiate Merrill's position. Pinches refers to a creature named Musaros Oannes, the Annedotos who was half man and half fish that had divine features in the shape of a man clothed with a fish's skin. According to Pinches there are some statuettes and large sculptures in the British Museum that substantiate

---

[22] Ibid., 59.

this claim.²³ In addition to this, Pinches offers proof that the name of Nineveh may be derived from Nina, the daughter of Engur, who was the god of the Abyss.²⁴ Merrill also sees great significance in the name of Nineveh:

> Nineveh was one of the most ancient of the Assyrian cities, with traceable roots going back to the Uruk period (ca. 4100–3100). Its name from earliest times was formed of the composite Sumerian logogram NINUA (=NINA), the interior sign of which is KU₆ or, in Akkadian, nūnu, "fish." The meaning of the outer sign is unclear since it no doubt underwent transformation in its composite orthographic development. A town of identical name (Nina) near Lagash worshipped the fish-goddess Nanshe, so it is suggested that she was also the chief deity of early Nineveh. The logogram NINUA can also be read NANŠE, an obvious support for this connection. The name of Nineveh, "Fishtown," is highly intriguing then in considering the meaning of Jonah as a sign to Nineveh, a matter to be elaborated presently.²⁵

Harper's Bible Dictionary adds that,

> The *Ninua* of cuneiform sources goes back to an earlier form, *Ninuwa,* which would seem to underlie the received biblical writing. In addition to the syllabic spelling, the cuneiform texts also occasionally use a pseudo logographic form, *Nina,* which is the combination of two

---

²³ Theophilus G. Pinches, *The Old Testament in the Light of the Historical Records and Legends of Assyria and Babylonia,* 2d. ed. (London, England: Society for Promoting Christian Knowledge, 1903), 62–63.
²⁴ Ibid., 64.
²⁵ Merrill, "The Sign of Jonah," 26–27.

signs (AB + HA) that represent an enclosure with a fish inside. This reading is of particular interest in light of the prophet Jonah being swallowed by a large fish (Jonah 1:17).[26]

Thus, the Ninevites likely interpreted Jonah's arrival to Nineveh in a unique way.

Perhaps one piece of irony is that Nineveh was the chief sanctuary of the goddess Ishtar whose sacred bird was the dove.[27] As already mentioned, Jonah's name means *dove*. Thus, the unwilling dove was sent to Nineveh, a city which held the dove to be sacred.

With respect to the god Oannes that Pinches mentioned, Trumbull considers this to be evidence for the historicity of Jonah. He writes, "While 'Oannes' is not the precise equivalent of the name 'Jonah' it is a form that might have been employed by Berosus, while writing in Greek, if he desired to give an equivalent of 'Jonah.'"[28] He defends this position as follows:

> This name, *Oannes*, as it stands in the Greek of Berosus, appears in the Septuagint and in the New Testament, with the addition of *I* before it—*Ioannes*. In the Septuagint this Greek word *Ioannes* is used to represent both the Hebrew name *Yohanan*, and the Hebrew name *Yona*.... Similarly, in the New Testament, the name Jonah is rendered both *Ionas* and *Ioannes*.... Professor Dr. Hermann V. Hilprecht, the eminent Assyriologist informs me that in the Assyrian inscriptions the J of

---

[26] Paul J. Achtemeier, Harper & Row Publishers., and Society of Biblical Literature., *Harper's Bible Dictionary*, 1st ed. (San Francisco, CA: Harper & Row, 1985), 707.
[27] W. O. E. Oesterley and Theodore H. Robinson, *An Introduction to the Books of the Old Testament* (London, England; New York, NY: Society for Promoting Christian Knowledge, 1960), 377.
[28] Trumbull, "Jonah in Nineveh," 58.

foreign words becomes an I, or disappears altogether; hence Joannes, as the Greek representative of Jonah, would appear in the Assyrian either as Iōannes or as Oannes.[29]

Trumbull states the importance of this fact for understanding the book of Jonah:

> And if it were a literal fact that a man called 'Yonah' had come up out of the very mouth of a fish in the sea, claiming to be a messenger of the great God to the people of Nineveh, and had to suppose that Berosus, writing after that event, would connect the name Jonah with the primal divinity of Nineveh?[30]

Merrill discounts this theory but suggests the following:

> Oannes is the Greek equivalent of Ea (Akkadian) or Enki (Sumerian), god of the earth. His abode was in the Apsû, the fresh-water ocean. It may be tempting to see a linguistic connection between Greek Oannes and Hebrew Yônâ, a view suggested by L. Spence, for example, in *Myths and Legends of Babylonia and Assyria* (London, England: George G. Harrap, 1916) 87. More likely one should compare with Sumerian U-Anna or something similar.[31]

Merrill's approach is the most likely, but one cannot completely dismiss Trumbull's theory.

---

[29] Ibid.
[30] Ibid.
[31] Merrill, "The Sign of Jonah," 27.

Significance of Merrill's View for Jonah's Prophecy

Jonah was a sign to the Ninevites that resulted in repentance and faith. This also speaks to the possibility of repentance in Jonah's original prophecy. Why would God send a sign that would perfectly convey the possibility of repentance if His only intent was to destroy them? It seems more likely that God sent Jonah because He knew Jonah's experience in the fish as well as his preaching would be extremely persuasive evidence that would lead them to repentance, not destruction. This reflects God's sovereign plan and not a last-minute change of mind on God's part at seeing the attitude of the Ninevites. Furthermore, the polysemantic wordplay view lends more credence to the idea that both the possibility of repentance and destruction were in Jonah's original prophecy.

Thus, contrary to Lubeck's argument, Jonah accurately preached the word of Yahweh to the Ninevites because Jesus accredits Jonah and his preaching as being the primary reason for their repentance. In fact, Jonah is the only Old Testament character with whom Jesus Christ compared Himself directly.[32] Jesus also notes the irony of Gentiles repenting at the preaching of one Jewish prophet when the nation of Israel would not repent at the preaching of the Messiah who was greater than Jonah. Thus, the repentance of the Ninevites, as well as the possibility of their destruction, was an essential aspect of the sign of Jonah.

SUMMARY

This chapter reviews the Biblical references to Jonah in the New Testament. In Jesus' sermons, He provides the same opportunity to the Israelites of His day as the Ninevites of Jonah's: either repent in order to receive mercy or be destroyed. Jesus picks up on the key theme of repentance in the purpose

---

[32] Thomas Constable, "Notes on Jonah," http://www.soniclight.com/constable/notes/pdf/jonah.pdf (accessed December 29, 2008): 3.

and message of Jonah. Both repentance and destruction are essential themes for His message. Jonah is a sign to the Ninevites and later to the Israelites of repentance and destruction. Some archaeological evidence has been provided to document the Assyrian legend that Nineveh itself was named after Ishtar which was written with a sign depicting a fish inside an enclosure.[33] Furthermore, there are legends of Dagon and Oannes who were half man and half fish deities that were known for visiting men and teaching them about the arts and sciences. The Ninevites likely believed that on occasion these gods would send messengers to the sea to communicate truth to the people. When Jonah arrived in Nineveh after having been in the body of a large fish, the Ninevites would have likely considered him to be a messenger from the gods. The time period in the fish would have likely made easily identifiable physical marks, and the stench would have validated his claim. This may explain why the Ninevites responded to his claim to such a high degree. The fact that God would use a sign that would clearly capture the attention of the Ninevites lends more credibility to the implicit polysemantic wordplay view. Consequently, this background information is very helpful for demonstrating that an implicit condition was likely a part of Jonah's original prophecy in Jonah 3:4.

---

[33] For additional verification see also D. R. W. Wood and I. Howard Marshall, *New Bible Dictionary*, 3rd ed. (Leicester, England; Downers Grove, IL: InterVarsity Press, 1996), 825.

CHAPTER 6

SUMMARY AND CONCLUSION

This work has reviewed the arguments for the implicit polysemantic wordplay of נֶהְפָּכֶת which serves as a key textual indicator of implicit conditionality, and has taken a holistic, inductive approach to the issue. We have established a methodology for detecting implicitly conditional prophecy by utilizing the research of Grice and Walvoord. Grice and Walvoord's approach both emphasized the importance of authorial intent in implicature and prophecy respectively. This work also utilized the approaches to polysemy by Chisholm and Herzberg. Especially critical was Herzberg's argument that modern commentators often miss the artistry of Hebrew wordplay because they try to limit a word to one meaning in a given text when an author may have ironically intended both meanings at the same time. This does not negate the principle of single meaning since polysemantic wordplay is a literary device of the author which has a single intent of multiple meanings at the same time. Literal interpretation should take figures of speech like double entendre into account as part of the interpretive process.

The second chapter reviewed the different interpretations of the fulfillment of Jonah's prophecy to the Ninevites. Chapters three through five presented a case for the implicit polysemantic wordplay view by analyzing the lexical data, the immediate context, the historical context, the purpose, the message, the genre, and the canonical context.

The lexical context in chapter three demonstrated that both repentance and destruction are possible meanings of the word הָפַךְ. The evidence in the niphal pointed to turning, change, or repentance as the primary meanings in the niphal. In derivative forms the concept of destruction is emphasized more. The *futurum instans* participle pointed to an expectation of immediate fulfillment which would lend more credibility to the argument for the Ninevite repentance fulfilling the prophecy.

Chapter four discussed the immediate and larger context of Jonah. The immediate context supports the implicit polysemantic wordplay view. The narrator, the Ninevites, Jonah, and Yahweh provide indications of implicit conditionality in Jonah 3. The narrator indicates the implicit conditionality of the prophecy by emphasizing the importance of Nineveh to God and utilizing more positive descriptions of the situation. The Ninevites response paralleled that of Moses' in Exodus 32 which is a passage in which Moses appealed to Yahweh based on His prior covenantal promises. While the Ninevites paralleled Moses, Jonah showed more similarities with rebellious Israel. Like the Israelites in Exodus 14:12, he questions why he left his homeland. Like the Israelites of his time, Jonah prefers death over repentance. Whereas he once praised God for delivering him from death in Jonah 2, he now criticizes God for His mercy. He admits that he anticipated Yahweh's compassion to Nineveh and fled as a result. He patiently waits east of the city in order to see if Nineveh would be destroyed. This, combined with his prior admission of anticipating Ninevite deliverance, indicates that he recognized that both repentance and destruction were part of the original prophecy he gave. Now, it is a matter of seeing that prophecy fulfilled. When God does not destroy Nineveh, Jonah becomes even angrier with God. However, God uses nature to teach His rebellious prophet a powerful lesson about His sovereign authority to extend grace to the repentant and to judge unrepentant Jonah (and by implication, unrepentant Israel). The book of Jonah concludes with a gap in which the author of Jonah challenges his eighth century BC original audience to repent of their rebellion toward God in order to enjoy the same deliverance of Nineveh, or they too will be judged by the Assyrians.

The historical context also supports the implicit polysemantic wordplay view. Jonah prophesied during a time of great undeserved blessing. Jeroboam was a disobedient king who had been visited by several prophets during his reign with no repentance; yet, Yahweh continued to bless him and the nation. Rather than being humbled by God's grace, the Israelites became prideful. They offered sacrifices but withheld obedience. Despite God's requests for them to return, they refused to repent and return to the covenant. As a result, God had no choice but to judge them consistent with Deuteronomic law. Like the Ninevites, they had two choices: They could repent and once again receive God's mercy, or they could continue in sin and be judged by the Assyrians. The historical situation of the eighth century BC Israelites best fits within the purpose and message of Jonah. Furthermore, the historical situation points to the possibility of repentance and destruction in Jonah's prophecy in Jonah 3:4. Both options were possible for Israel as they originally were for Nineveh.

The purpose, message, and genre of Jonah also point to implicit conditionality. The purpose and message were summarized as follows, "The book of Jonah was written to Israel in order to describe Yahweh's compassion to Nineveh in response to their repentance. This was done in order to demonstrate to the nation of Israel, which was symbolized by the prideful and disobedient prophet Jonah, that they too could enjoy the same deliverance if they would repent." Since repentance is critical to both the purpose and message of the book, it must have been implicit in the prophecy in Jonah 3:4. The implicit polysemantic wordplay gives the best way for textually indicating this implicit condition. Furthermore, the tragicomedy genre also points to the possibility of both repentance and destruction since both the Ninevites (comedy) and Jonah (tragedy) play important roles.

Chapter five discussed the relationship between Jesus' sermons regarding Jonah and his prophecy. Jesus affirmed that Jonah was a sign of repentance to the Ninevites but a sign of judgment and destruction to the Israelites. Like the original author of Jonah, Jesus argued that if the wicked Ninevites repented at the prophecy of a lesser prophet, how much more should the Israelites repent (especially now that they had seen the Messiah)? The sermons of Jesus pick up on the possibility of both repentance and destruction in the original preaching of Jonah which lends credibility to the implicit polysemantic wordplay view of Jonah 3:4.

SIGNIFICANCE AND AREAS OF FURTHER STUDY

This research addressed the common appeal to Jonah 3:4 in order to argue for the open view of God, fallible prophets, and the view that prophecy often has unstated conditions. The implicit polysemantic wordplay view is linguistically preferable, and most consistent with the immediate context, as well as the overall purpose and message of Jonah. Furthermore, the preaching of Jesus on the fact that Jonah was a sign of repentance to the Ninevites and judgment to the Jews supports the view, and cautions scholars to exercise more caution in using Jonah 3:4 to support those views.

Perhaps this work may also lead to more research and study of implicit conditionality. While this work forcefully addressed the need to ensure that one can prove that the implicature was the intent of the original author, much more work is needed on the nature of implicature and how it relates to a systematic theology of prophetic fulfillment.

Further, there is need that more expositors recognize the artistry and irony of the book of Jonah and heed its message. If we simply view the book as a discussion on the importance of foreign missions or a theological treatise on how God changes His mind, we will miss the point. Jonah was a challenge to the Israelites of his day to not pridefully assume: (1) the blessing they received was merited and (2) repentance was not necessary. The challenge was to have compassion for other nations and not to assume that God's judgment was only for them. Finally, like Jonah, many Christians have a tendency to assume that they can somehow avoid God's sovereign plan or question Him when they do not like His will. Jonah is a book that should encourage the church to repent of any prideful attitudes to avoid God's discipline. God is sovereign and omniscient in what He desires to bring to pass, whether in His prophetic word or His sovereign calling. The Christian's job is to obey and repent in the areas in which we are disobedient.

Overall, further research in the area of implicitly conditional prophecy would be beneficial. More work on the nature of the relationship between the conditional Mosaic Covenant and implicitly conditional prophecy might shed more light on why the original author and audience might have assumed some conditions in certain prophecies. While some of Sandy and Chisholm's conclusions are flawed (as well as the extent of application of some of their conclusions), they have helped Christian scholarship by bringing some of these concerns to the forefront. Perhaps more research can be done on the specific passages that they pointed out, such as Micah 3, Huldah's prophecy to Josiah, and Elijah's prophecy of Ahab's death. Although a more extensive treatment might be helpful, Master's previously cited work on Exodus 32[1] provides a more holistic approach to determining how Exodus 32 fits into the overall argument, purpose, and context of Exodus. While Chisholm's labels of decree and announcement are errant, more study on the nature of prophets giving conditional forthtelling warnings as opposed to predictive prophecy deserves more consideration. More elaboration on how to detect a warning would allow scholars to more easily distinguish between

---

[1] Jonathan Master, "Exodus 32 as an Argument for Traditional Theism," *Journal of the Evangelical Theological Society* 45, no. 4 (2002): 585–98.

unconditional promises and conditional warnings. While this research may be helpful to that end, resolving Jonah alone does not solve the dilemma. Sandy and Chisholm have raised some important issues related to prophecy that merit further research and consideration. It is hoped that continued research expands the work on implicature beyond Gricean and neo-Gricean theory in order to demonstrate how modern advancement in this area of study might contribute to our understanding of implicature.

Ultimately, the book of Jonah was written to Israel for Israel. While Jonah was a prophet sent to Nineveh, he had impact on the Northern Kingdom through his message and example. The implicit polysemantic wordplay and implicit conditionality evident in the book of Jonah are exegetically derived (and thus important) evidences against the open view of God, and are helpful for our broader understanding of God and His character.

APPENDIX A

TOWARD A METHODOLOGY FOR INTERPRETATION OF PROPHECY

This book utilized Walvoord's methodology for interpretation of prophecy as the basis for the implicit polysemantic wordplay interpretation of Jonah's prophecy to the Ninevites.[1] However, other scholars espouse different approaches from Walvoord's view to the prophetic view interpretation. In this appendix I will review conservative approaches to prophetic interpretation that fall under the following categories: covenant theology, progressive dispensationalism, and traditional dispensationalism.[2]

Interpretation of Prophecy in Covenant Theology
While covenant theologians take a diverse approach to interpreting prophecy, this section focuses on two covenant theologians: John Calvin and Vern Poythress. John Calvin was

---

[1] For more information on Walvoord's approach, see page ten of this book.
[2] This survey is not exhaustive. Time and space will only permit a discussion of a few representatives of each approach. Since critical scholars take such a wide variety of approaches, there is not enough space to discuss them here. This appendix is really focusing on conservative approaches to prophecy. However, chapter two does discuss critical approaches to Jonah and one can derive certain principles for prophetic interpretation from a critical perspective from that discussion.

chosen because his method was foundational for future covenant theologians. Also, his view of literal interpretation merits assessment. Since dispensationalism as a formal theological system did not exist when Calvin wrote, I have decided to address Poythress' critique of the traditional dispensational approach to prophecy espoused by individuals like Walvoord.

John Calvin
Calvin's Discussion of Jonah's Prophecy

In his commentary on Jonah 3:4, Calvin does not discuss the fulfillment of Jonah's prophecy to the Ninevites. Instead, he focuses on the great courage it took for Jonah to obey God in order to deliver that prophecy. However, he does discuss the fact that Jonah delivered a message of destruction that resulted in the faith of the Ninevites:

> We hence gather that the preaching of Jonah was not so concise but that he introduced his discourse by declaring that he was God's Prophet, and that he did not proclaim these commands without authority; and we also gather that Jonah so denounced ruin, that at the same time he showed God to be the avenger of sins that he reproved the Ninevites, and, as it were, summoned them to God's tribunal, making known to them their guilt; for had he spoken only of punishment, it could not certainly have been otherwise, but that the Ninevites must have rebelled furiously against God; but by showing to them their guilt, he led them to acknowledge that the threatened punishment was just, and thus he prepared them for humility and penitence. Both these things may be collected from this expression of Jonah, that the Ninevites believed God; for were they not persuaded that the command came from heaven, what was their faith? Let us then know, that Jonah had so spoken of his vocation, that the Ninevites felt assured that he was a celestial herald: hence was their faith: and further, the

Ninevites would never have so believed as to put on sackcloth, had they not been reminded of their sins. There is, therefore, no doubt but that Jonah, while crying against Nineveh, at the same time made known how wickedly the men lived, and how grievous were their offenses against God. Hence then it was that they put on sackcloth, and suppliantly fled to God's mercy: they understood that they were deservedly summoned to judgment on account of their wicked lives.

But it may be asked, how came the Ninevites to believe God, as no hope of salvation was given them? For there can be no faith without an acquaintance with the paternal kindness of God; whosoever regards God as angry with him must necessarily despair. Since then Jonah gave them no knowledge of God's mercy, he must have greatly terrified the Ninevites, and not have called them to faith. The answer is, that the expression is to be taken as including a part for the whole; for there is no perfect faith when men, being called to repentance, do suppliantly humble themselves before God; but yet it is a part of faith; for the Apostle says, in Hebrew 11:7, that Noah through faith feared; he deduces the fear which Noah entertained on account of the oracular word he received, from faith, showing thereby that it was faith in part, and pointing out the source from which it proceeded. At the same time, the mind of the holy Patriarch must have been moved by other things besides threatening, when he built an ark for himself, as the means of safety. We may thus, by taking a part for the whole, explain this, place, — that the Ninevites believed God; for as they knew that God required the deserved punishment, they submitted to him, and, at the same time, solicited pardon: but the Ninevites, no doubt, derived from the words of Jonah something more than mere terror: for had they only apprehended this — that they were guilty before God, and were justly summoned to punishment, they would have been confounded and stunned with dread, and could never have been encouraged to seek forgiveness. Inasmuch then as they suppliantly prostrated themselves before God, they must certainly have conceived some hope of grace. They were not, therefore, so touched with penitence and the fear of God, but that they had some knowledge of divine grace: thus they believed God; for though they were aware that they were most worthy of death, they yet despaired not, but retook themselves to prayer. Since then we see that the Ninevites sought this, remedy, we must feel assured that they derived more advantage from the preaching of Jonah than the mere knowledge that they were guilty before God: this ought certainly to be understood.[3]

In Calvin's view, Jonah's preaching likely contained more than the simple prophecy that is recorded in Jonah 3:4. In his opinion, the Hebrew writers often introduced concepts in simple brief terminology and later expanded upon it. Calvin also considers God's repentance in Jonah 3:10 to be an example of His accommodation. He writes:

Strictly speaking, no repentance can belong to God: and it ought not to be ascribed to his secret and hidden counsel. God then is in himself ever the same, and consistent with himself; but he is said to repent, when a regard is had to the comprehension of men: for as we conceive God to be angry, whenever he summons us to his tribunal, and shows to us our sins; so also we conceive him to be placable, when he offers the hope of pardon. But it is according to our perceptions that there is any change, when God forgets his wrath, as though he had put on a

---

[3] Jean Calvin and Calvin Translation Society, *Calvin's Commentaries*, vol. 14, 22 vols., (Grand Rapids, MI: Baker Books, 1999), 98–100.

new character. As then we cannot otherwise be terrified, that we may be humbled before God and repent, except he sets forth before us his wrath, the Scripture accommodates itself to the grossness of our understanding. But, on the other hand, we cannot confidently call on God, unless we feel assured that he is placable. We hence see that some kind of change appears to us, whenever God either threatens or gives hope of pardon and reconciliation: and to this must be referred this mode of speaking which Jonah adopts, when he says that God repented.

We hence see that there is a twofold view of God, — as he sets himself forth in his word, — and as he is as to his hidden counsel. With regard to his secret counsel, I have already said that God is always like himself and is subject to none of our feelings: but with regard to the teaching of his word, it is accommodated to our capacities. God is now angry with us, and then, as though he were pacified, he offers pardon, and is propitious to us. Such is the repentance of God.

Let us then remember that it proceeds from his word, that God is said to repent; for the Ninevites could form no other opinion but that it was God's decree that they were to be destroyed, — how so? Because he had so testified by his word. But when they rose up to an assurance of deliverance, they then found that a change had taken place, that is, according to the knowledge of their own faith: and the feelings both of fear and of joy proceeded from the word: for when God denounced his wrath, it was necessary for the wretched men to be terrified; but when he invited them to a state of safety by proposing reconciliation to them, he then put on a new character; and thus they ascribed a new feeling to God.

This is the meaning.[4]

Calvin argues that God does not literally repent; instead God accommodates Himself to communicate of this repentance through the human author Jonah because that is how the situation appeared from a human perspective.

Calvin's View of Literal Interpretation

Some have called Calvin the founder of grammatical historical exegesis. Since this approach was so critical to the history of Bible interpretation, one must understand how Calvin defined a literal approach to the Scriptures. For Calvin, the literal meaning was consistent with the author's intent, took into account historical as well as grammatical factors of the original languages, and presented the clear sense of the passage.

For instance, Calvin stressed the importance of authorial intent in Psalm 135:13 when he said, "This may recommend itself the more to be the true meaning, because the Psalmist seems to allude to the expression of Moses (Deuteronomy 32:36), whose very words indeed, he quotes."[5] The humanist model heavily emphasized authorial intent which greatly impacted Calvin's understanding of the human author of Scripture. In his commentary on Isaiah 29:7, Calvin noted the importance of context, "Sometimes it happens that, when a sentence is beautiful, it attracts us to it, and causes us to steal away from the true meaning, so that we do not adhere closely to the context, or spend much time in investigating the author's meaning. Let us therefore inquire if this be the true meaning of the Prophet."[6] Here Calvin clarified that the author's meaning was best ascertained by the context. Calvin also argued that the true meaning of Isaiah 33:11 was clear from the text itself, "But that

---

[4] Ibid., 115–116.
[5] Ibid., volume 6, 178.
[6] Ibid., vol. 7, 316.

is an unsuitable and even absurd comparison, and the true meaning readily suggests itself, 'The fire kindled by your breath shall devour you.'"[7] For Calvin, the true meaning was also revealed by grammar as he indicated in Jeremiah 40:10, "The verb here is ambiguous; but I prefer its most literal meaning, which ye have taken."[8] Therefore, Calvin espoused a literal approach, which emphasized historical and grammatical factors as well as authorial intent.

Calvin's View of Allegory

Calvin did not approve of the allegorical method of interpretation. Calvin called Origen's appeal to allegory diabolical. For instance, he said:

> We must, however, entirely reject the allegories of Origen, and of others like him, which Satan, with the deepest subtlety, has endeavored to introduce into the Church, for the purpose of rendering the doctrine of Scripture ambiguous and destitute of all certainty and firmness. It may be, indeed, that some, impelled by a supposed necessity, have resorted to an allegorical sense, because they never found in the world such a place as is described by Moses: but we see that the greater part, through a foolish affectation of subtleties, have been too much addicted to allegories. As it concerns the present passage, they speculate in vain, and to no purpose, by departing from the literal sense.[9]

In light of this criticism, how did he deal with the fact that the church fathers (even Augustine) used it? He wrote:

---

[7] Ibid., vol. 8, 23.
[8] Ibid., vol. 10, 452.
[9] Ibid., vol. 1, 114.

> There can be no doubt that the Fathers invented it contrary to the genuine sense of the parable. Allegories ought to be carried no further than Scripture expressly sanctions: so far are they from forming a sufficient basis to found doctrines upon. And were I so disposed I might easily find the means of tearing up this fiction by the roots."[10]

Calvin argued against the allegorical method of exegesis because of its tendency to try to find multiple hidden meanings that the text did not make clear:

> For many centuries no man was considered to be ingenious, who had not the skill and daring necessary for changing into a variety of curious shapes the sacred word of God…Scripture, they say, is fertile, and thus produces a variety of meanings. I acknowledge that Scripture is a most rich and inexhaustible fountain of all wisdom; but I deny that its fertility consists in the various meanings which any man, at his pleasure, may assign. Let us know, then, that the true meaning of Scripture is the natural and obvious meaning; and let us embrace and abide by it resolutely.[11]

Therefore, Calvin felt that the applications of the wisdom were multiple, but the interpreter did not have the right to assign a meaning that was not found in the text. For Calvin, the true meaning is the natural and obvious literal meaning of the text.

How did Calvin deal with the fact that Scripture said even the Apostle Paul allegorized? He wrote:

> But as the apostle declares that these things are

---

[10] Calvin, *Institutes of the Christian Religion*, trans. Henry Beveridge, vol. 1, 2 vols. (Grand Rapids, MI: Eerdmans, 1970), 291.
[11] Calvin, *Calvin's Commentaries*, vol. 21, 135.

allegorized, (ἀλληγορούμενα) Origen, and many others along with him, have seized the occasion of torturing Scripture, in every possible manner, away from the true sense. They concluded that the literal sense is too mean and poor, and that, under the outer bark of the letter, there lurk deeper mysteries, which cannot be extracted but by beating out allegories. And this they had no difficulty in accomplishing; for speculations which appear to be ingenious have always been preferred, and always will be preferred, by the world to solid doctrine.[12]

Calvin distinguished between allegorical interpretations that were consistent with the meaning of Scripture and those which did not approximate the meaning of Scripture. While he acknowledged the Scripture has a divine origin, Calvin argued that the human author's true meaning had a right to be interpreted.

Even though Calvin heavily criticized others for allegorical interpretation, he himself used an allegorical method of interpretation on occasion. For instance, Calvin said in his interpretation of Daniel 4:18:[13]

It is now added, the birds of heaven dwelt amidst the branches, and the beasts lived by its sustenance—which ought to be referred to mankind. For although even the beasts of the field profit by political order, yet we know society to have been ordained by God for the benefit of men. There is no doubt at all of the whole discourse being metaphorical, —nay, properly speaking, it is an allegory, since an allegory is only a continued metaphor. If Daniel

---

[12] Ibid.
[13] David Lee Puckett, *John Calvin's Exegesis of the Old Testament*, 1st ed., Columbia Series in Reformed Theology (Louisville, KY: Westminster John Knox Press, 1995), 110 for Calvin's use of allegory in Daniel 4:10-18.

had only represented the king under the figure of a tree, it would have been a metaphor; but when he pursues his own train of thought in a continuous tenor, his discourse becomes allegorical."[14]

Calvin argued at times that an allegory was simply an extended metaphor. He applied the same logic to his interpretation of Isaiah 30:25:

> When the prophets describe the kingdom of Christ, they commonly draw metaphors from the ordinary life of men; for the true happiness of the children of God cannot be described in any other way than by holding out an image of those things which fall under our bodily senses, and from which men form their ideas of a happy and prosperous condition. It amounts therefore to this, that they who obey God, and submit to Christ as their king, shall be blessed. Now, we must not judge of this happiness from abundance and plenty of outward blessings, of which believers often endure scarcity, and yet do not on that account cease to be blessed. But those expressions are allegorical, and are accommodated by the Prophet to our ignorance, that we may know, by means of those things which are perceived by our senses, those blessings which have so great and surpassing excellence that our minds cannot comprehend them.[15]

It is important to note that Calvin made a methodological distinction of when to use allegory and when to avoid allegory.

How then did Calvin distinguish his form of allegory from the church fathers? Puckett says:

---

[14] Calvin, *Calvin's Commentaries*, vol. 12, 257.
[15] Ibid., vol. 7, 375.

Calvin indicates that the difference between his approach and that of the allegorists is one of degree—he is moderate; they are excessive. In his passage on Isaiah 55:13...he distinguishes his spiritual exegesis from the allegorical approach which he opposes. The passage is rightly interpreted as a promise of the spiritual kingdom of Christ...But when the allegorists begin to draw meanings out of each of the particulars of the text, they have gone too far. "In expositions of that kind ingenuity is carried to excess."[16]

Thus, Calvin distinguished between allegory that went beyond the author's intended meaning and allegory which could be found within the divine Author's intention.

This section demonstrated that Calvin emphasized literal interpretation and a grammatical historical approach. For Calvin, the locus of meaning was the original author's intended meaning. He rejected most allegorical approaches to Bible interpretation.

Calvin's View of Prophecy

Calvin's approach to Old Testament prophecies reflected his attempt to resolve the tension between a literal fulfillment and the present reality. Calvin believed that God would be faithful to his original covenants to the Israelites. However, he recognized that not all prophecies had been fulfilled. Calvin resolved this tension by seeing an original physical fulfillment of many earthly promises in the Israelite's return from captivity in Babylon and a more complete spiritual fulfillment at Christ's second coming. Calvin ultimately rejected the notion that Old Testament prophecies either had to have a literal fulfillment on earth by the Israelite nation or a spiritual fulfillment in the church age. Instead, he preferred a both/and approach that

---

[16] Puckett, *John Calvin's Exegesis of the Old Testament*, 113.

enabled him to argue for a literal fulfillment, as expected by the human author/prophet, as well as a spiritual fulfillment that was intended by the divine Author.

For instance, Calvin believed that God must be faithful to his original covenant with Israel because the Old Testament promises made to the Jews were eternal:

> He then adds, 'This covenant *shall not be forgotten.*' We hence conclude that the perpetuity of which he speaks, was founded rather on the mere benevolence of God than on the virtue of the people. He calls then the covenant which God would never forget, perpetual, because he would remember his mercy towards the chosen people; and though they were unworthy to receive such a favor, yet he would continue perpetually his mercy towards them to the coming of Christ; for the passage clearly shows that this prophecy cannot be otherwise explained than of Christ's spiritual kingdom. The Jews indeed returned to their own country, but it was only a small number; and besides, they were harassed by many troubles; God also visited their land with sterility, and they were lessened by various slaughters in wars: how then came the prophets thus to extol in such high terms the favor of God, which yet did not appear among the people? Even because they included the kingdom of Christ; for whenever they spoke of the return of the people, they ascended, as we have said, to the chief deliverance. I do not yet follow our interpreters, who explain these prophecies concerning the spiritual kingdom of Christ allegorically; for simply, or as they say, literally, ought these words to be taken, — that God would never forget his covenant, so as to retain the Jews in the possession of the land. But this would have been a very small thing, had not Christ come forth, in whom is founded the real perpetuity of the covenant, because God's covenant cannot be separated from a state of

happiness; for blessed are the people, as the Psalmist says, to whom God shows himself to be their God. (Psalm 144:15.) Now, then, as the *Jews* were so miserable, it follows that God's covenant did not openly appear or was not conspicuous; we must therefore come necessarily to Christ, as we have elsewhere seen, that this was commonly done by the Prophets.[17]

However, Calvin considered the eternality of the covenants to only be operative until the better covenant that Christ ushered in. Consequently, he tried to find literal fulfillment prior to Christ's coming to earth for the first time and spiritual fulfillment after Christ's coming. This perspective forced Calvin to find fulfillment of some Old Testament prophecies in the return from Babylonian captivity. For Calvin, the Old Testament prophecy was fulfilled literally in kind in the deliverance of his people from Babylonian captivity and it will be fulfilled spiritually in extent at Christ's second coming. He criticized the Jews for limiting the perceived fulfillment to the deliverance from Babylonian captivity and Christians for only seeing a spiritual fulfillment. Why would Calvin take this approach? Puckett writes:

> Old Testament texts that, if taken literally, promise a time of great earthly blessing for God's people, are usually given a spiritual (or allegorical) interpretation by Calvin. He usually demonstrates the validity of his spiritual exegesis by pointing out that the prophecy in question has not had literal fulfillment.[18]

Puckett defends this assertion by referring to Calvin's interpretation of Jeremiah 31:38:

---

[17] Calvin, *Calvin's Commentaries*, vol. 11, 131–32. Emphasis his.
[18] See Puckett, *John Calvin's Exegesis of the Old Testament*, 110.

> The meaning is that God would again care for that city, as the Temple would become as it were his royal throne and earthly sanctuary. At the same time when the Prophet affirms that the extent of the city would not be less than it had been, we see that this prophecy must necessarily be referred to the kingdom of Christ: for though Jerusalem before Christ's coming was eminent and surrounded by a triple wall, and though it was celebrated through all the East, as even heathen writers say that it excelled every other city, yet it was never accomplished, that the city flourished as under David and Solomon. We must then necessarily come to the spiritual state of the city, and explain the promise as the grace which came through Christ.[19]

This quote illustrates a critical distinction between Calvin's interpretive method and Walvoord's method cited in chapter one. When Calvin found an Old Testament prophecy that had not yet had literal fulfillment (even in the judgment of the heathens), he assumed a spiritual fulfillment in the church age that would ultimately be realized in Christ's second coming. When dispensationalists see a promise in the Old Testament that has yet to be fulfilled in kind and extent, they argue that the fulfillment must be yet future (in the earthly millennial kingdom or in the eschaton most of the time). This methodological assumption on the part of Calvin is one reason why he saw no need for a literal earthly kingdom.

Calvin's Eschatology

Calvin's views of eschatology were influenced by Augustine's amillennial view of the kingdom. Augustine taught the following regarding premillennialists:

---

[19] Calvin, *Calvin's Commentaries*, vol. 10, 150–51.

> But in fact those people assert that those who have risen again will spend their rest in the most unrestrained material feasts, in which there will be so much to eat and drink that not only will those supplies keep within no bounds of moderation but will also exceed the limits of incredibility. But this can only be believed by materialists; and those with spiritual interests give the name 'Chiliasts' to believers in this picture, a term which we can translate by a word derived from the equivalent Latin, 'Millenarians.'[20]

One can note Augustine's disdain for the Chiliasts because of their belief in a literal material kingdom. Calvin also shared the same concern as Augustine:

> Those who assign only a thousand years to the children of God to enjoy the inheritance of future life, observe not how great an insult they offer to Christ and his kingdom. If they are not to be clothed with immortality, then Christ himself, into whose glory they shall be transformed, has not been received into immortal glory; if their blessedness is to have an end, the kingdom of Christ, on whose solid structure it rests, is temporary."[21]

Because Calvin believed that the kingdom began with Christ's first coming, he thought that the Chiliasts did not believe in an eternal state. Hence, he accused premillennialists of being "either most ignorant of all divine things or they maliciously aim at subverting the whole grace of God and power of Christ, which cannot have their full effects unless sin is obliterated, death swallowed up, and eternal life fully renewed."[22]

---

[20] Augustine, *The City of God*, trans. Henry Bettenson, Penguin Classics (London, England: Penguin Group, 2003), 907.
[21] Calvin, *Institutes of the Christian Religion*, vol. 2, 266.
[22] Ibid.

Why would Calvin say such a thing? For one, Calvin's view of accommodation as well as his presupposition that the New Testament should inform the interpretation of the Old Testament affected his understanding of the kingdom. For instance, he wrote:

> Let us then lay it down confidently as a truth which no engines of the devil can destroy—that the Old Testament or covenant which the Lord made with the people of Israel was not confined to earthly objects, but contained a promise of spiritual and eternal life, the expectation of which behaved to be impressed on the minds of all who truly consented to the covenant. Let us put far from us the senseless and pernicious notion, that the Lord proposed nothing to the Jews, or that they sought nothing but full supplies of food, carnal delights, abundance of wealth, external influence, a numerous offspring, and all those things which our animal nature deems valuable. For, even now, the only kingdom of heaven which our Lord Jesus Christ promises to his followers, is one in which they may sit down with Abraham, and Isaac and Jacob, (Matthew 8:11) and Peter declared of the Jews of his day, that they were heirs of gospel grace because they were the sons of the prophets, and comprehended in the covenant which the Lord of old made with his people, (Acts 3:25)…or would the stupidity of the whole nation in the present day, in expecting an earthly reign of the Messiah, be less wonderful, had not the Scriptures foretold this long before as the punishment which they were to suffer for rejecting the Gospel, God, by a just judgment, blinding minds which voluntarily invite darkness, by rejecting the offered light of heaven.[23]

---

[23] Ibid., vol. 1, 385.

Thus, like Augustine, Calvin considered earthly promises to be carnal. Calvin took it a step further and argued that the earthly promises were designed to point to the spiritual truth. He argued that God used these earthly promises to bring the ancient Israelites to him and that the goal was ultimately to bring the church to Christ which would cause them to rest in the spiritual promises of his kingdom.

Calvin then used this presupposition to argue for a spiritual kingdom. In his commentary on Daniel 7:27 he said:

> As often as Scripture says 'God reigns,' according to this argument God must be transfigured into human nature, otherwise there will be no kingdom of God except it is earthly, and if earthly it is temporal, and therefore perishable. Hence, we must infer that God changes his nature. [24]

Calvin argued that any kingdom on earth by nature is temporal and could not speak of God's kingdom. After this he concluded:

> But we know the reign of God and of Christ, although existing in the world, not to be of it, (John 18:36) the meaning of the two expressions is exactly the opposite. God, therefore, still exercises his heavenly reign in the world, because he dwells in the hearts of his people by his Spirit... The saints began to reign under heaven, when Christ ushered in his kingdom by the promulgation of his Gospel."[25]

This passage illustrates Calvin's methodology. He began by interpreting an Old Testament text as literally as possible. He then imported an idea from John 18:36 that trumped the literal

---

[24] Calvin, *Calvin's Commentaries*, vol. 13, 75.
[25] Ibid.

interpretation of the Old Testament text. He synthesized the two by providing for a spiritual fulfillment by the saints in the church who are doing the work of the Gospel.

Calvin's Ecclesiology

Calvin's definition of the marks of the church was essential to his ecclesiology. Calvin argued that the marks of the church were the ministry of the word and the administration of the sacraments instituted by Christ.[26] Those who forsake the church which was distinguished by these marks forsook the Church distinguished by such marks "are apostates, deserters of the truth and of the household of God, deniers of God and Christ, violators of the mystical marriage."[27]

Ironically, Calvin included Old Testament Saints from Israel in the church:

> The prophets, however, did not therefore either form new churches for themselves, or erect new altars on which they might have separate sacrifices, but whatever their countrymen might be, reflecting that the Lord had deposited his word with them, and instituted the ceremonies by which he was then worshipped, they stretched out pure hands to him, though amid the company of the ungodly.[28]

Calvin applied the marks of the church to Old Testament saints because they had the word of God deposited in them and had their own ceremonial sacrifices. Since Calvin's view of the marks of the church required perseverance, the Jewish nation would no longer qualify as part of the church since they did not persevere:

---

[26] Calvin, *Institutes of the Christian Religion*, vol. 2, 280.
[27] Ibid.
[28] Ibid.

> So long as the Jews and Israelites persisted in the laws of the covenant, a true Church existed among them; in other words, they by the kindness of God obtained the benefits of a Church. True doctrine was contained in the law, and the ministry of it was committed to the prophets and priests. They were initiated in religion by the sign of circumcision, and by the other sacraments trained and confirmed in the faith. There can be no doubt that the titles with which the Lord honoured his Church were applicable to their society. After they forsook the law of the Lord, and degenerated into idolatry and superstition, they partly lost the privilege. For who can presume to deny the title of the Church to those with whom the Lord deposited the preaching of his word and the observance of his mysteries? On the other hand, who may presume to give the name of Church, without reservation, to that assembly by which the word of God is openly and with impunity trampled underfoot – where his ministry, its chief support, and the very soul of the Church, is destroyed?[29]

Calvin believed that God replaced the unfaithful Jewish nation with the present church and argued for the covenant theology position that the church replaced Israel.

This blurring of the distinctions had several implications on his integration of Biblical texts. For instance, in his discussion of Luke 17:21 he wrote that,

> They are greatly mistaken who seek with the eyes of the flesh the kingdom of God, which is in no respect carnal or earthly, for it is nothing else than the inward and spiritual renewal of the soul. From the nature of the kingdom itself he shows that they are altogether in the

---

[29] Ibid., vol. 2, 310.

wrong who look around here or there, in order to observe visible marks. "That restoration of the Church," he tells us, "which God has promised, must be looked for within; for, by quickening his elect into a heavenly newness of life, he establishes his kingdom within them."[30]

In this discussion of Luke 17:21, Calvin applied the notion of the kingdom to the restoration of the church and placed a spiritual interpretation upon it.

In another instance, Calvin took the promises of the Davidic Covenant that originally governed the nation of Israel and applied them to the church, saying,

> Therefore, though the kingdom was broken up by the revolt of the ten tribes, yet the covenant which God had made in David and his successors behaved to stand, as is also declared by his Prophets, 'Howbeit I will not take the whole kingdom out of his hand: but I will make him prince all the days of his life for David my servant's sake,' (1 Kings 11:34).[31]

Calvin then applied this benefit to the church:

> Accordingly, David exclaims, 'The Lord is their strength, and he is the saving strength of his anointed;' and then prays 'Save thy people, and bless thine inheritance;' intimating, that the safety of the Church was indissolubly connected with the government of Christ…Here it is obvious that believers are invited to Christ, in the assurance that they will be safe when entirely in his hand. To the same effect is another prayer, in which the whole Church implores the divine mercy "Let thy hand be

---

[30] Calvin, *Calvin's Commentaries*, vol. 16, 212.
[31] Calvin, *Institutes of the Christian Religion*, vol. 1, 294.

upon the Man of thy right hand, upon the Son of man, whom thou madest strong (or best fitted) for thyself," (Psalm 80:17).[32]

How did he justify this replacement theology? Calvin appealed to the covenant of grace:

> Towards the conclusion, he declares it to be for the good of the Church that God should grant his request; and, indeed, when the peculiar manner in which God had deposited his covenant of grace with David is considered, it could not but be felt that the common hope of the salvation of all must have been shaken on the supposition of his final rejection.[33]

For Calvin, the covenant of grace covered both Old Testament saints and the New Testament believers who worship God.[34] Calvin avoided the distinction between the church and Israel because the covenant of grace applied to all believers of all ages who compose the church.

This brief discussion revealed Calvin's method for interpreting prophecy. Calvin's view of the divine and human nature of Scripture allowed for him to make literal and spiritual interpretations of the text. Calvin's marks of the church justified God's doing away with Israel for their disobedience to the covenant. Based on this replacement theology, Calvin applied the Davidic Covenant and other promises to the Church that were originally promised to Israel. Because his Old Testament interpretation was informed by the New Testament, he could easily substitute the church for any text that was originally given to the Jews while still maintaining in his mind a literal,

---

[32] Ibid., 1:295.
[33] Calvin, *Calvin's Commentaries*, vol. 5, 281–82.
[34] Ibid., vol. 4, 121.

historical, grammatical meaning.

Vern S. Poythress

Vern Poythress' method for interpreting prophecy is similar to Calvin's. Both emphasize the priority of the New Testament and argue for fulfillment of some Old Testament prophecies by the church. As opposed to thoroughly covering his methodology, I will address some of his specific arguments dispensationalism's view of prophecy.

For instance, Poythress argues for three categories of literal interpretation. The first is what he calls the "first-thought meaning." The "first-thought meaning" is "the meaning native speakers are most likely to think of when they are asked about a word in isolation."[35] According to Poythress, the first thought meaning is the opposite of any and all figurative meanings. Poythress' second category involves recognizing obvious figures of speech but nothing beyond the obvious. Thus, one "would ignore the possibility of poetic overtones, irony, wordplay, or the possibility of figurative or allusive character of whole sections of material."[36] Poythress labels this "literal if possible" category "flat interpretation."[37] The third category of the use of literal, which Poythress labels as grammatical historical interpretation, "reads passages as organic wholes and tries to understand what each passage expresses against the background of the human author and the original situation."[38] Poythress rightly recognizes that the literal method that dispensationalists advocate recognizes figures of speech and should be properly understood as his third category of grammatical historical

---

[35] Vern S. Poythress, *Understanding Dispensationalists* (Grand Rapids, MI: Academie Books, 1987), 82. These three categories were cited in Mike Stallard, "Literal Interpretation: The Key to Understanding the Bible," *Journal of Ministry and Theology* 4, no. 1 (Spring 2000): 25–26.
[36] Poythress, *Understanding Dispensationalists*, 83.
[37] Ibid.
[38] Ibid., 184.

interpretation. However, he cautions dispensationalists against using literal too much because others might confuse it for one of the first two categories.

After discussing the historical grammatical approach, Poythress argues that one must distinguish between actual interpretation of the Old Testament audiences and justified or warranted interpretation. Since scholars have little information about how the original audience actually interpreted the Old Testament and a flat interpretation might have caused them to miss the significance of the messianic passages, one must shift the discussion to what the original audience should have interpreted. According to Poythress, the Old Testament gave several indications that prophecy might have a symbolic or what Poythress calls a "vertical" significance.[39] Furthermore, the prophets had a connection with Moses until one who was greater than Moses would come to change the character of prophetic fulfillment.[40]

Poythress then discusses typology. He argues that grammatical historical interpretation can uncover symbolic significance in the Old Testament which corresponds to the New Testament use of them. Furthermore, according to Poythress, Old Testament prophecy is written against the backdrop of the Mosaic legislation. Consequently, Poythress argues that dispensationalists should reconsider how they define fulfillment. Poythress states that Old Testament prophecies may have partial fulfillment in the immediate future with a greater fulfillment in the latter days when "that which is partial and shadowy about Old Testament revelation will be superseded by that which is final and real."[41] Since the significance of types is not fully discernable until the time of fulfillment, one must compare later Scripture to earlier Scripture to understand

---

[39] Ibid., 111.
[40] Ibid., 110.
[41] Ibid., 113.

everything. Thus, according to Poythress, grammatical historical interpretation is not "all there is to interpretation."[42]

As a result, Poythress challenges dispensationalists to:

> (1) develop a conception of grammatical-historical interpretation that takes seriously symbolic overtones of both Old Testament history and Old Testament prophecy; (2) to be willing to enrich the results of grammatical-historical interpretation with insights that derive only from considering earlier and later Scriptures together. And they must learn to do the latter, not only when it is a matter of typology within the Old Testament historical passages, but also when it is a matter of typological or allusive material within Old Testament *prophetic* passages.[43]

Dispensationalists should take Poythress' appeal seriously. He has presented a balanced perspective of dispensationalists and raised some significant issues.

While a stronger defense of the traditional dispensational approach will occur later in this appendix, some of Poythress' arguments merit review. First, he tends to emphasize the connection of Old Testament prophecy with Moses. However, many of those prophecies were based on royal grant covenants like the Abrahamic and Davidic Covenants which God affirmed by His own character that He would literally fulfill (cf. Jeremiah 31:36–40 and Psalm 89:3–4). The Abrahamic Covenant, in particular, preceded the Mosaic Covenant.

Additionally, he overextends the role of typology into the realm of prophecy. The New Testament authors used the Old

---

[42] Ibid., 116.
[43] Ibid., 116–17.

Testament in five principal ways: exegesis, exposition, application, allusion and illustration. Exegesis is that process which is closest to the author's original intent whereas illustration is furthest. Exegesis is that practice whereby the New Testament author is focusing on explaining the author's original intent as described to the original audience. Paul's use of Genesis 15:6 in Romans 4:3 is a good example of this. Exposition refers to the preaching of an Old Testament text to a contemporary audience. Peter's use of Deuteronomy 18:18 in Acts 3:22 is a good example. Application deals with instances when an author applies a particular principle of an Old Testament text to a New Testament situation. Paul's use of Deuteronomy 25:4 in 1 Timothy 5:18 provides a good example of application. Allusion occurs when an author borrows terminology from an Old Testament text in order to make a specific point. This can be done in an analogical use of the Old Testament as Amos 9 is used in Acts 15. It can also be used in certain terms (for example in Revelation where the OT is not directly quoted but alluded to). The final type of use of the Old Testament in the New is illustration. Perhaps the most famous use is Paul's illustration of the two sons of Abraham in Galatians 4:27-31 as a comparison to the Judaizers. In this type of use, the author is simply using an image of the text (sometimes apart from its original context) in order to illustrate a point. Typology often fits in this category.

Some covenant theologians, like Poythress, derive exegetical principles from Old Testament typological illustrations even if the author is not specifically exegeting the text. In some instances, the author even notifies the reader of this (cf. Galatians 4:24 and Revelation 11:8). One should derive exegetical principles from the cases in which the New Testament author actually exegetes the Old Testament text.[44]

---

[44] One interesting study would be on the use of the New Testament in the New Testament. In some cases, the New Testament is applied apart in a way that is distinct from its originally intended meaning (Luke 10:7

Progressive Dispensationalism

Progressive dispensationalism provides an alternative to the methods espoused by covenant theology and traditional dispensationalism. For the most part, progressive dispensationalists prefer to use alternate terms and methods to the literal interpretation of traditional dispensationalists. This section will describe the method of Blaising and Bock[45] as well as Sandy.

Blaising and Bock's View of Literal Interpretation

Blaising and Bock argue that Ryrie's definition of literal interpretation as clear, plain and normal interpretation was prior to several advancements in scholarly research. As a result, Blaising and Bock prefer to substitute the phrase grammatical historical for literal or the clear, plain, and normal interpretation. They argue that classical dispensationalism cannot claim to employ this method "since they did not seek to practice such a hermeneutic consistently or exclusively."[46] Progressive dispensationalists also believe that historical-grammatical interpretation is preferable to the term "literal" because not even revised dispensationalists apply it consistently. They also argue that "consistently grammatical-historical interpretation, in the sense in which grammatical-historical is meant today, is much closer to being realized in the

---

refers to Jesus' instruction to the apostles to stay in one house but Paul uses it in 1 Timothy 5:18 to appeal for compensation of elders), or quoted differently (Acts 10:4–6 in Acts 10:31–32). Surely one would not derive all of the principles for New Testament exegesis from these cases.

[45] Portions of the discussion on Blaising and Bock are taken from Joseph Parle, "The Life and Theology of Lewis Sperry Chafer with Special Emphasis on His Contributions to Dispensationalism and Continuity with Essentialist Dispensationalism" (Th.M. Thesis, Baptist Bible Seminary, 2007), 26–35.

[46] Craig A. Blaising and Darrell L. Bock, *Progressive Dispensationalism* (Wheaton, IL: BridgePoint, 1993), 37.

hermeneutics of progressive dispensationalism."[47]

As previously mentioned, Blaising and Bock believe that the traditional literal or clear, plain and normal view of interpretation is somewhat outdated. Consequently, they suggest the historical-grammatical-literary-theological approach as the appropriate method. They believe that this "fourfold description of hermeneutics is really what most mean when they speak simply of the historical-grammatical method."[48]

In contrast to traditional dispensationalists, Bock and Blaising define the historical approach as that "which seeks to be sensitive to the message as it came to the initial audience, understanding original terms and ideas."[49] They define the grammatical approach as "how the terminology of that message is laid out."[50] According to Bock and Blaising, this is necessary because terms cannot be understood in isolation from each other. Third, they define the need for the literary theological approach based on their belief that "there is an abiding message and unity in the text, which is laid out literarily in various ways called genres."[51] They also believe that the interpreter must consider "the changing nature of the terrain within the text, as well as an appreciation of the various angles to present the truth."[52]

Bock and Blaising also argue that a text can have multiple meanings. They do not distinguish between interpretation and application as strongly as traditional dispensationalists do.[53] They utilize Hirsch's concepts of

---

[47] Ibid.
[48] Ibid., 77.
[49] Ibid.
[50] Ibid.
[51] Ibid.
[52] Ibid.
[53] A defense of single meaning as is found in Appendix B. Their title for chapter two of *Progressive Dispensationalism* on hermeneutics is "Interpreting the Bible–How We Read Texts" [meaning] and their title

meaning and significance but argue that "textual meaning is not really limited to reproducing what the reader thinks the author might have meant."[54]

Perhaps the most significant difference in the Old Testament deals with the already-not-yet approach to Old Testament prophetic fulfillment. Blaising and Bock write:

> It is possible to get fulfillment "now" in some texts, while noting that 'not yet' fulfillment exists in other passages. In fact, in some texts, fulfillment can be initial or partial as opposed to being final and total. As a result, one can speak of inaugurated eschatology without denying either what the Old Testament indicates about the future, earthly kingdom or what the New Testament asserts about the arrival of the kingdom as part of fulfillment in the first coming of Jesus.[55]

Bock and Blaising approach prophecy with both a New Testament and an Old Testament lens. Bock argues that meaning "involves the sense of a passage and not primarily the referents of a passage; but the language of an Old Testament passage and its New Testament fulfillment can be related in terms of referents in one of several ways."[56] Consequently, the progress of revelation requires both the New and the Old Testament for understanding the meaning of the text. Bock writes:

> The progress of revelation affects the detailed

---

for chapter three is "Interpreting the Bible–How the Texts Speak to Us" [application].
[54] Blaising and Bock, *Progressive Dispensationalism*, 64.
[55] Ibid., 97–98.
[56] Darrell L. Bock, "Part 2: Evangelicals and the Use of the Old Testament in the New," *Bibliotheca Sacra* 142, no. 568 (October – December 1985): 315.

understanding of Old Testament passages in specifying details about the completion of the promise and the completion of salvific patterns in God's revelation. But one should always be aware of (a) what was originally understood by the human author at the time of the original revelation and (b) what God disclosed about the details of that revelation through later revelation or through events in Jesus' life.[57]

Thus, from Bock's perspective, the focus should not only be on the literal interpretation of the passage at the time of the writing that is reflected in the intent of the human author but the overall intent of the Divine Author. Bock rejects a "total" identification between the divine intent and the human author's intent because "in certain psalms, as well as in other Old Testament passages, theological revelation had not yet developed to the point where the full thrust of God's intention was capable of being understood by the human author."[58] As a result, the distinction between the intention of the human author and the intent of the Divine Author requires a different interpretive technique.

With respect to the genre of prophecy, Blaising and Bock argue that Old Testament prophecy is not primarily prediction but instead prophecy is the story of confrontation and fresh perspective.[59] Since the prophets rely so heavily on symbolic imagery, one must interpret prophecy in light of a background of metaphors.[60] They argue that as dispensationalists begin to study the literary features of prophecy an apocalyptic they must understand the pattern of prophecy and fulfillment in Biblical history. This will lead the interpreter to call into question the assumption that prophetic language gives "one concrete

---

[57] Ibid., 315–16.
[58] Ibid., 309.
[59] Blaising and Bock, *Progressive Dispensationalism*, 89.
[60] Ibid.

historical scenario in partially codified form."[61]

In sum, Blaising and Bock argue that the traditional historical-grammatical approach to prophetic interpretation is outdated. Instead, they advocate a historical-grammatical-literal-theological approach. They question whether prophecies always have one fulfillment. Instead, they prefer an already-not-yet approach to prophecy that recognizes original fulfillment with a more complete fulfillment yet to come.

D. Brent Sandy

Sandy also proposes an alternate approach to prophecy. He agrees with Blaising and Bock that prophecy is not primarily predictive but intended to appeal to the heart of the recipients. He also argues that a metaphorical view of language should drive prophetic interpretation. Sandy prefers to define prophetic fulfillment in light of patterns of New Testament fulfillment of Old Testament prophecy.

To begin with, Sandy takes a philosophical approach to prophecy based on its symbolic nature. He says:

> For another perspective on the power of prophecy, we need to slow down and think more philosophically. Language originates in humankind's fundamental need to communicate. It is a way to express what humans experience and need to voice. In rudimentary form, words are symbols for things we want to talk about.[62]

According to Sandy, this symbolic nature of language creates a dilemma for God on how to communicate to humans in different languages and cultures. This challenge is compounded by God's desire to communicate heavenly concepts in ways that human

---

[61] Ibid., 294. Emphasis in original text.
[62] D. Brent Sandy, *Plowshares & Pruning Hooks: Rethinking the Language of Biblical Prophecy and Apocalyptic* (Downers Grove, IL: InterVarsity Press, 2002) 25.

beings can understand. Since language is imperfect, the description of concepts such as the Trinity and the agenda of eternity are challenging for God in Sandy's view. According to Sandy, God solves this problem through "the creative use of language."[63] Much like Calvin's concerns about Chiliasts, Sandy expresses concerns that a literal interpretation of some symbols of prophecy such as "streets of gold" will lead to a lowered view of the heavenly state. Sandy writes, "Will we walk streets of gold? We can be sure heavenly existence is something like what they describe, but if we think it is exactly what they describe we will have lowered the spirit world of God and heaven to the physical world we have experienced."[64]

In a related matter, Sandy claims that one must determine whether the prophecy should be interpreted exactly or hyperbolically in light of emotive undertones. He writes:

> Most prophecy is full of emotion, because the prophets are addressing a desperate situation…The hyperbole gets the point across better…Of course sometimes an emotional statement can be exact, but the pattern is that the stronger the emotion, the more likelihood of the inexactness. Hyperboles, in effect, stretch the truth in order to increase the impact of words.[65]

While one must question Sandy's argument that hyperbole is stretching the truth (especially in light of the fact that God cannot lie as per Titus 1:2 and Hebrews 6:18), his primary point is that surface meanings may not always be the correct meanings. Sandy cites examples of judgment and the use of the word "forever" to underscore his point that the prophets often take poetic license to shock their listeners.

---

[63] Ibid., 27.
[64] Sandy, *Plowshares & Pruning Hooks: Rethinking the Language of Biblical Prophecy and Apocalyptic*, 28.
[65] Ibid., 41.

Sandy then makes an argument that prophecy is primarily metaphorical:

> Prophecy is powerful and problematic for one tall reason: the creative use of language, poetic expression, arresting and emotive metaphors. If figures of speech were sequoias on the landscape of prophecy, prophecy would be densely forested, and the most common tree in the woods is metaphor.[66]

He argues this from a philosophical view of language:

> This new understanding of metaphor charted the course for the research of more recent decades. The reasoning went like this: if language is essentially a medium for expressing reality, then language itself is metaphorical. And if language is in essence the making of metaphors, then metaphors not only express what we perceive but influence what we perceive.[67]

As a result, Sandy believes that the readers in the current age are too far removed to understand some of the metaphors used in the original language and culture.

Consequently, he urges a reconsideration of the premillennial and amillennial views of prophecy:

> Central to amillennialism is the belief that many Old Testament prophecies regarding Israel will be fulfilled in the church. Central to premillennialism is the belief that many Old Testament prophecies will be fulfilled in a future nation of Israel. In both cases there may be a limited understanding of how prophecy speaks. When it

---

[66] Ibid., 58.
[67] Ibid., 60.

seems improbable that Old Testament prophecies will be literally fulfilled in the future Israel, amillennialists assume they were meant to be spiritualized and fulfilled in the church. When certain Old Testament prophecies seem not to have been literally fulfilled before the first advent, premillennialists assume that they will be fulfilled in a future Israel. For the chosen people, especially messianic Jews, descriptions of a regathering in Jerusalem are assumed to predict a great day when everywhere will recognize their Messiah. However, in light of how the language of destruction and blessing works—illocution, visualization, conditionality, stereotypical features and the like (see pp. 83–97)—these viewpoints need to be reevaluated carefully.[68]

In other words, Sandy argues that the actual fulfillment in a spiritualized or literal sense should not always be expected since much of prophecy is metaphorical and should not be taken in this vein. Part of the reason for Sandy's approach is to promote unity instead of the divisiveness that results from debates about prophecy.[69]

Sandy summarizes his hermeneutical method for interpreting prophecy as:

1. Since prophecy is powerful language that is designed for dramatic impact on its hearers, one should listen with the heart and not just the head;
2. Since the prophets were prosecuting attorneys pronouncing God's wrath on guilty sinners, look for evidence in the prophetic and historical books for the condition of the people at that time;
3. Since prophecy promises incredible rewards for

---

[68] Ibid., 206.
[69] Ibid., 208–09.

overcomers, explore the full range of what heaven on earth will be like;
4. Since prophecy is poetic, seek to understand what a prophet meant by taking into account literary features like metaphors and hyperbole, rhetorical techniques, unexpressed conditions, stereotypical language, and rich symbolism. Do not take the nature of the words superficially, but focus on the function of the language. Since biblical prophecies were not understood until they were fulfilled, do not expect prophecy to provide a blueprint for the future;
5. Since prophecy may describe the same idea with a variety of images, look for overarching themes. If you do not understand the intent of the prophetic expression, it may be time to step back and take in the big picture. Not understanding some things does not imply not understanding everything;
6. Since prophecy draws on present and earthly language to describe future and heavenly scenes, expect the future reality to exceed your wildest imagination;
7. Since prophecy has been subjected to different interpretations, focus on what we can agree on by being humble and considerate of other views of prophetic fulfillment.[70]

One can note from Sandy's method that systematic theological assumptions precede the exegetical process of interpreting the prophecy. Sandy's method, like Bock and Blaising's, is not only historical and grammatical but literary and theological as well. Speech act theory has a high priority in how prophecy is interpreted. Consequently, he introduces the process of interpreting prophecy with the emotions of the heart at a hermeneutical level which would incorporate the reader's

---

[70] Ibid., 199–200.

response in the interpretive process. This method leads one to question how he can validate whether he actually has the right interpretation. How exactly does an interpreter determine if he has truly listened with the heart and not just the head? Sandy also says that if one does not understand the details of the prophecy, one should focus on the big picture of the prophecy itself. This understanding of the big picture of prophecy should preclude one from thinking prophecy will provide a blueprint for the future. Sandy also places the process of interacting with contrary views in his interpretive method.

Sandy's view of the philosophy of communication causes him to emphasize the function of prophecy more than the content of prophecy. Based on speech act theory, he asserts that prophetic illocutions are more performative than instructive in nature. As a result, most prophecies should not be taken literally but metaphorically. Sandy's metaphorical view of prophecy leads him to emphasize understanding the overall message of the prophecy as opposed to the specific identification of details. Sandy concludes that one cannot specifically determine whether a prophecy has been fulfilled or is unfulfilled, is conditional or unconditional, or is intended to be taken literally or figuratively until after fulfillment. Therefore, one should simply obey the message that the prophet was intending to communicate and not pay too much attention to how the details will be worked out.

Defense of a Traditional Dispensational Approach to Prophecy

The dispensational system is the most logical and Biblical way of interpreting prophecy. Wolfe gives four criteria for validating epistemological systems: consistency (freedom from contradiction in the interpretive scheme), coherence (internal relatedness of the statements within the interpretive scheme), comprehensiveness (applicability of the interpretive scheme to all experience), and congruity (appropriateness of the interpretive scheme to the experience it covers).[71] Traditional dispensationalism provides a consistent approach to prophecy with clear guidelines for interpretation. Traditional dispensationalism comprehensively applies a hermeneutic to all aspects of Scripture. Traditional dispensationalism offers an appropriate explanation for the vast majority of prophecy that has already been fulfilled (especially Messianic prophecies that were fulfilled in literal fashion). Finally, the dispensational framework can coherently explain how the Bible fits together in the past, present, and future. As a result, there is no warrant for a change in the hermeneutical approach to prophecy of traditional dispensationalism.

Stallard proposes a theological method that summarizes the methodology of many traditional dispensationalists. Stallard's method addresses Poythress' request for an alternative grammatical historical approach that takes seriously the symbolic overtones as well as the New Testament. Following is the logical order of priority that Stallard proposes:

1. The recognition of one's own preunderstanding
2. The formulation of a biblical theology from the Old Testament based upon literal interpretation (grammatical-historical method of interpretation) of the Old Testament text
3. The formulation of a biblical theology from the New Testament based upon literal interpretation (the grammatical-historical method of interpretation) of the New Testament text, which method includes the backgrounds arrived at via point 2 above
4. The production of a systematic theology by harmonizing all inputs to theology including points 2 and

---

[71] David L. Wolfe, *Epistemology, the Justification of Belief*, Contours of Christian Philosophy (Downers Grove, IL: InterVarsity Press, 1982), 55.

3 above[72]

Stallard emphasizes the distinctiveness of the dispensational approach as follows:

> The proper sequence of theological method based upon a correct understanding of the progress of revelation prohibits the reading of the New Testament into the Old, although expansion and enhancements are allowed. This is not literal interpretation of the Bible in general, but the guaranteeing of literal interpretation of the Old Testament through the use of a correct theological method. Thus, literal interpretation tied to correct theological method is a distinctive of dispensationalism.[73]

Stallard's argument helps demonstrate some of the distinctions between the approach in covenant theology and progressive dispensationalism. Both covenant theology and progressive dispensationalism emphasize the interpretation of the Old Testament in light of the New Testament. However, Stallard rightly prioritizes the progress of revelation as the proper approach to systematic theology from inputs of the Old Testament and New Testament. The original Jewish audience of the New Testament books would likely have had the Old Testament books as background material while reading the New Testament books.

Stallard's approach seems to be consistent with how Old Testament prophecies were interpreted by Jewish audiences. Daniel looks for a literal fulfillment of Jeremiah's seventy-year prophecy (Daniel 9:2). Jesus expected a literal fulfillment of Daniel's prophecy regarding the abomination of desolation

---

[72] Mike Stallard, "Literal Interpretation, Theological Method, and the Essence of Dispensationalism", *Journal of Ministry and Theology* 1, no. 1 (Spring 1997): 35. All emphasis his.
[73] Ibid. All emphasis is his.

(Matthew 24:15). The disciples themselves waited for a literal restoration to the kingdom to Israel (Acts 1:6). While Jesus tells them that they will not know the timing of the restoration, he does not tell them it will not happen.

Walvoord's approach as described in chapter one also best accounts for the use of figurative language in the Bible. Walvoord argues that the natural sense is to be preferred unless there is firm evidence to the contrary. He also says that the context alone and not a priori considerations determine whether the language is figurative. In contrast, Sandy asserts on the basis of speech act theory that prophecies are generally metaphorical and one cannot be certain whether or not they were to be taken literally until after their fulfillment (which would be difficult for the original audience to determine). In contrast to the claims of some critics of the dispensational way of interpreting prophecy, Walvoord's interpretation does not leave everything completely to the future (in fact, he argues that one half of prophecies have already been fulfilled),[74] but allows for the divine inspiration of Scripture and grammatical considerations to determine the nature of the fulfillment.

Walvoord also argues that the pattern of fulfillment of prophecies from Christ's first coming points to literal interpretation. Prophecies about his place of birth, the timing of his Triumphal entry, and his death were literally fulfilled. Not only that, but the fact that God can make predictions and bring them to pass is one of the things that makes Him greater than all false gods. Isaiah 46:9–11 in the New American Standard Translation says:

> Remember the former things long past, For I am God, and there is no other; I am God, and there is no one like Me, Declaring the end from the beginning, And from ancient

---

[74] John F. Walvoord, "Interpreting Prophecy Today Part 1: Basic Considerations in Interpreting Prophecy," *Bibliotheca Sacra* 139, no. 553 (January 1982): 8.

times things which have not been done, Saying, "My purpose will be established, And I will accomplish all My good pleasure"; Calling a bird of prey from the east, The man of My purpose from a far country. Truly I have spoken; truly I will bring it to pass. I have planned it, surely I will do it.

In this passage, God says He will bring everything that He has predicted to pass. He does this by His authority, and it is not conditioned on man's response. As opposed to arguing that the patterns of Old Testament prophetic fulfillment are not clear, traditional dispensationalists argue that prophetic fulfillment presents one of the best apologetic arguments.

Furthermore, one must question whether scholars like Sandy overemphasize language theory in their description of how God communicates. Nowhere does Scripture report this dilemma God was allegedly faced with in communicating with mankind. One must remember that God created mankind and the He created means to communicate with him. God is fully capable of communicating in a language that is completely understandable and accurately portrays reality. Ryrie asserts that God communicates in the way that is most comprehensible to man, and can be interpreted in a clear, plain and normal way.[75] If even his invisible attributes can be clearly seen in the natural world (cf. Romans 1:20), would it not make sense that He can communicate those attributes in words as well? From the very beginning, God communicated clearly with Adam without using metaphorical language in every statement. Grice's aforementioned cooperative principle illustrates that the intent of most speakers is to communicate clearly unless the speaker has strong reason to violate a conversational maxim. It only seems logical to assume that God operates in the same way.

---

[75] Charles Caldwell Ryrie, *Dispensationalism Today*, Eighth ed. (Chicago, IL: Moody Press, 1973), 158.

In terms of the portrayal of divinity, the traditional dispensational model preserves the glory of God as the Divine Communicator who is completely capable of communicating to humanity in plain language. With respect to the Scriptures, the traditional dispensational model is the most consistent with the promissory nature of the royal grant covenants made to Israel and the clear statements in Deuteronomy 18 that establish a test of a true prophet.

Additionally, literal interpretation of prophecy best preserves objective interpretation. Ryrie writes, "To try to see meaning other than the normal one would result in as many interpretations as there are people interpreting. Literalism is a logical rationale."[76]

Furthermore, literal interpretation is the most consistent approach throughout the Bible. Stallard emphasizes the consistency of the dispensational approach as follows:

> An interpreter cannot pick and choose what he wants to be literal and what is figurative when there is no evidence of a figure of speech or extended metaphor…To do so is inconsistency at its best. One of the reasons that dispensationalists focus on prophecy is that its interpretation almost becomes a barometer by which one's overall approach to the text can be stabilized."[77]

Thus, in a dispensational hermeneutic, prophecy should not be interpreted metaphorically unless the text clearly indicates so.

Not only is the traditional dispensational approach to prophecy the most consistent approach to prophecy but it is also the most comprehensive. Ryrie writes:

---

[76] Ibid., 88–89.
[77] Mike Stallard, "Why Are Dispensationalists So Interested in Prophecy?" (paper presented at the annual meeting of the Conservative Theological Society, Fort Worth, TX, August 2005), 4.

> The hermeneutical principle is basic to the entire dispensational system, including its eschatology... Dispensationalism is the only system that practices the literal principle consistently. Other systems practice literalism but not in every area of theology or on all parts of the Bible...Consistent literalism is at the heart of dispensational theology.[78]

Ryrie's point is that all conservative Christian systems interpret the Bible literally to some degree. What differentiates dispensationalism from others is that dispensationalists try to interpret the entire Bible as literally as possible.

A literal method of interpretation best preserves a conservative approach to the Bible. Stallard recounts a discussion he had with Walvoord on literal interpretation:

> In our discussion I finally asked him this question: 'What is the greatest issue facing dispensationalism today?' His answer, without hesitation was the following: 'It is what it has always been, the inerrancy of the Bible.' What he meant was the literal hermeneutic followed by dispensationalists was the only approach which allows the Bible to be harmonized properly so that its inerrancy could be fully established. This fit well with earlier statements by Walvoord to the effect that one can be a liberal and be an amillennialist and perhaps a postmillennialist. However, it is impossible to be a liberal and at the same time a dispensational premillennialist.... At least part of Walvoord's view stems from dispensationalism's attempt to let distinctions stand throughout the Bible so as not to produce a false and

---

[78] Charles Caldwell Ryrie, *Dispensationalism*, Rev. and expanded. ed. (Chicago, IL: Moody Press, 1995), 146–47.

forced unity.[79]

As one steers away from a literal interpretation of the Bible, it becomes much easier to spiritualize interpretations in order to suit one's assumptions. A strong, consistent, literal approach prevents that from happening.

Summary

Covenant theology interprets Old Testament prophecy in light of the New Testament. As a result, the Church now fulfills certain prophecies that God originally gave to Israel. The support for spiritualizing the prophecies and applying them to the church comes from a conditional understanding of God's covenant with Israel as well as an overarching principle of the covenant of grace.

Progressive dispensationalism argues that the traditional historical-grammatical approach to prophecy requires revision. As a result, progressive dispensationalism incorporates theological and literary aspects to the interpretive process. Due to the performative nature of language, progressive dispensationalism generally assumes more symbolism and metaphor than traditional dispensationalism.

This book defends the traditional approach to prophecy based on its consistency, coherence, comprehensiveness, and congruity. The literal approach to prophecy is more consistent with the literal approach to other parts of the Bible. It is comprehensive in nature since it provides an interpretive process that can apply to the entire Bible. The literal approach is coherent with the fulfilled prophecies regarding Christ's first coming and statements about God's predictive powers. The literal approach also is congruent with the normal communicative process as described by Grice's cooperative

---

[79] Mike Stallard, "Why are Dispensationalists so Interested in Prophecy?" 9.

principle which emphasizes clarity of speech among rational agents.

APPENDIX B

A BRIEF DEFENSE OF SINGLE MEANING AS INTENDED BY THE AUTHOR

In chapter one, I argued that single meaning as intended by the author is critical to interpretation of prophecy as well as implicit conditionality. This debate is not new. Even in the first century AD, the apostle Peter complained of individuals who distorted the original meaning of Paul's letters (1 Peter 3:16). This appendix will attempt to define authorial intent, defend its importance, and work to overcome objections to it.

Definition of Authorial Intent

This section will address the various ways individuals have defined authorial intent and how it should be appropriately defined. Fowl addressed the challenge involved in defining this issue in his article entitled "The Role of Authorial Intention in the Theological Interpretation of Scripture" as follows:

> Limiting a text's meaning to the author's intention presupposes a definitive account of what the meaning of a text is (or ought to be). Of course, a quick survey of the critical landscape makes it pretty clear that our situation is marked by interminable debate and disagreement

about just what the meaning of a text is.¹

Fowl aims to overcome the objection that an author's intention is the "meaning" of a text, "especially if this claim is made at the expense of other approaches to texts that do not accord privilege to authorial meaning."² He argues that if the author's intent is to be pursued, he wishes to see it done in a way that does not "presume that via an analysis of a text we can climb inside an author's head and share with the author an immediate and unfettered access to the author's intentions."³

Norm Geisler, on the other hand, argues that authorial intention is paramount to interpretation. He notes that the word intent can be used in four different ways: (1) plan, as in: "I intend to go tomorrow"; (2) purpose, as in: "My intention was to help you"; (3) thought in one's mind, as in: "I didn't intend to say that"; (4) expressed meaning, as in: "The truth intended in John 3:16 is clear."⁴ Regarding the third point Geisler writes, "First, evangelicals who believe in verbal inspiration of Scripture should not use *intention* in the third sense when referring to the meaning of Scripture, for the locus of meaning (and truth) is not in the author's mind behind the text of Scripture."⁵ Consequently, he argues for the fourth option since in his view purpose does not determine meaning, but the opposite is true. This approach is more grounded in the text than Fowl's.

Elliott Johnson defines the intended meaning as "that

---

[1] Joel B. Green and Max Turner, *Between Two Horizons: Spanning New Testament Studies and Systematic Theology* (Grand Rapids, MI: W.B. Eerdmans, 2000), 78.
[2] Ibid., 73.
[3] Joel B. Green and Max Turner, *Between Two Horizons: Spanning New Testament Studies and Systematic Theology* (Grand Rapids, MI: W.B. Eerdmans, 2000), 74.
[4] Norman L. Geisler, "The Relation of Purpose and Meaning in Interpreting Scripture," *Grace Theological Journal* 5, no. 2 (1984): 230.
[5] Ibid. Emphasis his.

meaning which the Author/author has expressed in the written text" and in another work as "the sense of the whole by which the author arranges and relates each particular meaning of his composition."[6] Johnson makes three critical qualifications to this definition. First, he argues that the intention is not to be identified with the psychological experience of the author. Second, he says that intention does not distinguish between the meanings expressed and meanings merely desired and unsuccessfully expressed. Third, he asserts that intention does distinguish between what is meant based on what is written and what is not meant based on what is written.[7]

The first argument is critical for disputing the charge of Schleiermacher and even the deconstructionists who argue that the author cannot possibly know himself because he has too many biases and presuppositions he is ignoring. The influence on Freudian psychology with its emphasis on the subconscious has tainted the hermeneutical landscape because people like Schleiermacher believe that they can know the author better than he knows himself. Johnson rightly limits authorial intention to the text itself.

As previously mentioned, Johnson also argues that intention does not distinguish between the meanings expressed and meanings merely desired and unsuccessfully expressed. This counteracts the argument that sometimes one might be able to articulate what another is feeling better than they do themselves. While that may be true, the meaning can only be accurately determined by what the author wrote and not how the author wishes he would have said it.

---

[6] The first definition comes from Elliott E. Johnson, *Expository Hermeneutics: An Introduction* (Grand Rapids, MI: Academie Books, 1989), 26. The second comes from Earl D. Radmacher, Robert D. Preus, and International Council on Biblical Inerrancy., *Hermeneutics, Inerrancy, and the Bible: Papers from ICBI Summit II* (Grand Rapids, MI: Academie Books, 1984), 414.
[7] Johnson, *Expository Hermeneutics: An Introduction*, 26–30.

In sum, Johnson and Geisler's definitions of intentionality are the most convincing. They rightly restrict the intention of the author to the text. Johnson rightly qualifies the intention of the author by eliminating the allegedly subconscious thoughts of the author as well as the imprecision of the author's writing. Geisler rightly asserts that the purpose of the author is primarily defined by the meaning of the text rather than the meaning consistently being defined by the alleged purpose of the author.

Importance of Authorial Intent

Identifying the authorial intent is paramount for several reasons. The first reason is that authorial intent is the only method that can be objectively validated. Additionally, Scripture commands believers and holds them accountable for knowing and adhering to the true meaning of Scripture.

First, as E. D. Hirsch so effectively argued in *Validity in Interpretation*, the author's intended meaning is the only interpretation that can be objectively validated. All other methods fall into a hopeless sea of subjectivity. He argues that "to banish the original author as the determiner of meaning was to reject the only compelling normative principle that could lend validity to an interpretation."[8] Hirsh wisely argues that a text can only have one meaning or "what the author meant by a particular sign sequence."[9] However, a text may have multiple applications of forms of significance for the reader. For Hirsch, significance "names a relationship between that meaning and a person, or a conception, or a situation, or indeed anything imaginable."[10]

Secondly, the Bible itself commands individuals to seek the true meaning of the Scriptures. In 2 Timothy 2:15 Paul

---

[8] Hirsch, *Validity in Interpretation*, 5.
[9] Ibid., 8.
[10] Ibid.

admonishes Timothy to accurately handle the word of truth. In several passages, Paul clarifies what he is meaning in order to avoid misinterpretation (1 Corinthians 1:12; 5:9–11, 10:19, etc). Jesus admonished the religious leaders of Israel for not identifying the true meaning of the Scripture (Matthew 9:13, 12:3–8, 19:4, 22:31; Mark 12:10, 26; Luke 6:3, etc.). As previously mentioned, both Paul and Peter rebuked individuals for distorting the true meaning of Scripture (cf. Galatians 1:7 and 2 Peter 3:16). Thus, since correct theology is critical to the Christian life, one must comprehend the intended meaning of Scripture and not simply the one they wish to adhere to.

Third, even those who question the importance of the author's intended meaning for interpretation of the Bible recognize the importance of the author's intended meaning for their own writing. Ironically, many deconstructionists would not want their own books to be read in the way they are proposing for the Bible to be read. For instance, in his article entitled "The Sign of Jonah: A Fish-Eye View," Adam wrote this in a closing footnote, "My thanks to Richard Hays, for his helpful comments throughout my elaboration of this project, and to Stanley Fish, for emphatically (if not always successfully) correcting my misunderstandings concerning his work."[11] Apparently the very method of interpretation that Fish and even Adam would advocate of the Bible should not apply to any work written by Fish since he as the author has the ultimate say about what the text should mean.[12]

Common Objections

---

[11] A. K. M. Adam, "The Sign of Jonah: A Fish-Eye View," *Semeia* 51 (1990): 187.

[12] Radmacher raises the same argument from Hirsch's perspective in Radmacher, Preus, and International Council on Biblical Inerrancy., *Hermeneutics, Inerrancy, and the Bible: Papers from ICBI Summit II*, 434–35.

There are many common objectives to this argument. Hirsch addresses the following in *Validity in Interpretation*: the meaning of a text changes – even for the author; it does not matter what an author means, only what the text says; the author's meaning is inaccessible; and the author often does not know what he means. These all will be addressed in this appendix.

Regarding the first argument, Hirsch argues that the meaning of the author is limited to when he wrote the text. Where there is an authorial self-repudiation, if the work's meaning had changed, then a repudiation of meaning would not have been necessary. In Hirsch's opinion, the meaning of the work did not change, but the author's relationship to the meaning did. If the meaning had changed, the only way we could tell is by the author telling us, but this is usually not necessary because a revision of the text will usually take place in these situations. The significance may change for the author over time but not usually the meaning. Hirsch argues that "meaning is that which is represented by a text; it is what the author meant by his use of a particular sign sequence; it is what the signs represent."[13] He contrasts this with significance which "names a relationship between that meaning and a person, or a conception, or a situation, or indeed anything imaginable."[14] Thus, according to Hirsch, what changes for the author over time (provided that he did not change his opinion about what he was originally writing) was the significance of the text and not the meaning. Thus, he concludes that when critics argue for a change in meaning, they really mean a change in significance.

Furthermore, some of the arguments for the New Testament interpretation of the Old can be addressed in this fashion. The New Testament authors do not establish a new meaning of the Old Testament texts, but they see greater significance for some of them now that the Messiah has come. In

---

[13] Hirsch, *Validity in Interpretation*, 8.
[14] Ibid.

some cases, the Old Testament text is used as an allegorical illustration (cf. Galatians 4:24), but in those cases the author is not suggesting that the meaning of the Old Testament text has changed.

With respect to the second argument that the author's intention is not as relevant as the text itself, Hirsch does not consider the text and author to be mutually exclusive. He argues that validity of interpretation is not the same as inventiveness of interpretation. He believes that validity implies the correspondence of an interpretation to a meaning which is represented by the text. Thus, the best way to know what the text means is to ascertain what the author intended when he wrote the text. Hirsch, like Johnson, distinguishes between the intention to do something and the accomplishment of that intention. The author's desire to communicate meaning is not the same as his success at doing so.

Additionally, Hirsch addresses the question of whether the author's meaning is inaccessible. He addresses those who say that it is impossible for even the author to bring back his original meaning because it is impossible to reproduce his original meaning experience by arguing that irreproducibility of meaning experience (i.e. significance) is not the same as irreproducibility of meaning. He addresses those who believe that the author's intended meaning cannot certainly be known by saying that it is a logical mistake to confuse the impossibility of certainty with impossibility of understanding. According to Hirsch, it is not improbable for an author and interpreter to entertain identical meanings. This happens in everyday conversations.

Finally, the argument that the author himself cannot know the meaning of his own work is based on Freudian assumptions about the subconscious. There is no Biblical evidence for the subconscious. One can say that an individual may not be conscientious of all he does but that does not mean his conscience is not working. Even in sleep the conscience is still working. Song of Solomon 5:2 says, "I was asleep, but my heart was awake." All sinful actions are sourced in the thoughts and intents of the heart (cf. Mark 7:21–22). Thus, this argument is equally as invalid as the others.

Conclusion

This appendix addresses the issue of authorial intent. I agree with Geisler and Johnson's arguments for the locus of meaning in the intent of the author, and the author's intent is restricted to the information that can be identified in the text. Authorial intent is important because it is the only interpretation that can be objectively validated, and the Bible commands believers to seek it. Finally, the arguments against this view were addressed by citation of some of Hirsch's arguments from *Validity in Interpretation*.

APPENDIX C

A RESPONSE TO ARGUMENTS FOR A LATE DATE OF JONAH

Walvoord's method for interpreting prophecy requires an understanding of the historical context of the prophecy. The pre-exilic eighth century BC historical context helps substantiate the view that God was providing the Israelite audience with an opportunity to repent and avoid the judgment of exile or to be destroyed by the Assyrians. After the exile, a prophecy of repentance to avoid future destruction would not likely have the same effect. If Jonah was written after the destruction of Nineveh by the Babylonians, the audience would have likely questioned whether God had in fact delivered the Ninevites. At this point, the issue would not be conditional prophecy but fulfilled prophecy. The purpose and message of Jonah presented in chapter four was, "The book of Jonah was written to Israel in order to describe Yahweh's compassion to Nineveh in response to their repentance in order to demonstrate to the nation of Israel which was symbolized by the prideful and disobedient prophet Jonah that they too could enjoy the same deliverance if they would repent." Since the proposed message and purpose require an early date for Jonah, I will respond to arguments for a late date of Jonah in this appendix.

In "Studies in the Book of Jonah," Trible discusses some of the issues corresponding to the dating of Jonah. She argues that the book has no superscription that locates the book in the reigns of the kings of Israel and Judah, or in the exilic or post-exilic periods. Based on 2 Kings 14:25, she considers the dating of the reign of Jeroboam around 750 BC to be the *terminus a quo* for the book. She argues that the *terminus ad quem* is six centuries later when there is a statement by Jesus Ben Sirach who speaks of the twelve prophets in Sirach 49:10 as well as the fact that by 180 BC Jonah was part of the prophetic canon.[1]

As part of her discussion on the date of Jonah, Trible's informal survey of critical opinions reveals that critical scholars date the book anywhere from the eighth century to the second century BC. She cites Newcombe (who even considers a ninth century BC date possible), Kennedy, Pusey, Keil, and Godlhorn as advocates of an early eighth century BC date for Jonah.[2] She cites Eerdmans, Rosenmüller, Bertholdt, and Dijkema as advocating a seventh century BC date for Jonah. The advocates she lists of a sixth century date include Schmidt, Jäger, Kleinert, Orelli, and Bleck.[3] The advocates of a fifth century date are Driver, Cheyne, Cohen, Gaster, Blecker, and Delcor.[4] Moore, Cornill, Lancaster, and Wade date Jonah in the fourth century BC. Eiselen and Horton place the writing of the book in the third century BC while Hitzig places the writing in the Maccabean era in the second century BC.[5]

Trible argues that regardless of the century for a late date of Jonah, the arguments are essentially the same. She cites five major arguments for the late date.[6] The first argument is the author of Jonah's reliance on other Old Testament literature. The primary texts cited are the Elijah and Elisha stories, Jeremiah, Ezekiel, and Joel. The second issue is the theology of

---

[1] Phyllis Trible, "Studies in the Book of Jonah" (Ph.D. Dissertation, Columbia University, 1963), 104.
[2] Ibid., 105.
[3] Ibid., 105–106.
[4] Ibid., 106–107.
[5] Ibid.
[6] The following discussion is a summary of her pages 107–110 of her previously cited dissertation.

Jonah allegedly evolved late in Israel's history. Proponents of this view argue that Jonah emphasizes the universality of Yahweh's love which is likely influenced by Second Isaiah. According to them, this issue of nationalism versus universalism would likely represent the post-exilic times of Ezra-Nehemiah. The third argument is basically linguistic since the book allegedly has Aramaisms, late Hebrew words, and expressions that are supposedly characteristic of post-exilic times. The fourth argument is the historical markers that allegedly show that this story was composed after the existence of Nineveh. Advocates of this view assert that Jonah 3:3 speaks of the city in the past tense, the exaggerated size of Nineveh, as well as the use of the title "King of Nineveh." The fifth argument is that the literary form of Jonah may point to the post-exilic era. Trible concludes:

> There are words which can only be accounted for, so far as we know, in terms of the post-exilic era. This latter linguistic evidence indicates that the book cannot have been composed before the fifth century BC. The legendary portrayal of Nineveh supports this dating; the historical city lies in the distant past...All in all, however, a date in the fifth (or possibly fourth) century BC is feasible. Surely the burden of proof lies upon him who would place the composition before this time."[7]

This appendix addresses some of the issues raised by Trible. The discussion of genre was primarily addressed in the fourth chapter. An extensive discussion of genre is outside of the scope of this book. However, the fourth chapter argued for the historical narrative. One should not date the book on the basis of genre. With respect to the other views, the basic assumption of each argument will be evaluated. What the reader will soon

---

[7] Ibid., 116.

discover is that the arguments are based on a preconceived notion of the nature of theological development, how to identify an Aramaism, what sources if any the author of Jonah depended on, and how the city of Nineveh was described. Once these assumptions are contradicted, Trible's requirement for establishing the burden of proof will be satisfied.

With respect to her statement regarding the burden of proof, she overstated her case. Despite her arguments to the contrary, the connection between Jonah 1:1 and 2 Kings 14:25 places a clear historical marker on the book. As chapter four suggested, Jonah was likely addressed to the eighth century northern Israelite kingdom. Otherwise, the comparison between Jeroboam II and the king of Nineveh is completely lost. If the book was written after the destruction of Nineveh, the force of God's merciful sparing of the Ninevites would not be as strong. Additionally, the clear statements by Josephus and Jesus point to the book being a historical record and not a parable. One must question why God would inspire a false account of a prophet as an object lesson to the post-exilic community when he did not specifically condemn their bias against the Samaritans within those books themselves. In his article entitled "Jonah and Genre" Alexander addresses those who question the historicity of Jonah with the words of C. S. Lewis from pages 109 and 111 of his book *Fern-seed and Elephants*:

> Whatever these men may be as Biblical critics, I distrust them as critics. They seem to me to lack literary judgment, to be imperceptive about the very quality of the texts they are reading.... These men ask me to believe they can read between the lines of the old texts: the evidence in their obvious inability to read (in any sense worth discussing) the lines themselves. They claim to see a fern-seed and can't see an elephant ten yards away in

broad daylight.[8]

The internal evidence points to an early date for Jonah and the burden of proof is on the person who suggests otherwise.

The Reliance on other Old Testament Texts

As previously mentioned, this view assumes literary dependence of Jonah on later books such as I and II Kings, Jeremiah, Ezekiel, and Joel. Allen also argues that there is literary dependence on Genesis. However, as discussed later in this appendix, the evidence for dependence on sources is weak and not a sufficient argument for dating a book.

One strong advocate of the position that Jonah relied on several Old Testament texts is Leslie Allen. Allen relates the overturning of Nineveh to Sodom and Gomorrah in Genesis 19. He compares God's response to the violence of the Ninevites to Genesis 6:11–13. Jonah is like the divine messengers sent to announce the destruction of Sodom. As a result of this alleged dependence, Allen writes:

> This modelling of the story upon the old Genesis narratives leads one to question the nature of its links with the prophetic narratives of 1, 2 Kings and elsewhere. Did the author intend to set forth an imitation of prophetic narrative, presenting it *as if* it were an old story culled from a prophetic collection? If so, it would explain both the echoing of prophetic motifs and the way the narrative consistently pushes beyond anything that has gone before. It is significant that the elements of surprise and hyperbole are characteristics of the parable.[9]

Allen argues for additional Old Testament parallels in Jonah.

---

[8] Cited in T. Desmond Alexander, "Jonah and Genre," *Tyndale Bulletin* 36 (1984), 35.
[9] Ibid., 176–177. Emphasis his.

He believes that Jonah's words in 4:4, 8 are a parody of Elijah in I Kings 19:4. He also considers Jonah 3:9 and 4:2 to be similar to quotations from Joel 2:13–14. He also argues that Jonah 3:9–10 is dependent on Jeremiah 18:7–8 and 11 when he writes:

> The author is implicitly appealing to Jeremiah 18 as an accepted prophetic principle and claiming it as a warrant for an incident the audience would otherwise have found much harder to swallow than the fish found Jonah to be. In these and other cases…the narrator is copying…in order to create a contrast with the past or to use an act of accepted truth as a religio-psychological stepping-stone to an unwelcome revelation."[10]

These issues lead Allen to question the historicity of Jonah as well as the early date of its writing. Other scholars propose similar arguments. For Wolff, this is a decisive factor in dating Jonah. He considers the alleged verbal echo of 3:9a, 4:2b of Joel 2:13b to be a "clear milestone that helps toward a closer dating…Our study of Joel has shown that this means that the book of Jonah cannot have been written before the middle of the fourth century."[11]

Not all critical scholars consider this argument to be valid, however. Trible writes:

> An argument based on literary affinities is never decisive. From the observation that Jonah is similar to or identical with given OT passages, it does not necessarily follow that Jonah is dependent upon this literature and hence late. For instance, on the basis of the fact that Jon. 4:2b is like Joel 2:3 it cannot be established that Jonah is

---

[10] Ibid., 177.
[11] Hans Walter Wolff, *Obadiah and Jonah: A Commentary*, trans. Margaret Kohl (Minneapolis, MN: Augsburg Publishing House, 1986), 77–78.

therefore borrowing from Joel. One might argue just as well that Joel is dependent upon Jonah, or that these two borrowed from a third writer, or that the similarities between them exist independently and show only a general milieu of thinking in ancient Israel. In other words, literary similarities do not prove sources and hence cannot be employed as reliable criteria for dating. Since literary affinities may be accounted for in various ways, their value as an argument for the dating of Jonah, early or late, is to be minimized.[12]

Trible's argument is well taken. In some cases, one cannot be certain as to who borrowed from whom. Wolff argues that there is a developing reflection in Jonah of the function of the saying of judgment is directed toward Gentiles that is unknown in Joel. In his estimation, this argument proves that Jonah depends on Joel. However, he ignores the clear instances when similar statements of judgment occur in Amos. Additionally, the basis for the late date of Joel has been brought into question by several scholars and the uncertainty with which the book of Joel is dated should make one cautious on dating Jonah based on Joel.[13] Perhaps Sasson rightly concludes, "It makes little sense to solve a difficult problem (the dating of Jonah) by relying on an intractable issue (the dating of Joel)."[14]

---

[12] Trible, "Studies in the Book of Jonah", 110.

[13] For a refutation of common arguments against the critical dates for Joel see Douglas K. Stuart, *Hosea–Jonah*, vol. 31, 52 vols., Word Biblical Commentary (Waco, TX: Word Books, 1987), 225–226. Also see Duane A. Garrett, *Hosea, Joel* (Nashville, TN: Broadman & Holman, 1997), 286–94. For arguments for a ninth century BC date for Joel see Hobart E. Freeman, *An Introduction to the Old Testament Prophets* (Chicago, IL: Moody Press, 1969), 147–49.

[14] Jack M. Sasson, *Jonah: A New Translation with Introduction, Commentary, and Interpretation*, 1st ed. (New York, NY: Doubleday, 1990), 23.

Furthermore, the verses Allen alludes to for a clear echo may not be an echo at all. He argues that Jonah 3:9, which states, "Who can tell if God will turn and relent, and turn away from His fierce anger, so that we may not perish?" is based on Joel 2:13 which states, "So rend your heart, and not your garments; Return to the LORD your God, For He is gracious and merciful, Slow to anger, and of great kindness; And He relents from doing harm." Rather than viewing this as dependence on Joel, there is a better argument for dependence on Exodus 32:12 which was written long before Joel, "Why should the Egyptians speak, and say, 'He brought them out to harm them, to kill them in the mountains, and to consume them from the face of the earth'? Turn from Your fierce wrath, and relent from this harm to Your people." In addition to sharing some key words such as נחם and שוב this literary relationship also has a similarity in the result that the Joel passage does not have. As previously mentioned, Exodus 32:14 says, "So the LORD relented from the harm which He said He would do to His people." Jonah 3:10 similarly says, "Then God saw their works, that they turned from their evil way; and God relented from the disaster that He had said He would bring upon them, and He did not do it." This relationship would provide a greater irony to the fact that God relented from the destruction of Israel based on the intercession of Moses, and now the nations are repenting and receiving mercy while Israel refuses to do so.

This is not the only case where there is not a clear connection between the proposed passage in Jonah and its alleged referent outside of Jonah. Allen and Wolff argue for a relationship between Jonah 3:8–10 and Jeremiah 18:7–10. Stuart addresses this view:

> As to the possible dependence of Jonah on Jeremiah, it must be stated that the evidence is both minimal and ambiguous. The book of Jonah reminds its audience that God is willing to adjust his plans for a nation according to that nation's attitudes and actions before him, a concept

expressed propositionally in Jer 18:7–8. But sharing of concepts is not the same as a dependency of concepts. The widespread tendency of biblical scholars to think only in terms of the lineal generation of ideas (i.e., if two parts of the Bible say roughly the same thing, one part must have preceded and influenced the other part) has never had merit. The similarity of Jonah and Jeremiah is far more cogently attributable to the univocal nature of divine revelation throughout the Scripture than to a borrowing from Jeremiah on the part of the book of Jonah.[15]

At best, there is some similarity of language. However, to argue outright dependence is suspect. Jonah 3:9–10 shows that the author had a familiarity with Exodus 32:12–14. Therefore, it would be a logical deduction based on Exodus 34:6–7 that God would show mercy to repentant people.

Additionally, since Allen bases his view on a supposed relationship between Jonah and Genesis, this issue should be evaluated as well. Sasson is right in arguing that comparisons like these are "often superficial and do not adequately recognize how ideas and phraseology are transmitted in ancient Israel."[16] While the threat against Nineveh included a similar word choice of the Hebrew word הָפַךְ, this really has nothing to do with the date of Jonah since Genesis was written long before Jonah.[17] One has to assume a critical approach to the dating of Genesis in order to use it to argue for a late date for Jonah.

Arguments based on an alleged literary dependence are weak. Even advocates of the late date like Trible and Sasson acknowledge this. The major reason why these arguments do not

---

[15] Stuart, *Hosea–Jonah*, 433.
[16] Sasson, *Jonah: A New Translation with Introduction, Commentary, and Interpretation*, 23.
[17] For a critique of the critical view of the dating of the Pentateuch, see Gleason Leonard Archer, *A Survey of Old Testament Introduction*, Updated and Rev. ed. (Chicago, IL: Moody Press, 1994), 89–189.

prove a late date for Jonah is the fact that one cannot be certain who is borrowing from whom. Secondly, there is no clear evidence that the borrowing may be from an earlier book rather than a later one. This essay has shown that alleged borrowing from Joel and Jeremiah may have actually been influenced by antecedent theology in Exodus or other earlier writings.

The Alleged Theological Development of the Book

The next issue which advocates of the late date address is their belief that the theology of Jonah is too developed to have been written in the eighth century BC. They argue that God's universal love is the focus of the book of Jonah and the book was written to counteract the prejudice that allegedly occurred in the time of Ezra and Nehemiah. The theological argument, however, is based on inaccurate assumptions that should not affect the date of Jonah.

R. B. Y. Scott argues for this position when he writes:

> In the historical circumstances of Judaism, after the return from Babylonian exile, we can discern that which led to the writing of the Book of Jonah by one of the more perceptive prophets. There are various bits of evidence which point to its composition in that period. The literary genre to which the book belongs has no exemplar from the pre-exilic period.... The kind of Hebrew in which it is written is post-classical. Thus, when we find evidence that there developed in Judaism at the time a tendency toward rigidity in belief and religious exclusiveness, with a new note of bitterness toward non-Jews, the setting of such a book as Jonah and the need for it become apparent....The stringent measures taken by Nehemiah to prevent the total disappearance of the Jewish people through assimilation (Neh 13:23–25) may have been totally politically necessary, but they bore bitter fruit. The figure of Jonah is thus a portrait, exaggerated

doubtless for emphasis, of those among the writer's co-religionists who have given way to bitterness and unrighteous anger because of all they had suffered at the hands of their enemies.[18]

Thus, according to Scott, the basis for a late date of Jonah is the genre, the linguistic factors, and a reconstruction of the alleged theology.

In Scott's view, the theology of Jonah expresses God's love and was written to rebuke a prejudice among the Jews during Nehemiah's time. Scott's arguments focus on God's universal love for the church. However, not all critical scholars consider this position to be plausible. Allen says, "It used to be an axiom of critical orthodoxy to regard the book as propaganda directed against the work of Ezra and Nehemiah. But this view has rightly fallen into disfavor."[19] While conservative scholars may consider the phrase "critical orthodoxy" to be an oxymoron, Allen should be commended for his honesty on this matter. He quotes page 291 of Von Rad's *Old Testament Theology* as support that there is no knowledge of a universalistic opposition to particularistic measures taken by Ezra and Nehemiah. Von Rad also rightly argues that the book itself does not contain support for that theory.

Trible denies the alleged dependence on the alleged Second Isaiah as a source and also dismisses this argument on the basis of the presupposition of a theory of progressive revelation. She writes, "Such reasons, which were much used by the Wellhausenian school in dating the sources of the Pentateuch are today increasingly recognized as invalid. The OT itself denies a scheme of progressive revelation from lower to higher 'ideas.' In Israel's history low and high 'theologies' exist

---

[18] R. B. Y. Scott, "The Sign of Jonah," *Interpretation* (1965), 24–25.
[19] Allen, *The Books of Joel, Obadiah, Jonah and Micah*, 188.

side by side."[20] Conservative scholars recognize the progress of revelation but they do not do so on the basis of an alleged evolutionary assumption from the simple to the complex as the Wellhausenian school does.[21] Furthermore, the progress of revelation does not inherently occur based on what the people were capable of understanding but on what God chose to reveal at which time.

If this is true, critical scholars have no leg to stand on in using theology as a means to date the book. If Jonah was written in the post-exilic era, one must wonder what relevance the book would have for the original audience. As Clements was previously cited as mentioning, the book also does little to show how to apply that message. At best, Trible can argue that the "heart of the story is the proclamation that God is love (cf. 4:2). This love is manifested toward foreigners and towards the rebellious prophet himself."[22] One must question why God would choose to write a book of love during a time when Amos had prophesied in Amos 8:11 that there would be a famine of hearing the words of the Lord. Even Trible recognizes that theological arguments could equally be used to defend an early date of composition when she says:

> One might equally aver, as do Eerdmans and Dijkema, that the message of the book fits best the historical situation of the seventh century. In other words, to attempt to date Jonah on the basis of its theology or of its meaning is an unreliable procedure. Like arguments based on literary affinities, arguments from theology are not decisive in establishing the date of the book.[23]

---

[20] Trible, "Studies in the Book of Jonah", 111.
[21] For a description of the evolutionary assumptions in JEDP theory see Archer, *A Survey of Old Testament Introduction*, 95.
[22] Trible, "Studies in the Book of Jonah", Abstract, page 2.
[23] Ibid., 112.

While theological arguments are not decisive, how the text applied to the original audience who received the message would be decisive.

In light of this historical situation discussed in chapter four of this book, the eighth century BC northern tribes of Israel were the most likely to have received Jonah's message. Jonah represents the prideful disobedience of the Israelite nation during the eighth century. Jonah, like the Israelites, accepted the blessings of God's favor but he was not willing to demonstrate true repentance in order to avoid His judgment. While the love of God for all people is a theme of the book, it is not the overriding message. Neither is sharing the gospel in a missionary sense. At best that is an application of the book, but most critical scholars have the overall message wrong.

Essentially these arguments are based on assumptions of the complexity of theological issues in Jonah. Critical scholars who advocate this view believe that the book was written to emphasize God's universal love to post-exilic Jews in order to encourage them to love Gentiles more. Due to the lack of evidence to support this claim, this argument has lost support in the critical community as even Allen and Trible disagree with it. Thus, there is insufficient support for a late date of Jonah on the basis of theological arguments. If anything, the theology and message of Jonah point to an early date when one takes the eighth century BC historical situation into consideration. Consequently, one of the alleged arguments against the early date of Jonah is actually one of the strongest arguments for it.

Linguistic Issues in Jonah

One of the strongest arguments in support of a late date for Jonah is the linguistic issues that surface when dating the book. There are several suggested Aramaisms and late Hebrew words that proponents of the late date use to argue for Aramaic influence of the book. Some of the alleged Aramaisms include מָנָה (2:1, 4:6, 7, 8), רִבּוֹ (4:11), בְּשֶׁלְּמִי (1:7), יִתְעַשֵּׁת (1:6), הַסְּפִינָה (1:5), הַמַּלָּחִים (1:5). Some of the allegedly late Hebrew words include הַקְּרִיאָה

(3:2), וְיִשְׁתֹּק (1:11). Finally the expression "God of the heavens" (אֱלֹהֵי הַשָּׁמַיִם) is allegedly late since it is used in Jeremiah 18:7–8, 51:34, Joel 2:13–14, Ezekiel 1:2, 6:9, Nehemiah 1:4–5, and Daniel 2:18, 4:34.[24] Of all of the issues, this is the one that Sasson finds most convincing for dating the book of Jonah in the postexilic period.[25] Trible, Wolff, Allen, and other advocates of the late date also consider this argument to be one of the more convincing for disproving an early date of Jonah.

Alleged Aramaisms

One of the most significant treatments of this issue was George Landes' articles entitled "Linguistic Criteria and the Date of Jonah."[26] Although Landes dates the book in the sixth century BC, he provides some credible evidence to show that many of the alleged Aramaisms are not Aramaisms and that the author writes in pre-exilic Hebrew. Best of all, Landes provides a system that is based on the work of Kautzch by which Aramaisms can be evaluated. He basically utilizes Kautzch's work to establish three criteria by which a word can be rightfully established to be an Aramaism: 1. The word should be attested in a distinctly Aramaic form. 2. It should be known from the vocable stock of West Aramaic while at the same time not occur in either Canaanite or South Arabic. 3. It should not be found in pre-exilic literature or, if it is, the meaning should differ from its later usage.[27]

This methodology is a helpful starting point for analyzing some of the alleged Aramaisms in Jonah. However, some

---

[24] Index of words and expressions came from David Klingler, "Jonah: A Call for Repentance" (Th.M. Thesis, Dallas Theological Seminary, 2004),7.
[25] Sasson, *Jonah: A New Translation with Introduction, Commentary, and Interpretation*, 27.
[26] George M. Landes, "Linguistic Criteria and the Date of the Book of Jonah," *Eretz Israel* 16 (1981): 147–70.
[27] Ibid.

clarifications should be made. First, one has to determine what exactly pre-exilic literature is. In other words, many of the critical scholars who advocate a late date for Jonah also subscribe to the documentary hypothesis. Therefore, although several of the words appear in the Pentateuch, they are eliminated from consideration because of some of the inherent assumptions about the dating of those books.[28] Landes, while addressing the piel of מָנָה, refers to its use in Job 7:3 which would be determinative for a conservative scholar since most conservatives consider Job to be one of the first books written. However, Landes leaves open the possibility of Aramaic influence.[29] Thus, the very methodological criteria they espouse to prove a late date of Jonah is based on assumptions about the late date of other books.

Second, the third category should be exercised with caution. Just because a word develops a different meaning over time does not in any way prove that this meaning was borrowed from another culture. Words in the English language like "cool" and "bad" have undergone many developments that were cultural in nature and not necessarily linguistic borrowing from outside influences. The other challenge with this category is that oftentimes it is difficult to be certain of who borrowed from whom. Since there is only a small amount of extant written material in many of the written languages, one cannot make assumptions that these words were not used in common conversation long before the time period in which they were used. Klingler writes:

> Further, Loretz has demonstrated that the words הַמַּלָּחִים (1:5), הַסְּפִינָה (1:5), בְּשֶׁלְּמִי (1:7), and רִבּוֹ (4:11) are not Aramaisms but a north Israelite-Phoenician vocabulary.

---

[28] For more information on what assumptions drive these arguments, consult Mike Stallard, "An Essay on Liberal Hermeneutics," *Conservative Theological Journal* 3, no. 10 (1999): 290–303.
[29] Landes, "Linguistic Criteria and the Date of the Book of Jonah," 150.

The word מָנָה is attested in Ugaritic[30], שָׁתַק is used in Psalm 107:30 as well as Proverbs 26:20 (which is ascribed to Solomon), עֶשֶׁת is used in Song of Solomon 5:14, and although הַקְּרִיאָה; is only used in Jonah 3:2, the adjective קָרִיא. is attested in Numbers 1:16. Therefore, instead of pointing to a late date, Trible suggests that this evidence may "testify to possibly early linguistic influences."[31]

Third, Landes acknowledges that some of the alleged Aramaisms may actually come from a northern Israelite dialect which had Canaanite and Phoenician influence rather than an Aramaic influence. For instance, he argues that הַמַּלָּחִים; in Jonah 1:5 was likely a Phoenician term instead of an Aramaism.[32] Landes also cites evidence that the word סְפִינָה that is used in 1:5 had clear presence in Acadian form dating back to the seventh century BC. Douglas also recognizes the importance of the northern Israelite dialects:

> "Aramaisms" have increasingly disappeared, to be replaced by "Northwest Semitisms." That is, the vast majority of words and phrases once thought to be native only to Imperial Aramaic (and therefore, when found in the OT, proof of a date later than 587 BC) have now been found to belong to a far wider provenance in date and language grouping. So many "Aramaisms" have turned up in Ugaritic texts—which cannot be later than 1200 BC—that the arguments from silence on which such identifications are made can now be dismissed as spurious. Indeed, none of the total of seven Aramaisms variously identified in the book fits for certain the criteria

---

[30] Cyrus Herzl Gordon, *Ugaritic Manual; Newly Revised Grammar, Texts in Transliteration, Cuneiform Selections, Paradigms, Glossary, Indices* (Roma, Italy: Pontificium Institutum Biblicum, 1955).
[31] David Klingler, "Jonah: A Call for Repentance," 7–8.
[32] Landes, "Linguistic Criteria and the Date of the Book of Jonah," 152.

necessary to constitute a "genuine" Aramaism according to O. Loretz (*BZ* 5 [1961] 19–22).[33]

As previously mentioned, since Ugaritic texts dating to 1200 BC include many of the alleged Aramaisms, one must question the rationale behind this method of determining the dating of the book of Jonah. Even Trible says that "it is now known that Aramaic, like Hebrew, is but one dialect of Northwest Semitic, and that many words once thought to be Aramaisms are in reality pure Canaanite or Phoenician words of sometimes ancient origins. Thus the term 'Aramaisms' may not only be misleading but even inaccurate."[34]

Even once that criteria is established, Landes further relied on Kautzch's arguments to set some additional parameters by which a word could influence the dating of the book. Thus, for both Landes and Kautzch, even if the word has been determined to be an Aramaism, it is only important for dating purposes if: (1) It manifests phonetic or morphological peculiarity or is used in a syntactical construction that is characteristic of a well-defined period of the Aramaism. (2) It is attested in Aramaic texts of a specific period while in Hebrew it occurs in texts that are datable to a different period, yet in both it is used with the same meaning. (3) In probably early texts Biblical Hebrew employs a different word for specifying the same idea or object. (4) It has a fairly strong frequency of occurrence in Hebrew sources (Biblical or extra-Biblical) datable to a definite period, and also is associated in these sources with other linguistic features (whether or not Aramaisms) characteristic of the Hebrew of the same period.[35] As a result, Landes ultimately concludes, "In light of these criteria, it seems to me that a number of the words or forms in the book of Jonah

---

[33] Stuart, *Hosea–Jonah*, 432.
[34] Trible, "Studies in the Book of Jonah", 114–15.
[35] Landes, "Linguistic Criteria and the Date of the Book of Jonah," 148.

which are alleged to be Aramaisms are either significantly questionable or actually do not qualify."³⁶

After surveying the evidence, Landes ultimately concludes that there are only three possible cases for clear Aramaisms. They are in יִתְעַשֵּׁת in Jonah 1:6 which comes from the verb עֲשֵׁת. He also labels the noun טַעַם in Jonah 3:7 in this category as well as the use of the ל as a *nota accusative* particle in Jonah 2:11 and 4:6.³⁷

With respect to the first word, יִתְעַשֵּׁת, Landes rightly states that the verb form only occurs in Jonah 1:6 in the Hithpael and it means "to think." Outside of Biblical Hebrew he says this verb is only found in the Aramaic. He does argue based on the usage of עֲשֵׁת in the Elephantine texts and Daniel 6:4 that this word may possibly have an early model in the Akkadian which also means to think about. However, he fails to mention that the noun form עַשְׁתּוּת appears in Job 12:5 and is translated in the New King James Version as "A lamp is despised in the thought of one who is at ease; It is made ready for those whose feet slip." A similar word עֶשְׁתֹּנָה also appears and is translated as thought in Psalm 146:4. Since Job is likely one of the oldest books of the Old Testament, this word can be disqualified from consideration as an Aramaism.³⁸

Regarding the use of the noun טַעַם in Jonah 3:7, Landes argues that it is only used in the sense of meaning to order, decree, or command in Jonah 3:7. However, there is a very similar use of this noun in Job 12:20 which the New King James translates as "He deprives the trusted ones of speech, And takes away the discernment of the elders." To a certain degree a decree can represent the judgment of a leader which seems to be

---

³⁶ Ibid.
³⁷ Ibid., 155.
³⁸ For a defense of the early date of Job see Roy B. Zuck, "Job," in *The Bible Knowledge Commentary: An Exposition of the Scriptures*, ed. John F. Walvoord and Roy B. Zuck., vol. 1, 2 vols. (Wheaton, IL: Chariot Victor Publishing, 1985), 716.

reflected in Job 12:20. Once again, if Job is the oldest book in the Bible, one has to question whether טַעַם is an Aramaism.

Even if one were to prove that it was, Landes shows that this word had Neo-Assyrian origin that dates as far as the ninth century BC. According to Landes, the word was used in a letter that was addressed to King Sargon II (who ruled in 721–705 BC) from one of his subjects regarding the royal order he received.[39] One has to remember that Jonah was dealing with Assyrians in Nineveh so he may have borrowed the word from them rather than it being an Aramaism. Archer writes:

> While it is a common Hebrew word meaning "taste" or "understanding," it occurs only here in the governmental sense (Jonah 3:7). However, it is obviously related to the Assyrian word tēmu, which bears the same meaning and Jonah's use of it may therefore have a reminiscence of the actual wording of the Assyrian decree of the king of Nineveh. (It is also used in Ezra 6:14, an Aramaic passage, quoting a decree of the king of Persia).[40]

Archer's point illustrates the fact that what critical scholars consider to be an Aramaism was likely borrowed from the culture Jonah was interacting from.

Landes also cites a parallel situation in one of the inscriptions of Adad-nirari III who ruled from 811–784 BC. The inscription was addressed to his governor in Gozan who had reported a disaster. According to Landes, the king wrote an edict specifying what religious ceremonies should be carried out to assuage the anger of the God Adad who they thought was responsible for the disaster.[41] This situation is very similar to the very situation Jonah reported in Jonah 3. Thus, rather than

---

[39] Ibid., 156.
[40] Archer, *A Survey of Old Testament Introduction*, 348.
[41] Landes, "Linguistic Criteria and the Date of the Book of Jonah," 156.

demonstrating evidence for an author borrowing from a postexilic language, some words may lend credibility to an argument that Jonah wrote the book and included words that the Ninevites may have used.

With respect to the use of the ל as a *nota accusativa* particle Landes argues that it appears in post-exilic Biblical Hebrew in Ezekiel, Deutero-Isaiah, Chronicles, and Daniel.[42] Once again, the critics' own assumptions of the dating of the books drive the issue rather than the Biblical record. If one accepts the unity of Isaiah as well as the early date for the book, there should be no question that the word is not an Aramaism and was likely in use in Hebrew in the time of Jonah (Landes also shows that this use was found in Isaiah 14:2 which critical scholars would recognize as earlier than its appearances in Isaiah 53:11 and 61:1). Not only that, but Landes lends support for the use of the l as a *nota accusativa* particle in Job 5:2, 9:7, 12:23, 19:28, as well as 2 Samuel 3:20, 16:11, and Psalm 69:6.[43]

Landes thus concludes that of all of the alleged Aramaisms only the one in Jonah 1:6 "seems reasonably to have come into the Hebrew directly from Aramaic."[44] However, the previous study showed the noun with the meaning of thought appeared in Job 12:20 which would disqualify it as an Aramaism. Thus, the argument from alleged Aramaisms is an extremely weak foundation on which to base the dating of Jonah.

Late Hebrew Words

The second argument regarding the linguistic features of the dating of the book of Jonah involves the allegedly late Hebrew words. Once again, Landes' methodology is helpful. He writes that usually the key issues in judging whether a word is early or late is determined by special word usages, especially

---

[42] Ibid., 157.
[43] Ibid.
[44] Ibid.

when used in contrast to words they appear to replace. Secondly, grammatic-syntactic constructions which only turn up in indisputably dated post-exilic sources may point to a late writing.[45]

Perhaps some uniqueness in Jonah's writing can be attributed to the fact that he was from Galilee, and there is no other Old Testament book that is written by a Galilean. This may explain some of the unique words and expressions he uses. With respect to the use of הַקְּרִיאָה in Jonah 3:2, Landes argues that the word itself is clearly derived from קָרָא and "the formation alone cannot be used as an important clue for dating."[46] Ultimately, even though he argues that the book was not written before the sixth century BC, Landes acknowledges that there is a "paucity of characteristics" within Jonah of late Biblical Hebrew.[47] Even the characteristics he did find were basically based on the work of Robert Polzin who employs the literary-critical method which most conservative scholars reject. Of course, the argument for late Hebrew expressions is fairly suspect since critics consider evidences of early Hebrew within Jonah to be the author's attempt to imitate an early style to give the impression that the book was written within the time of Jonah. One must question why the author would intend to give this impression unless he truly was writing in that time.

The Expression "God of the heavens"

The Hebrew expression אֱלֹהֵי הַשָּׁמַיִם/ which is translated as "God of the heavens" has been cited as a linguistic argument for a late date because of its frequent use in Jeremiah (18:7–8, 51:34), Joel (2:13–14), Ezekiel (1:2, 6:9), Nehemiah (1:4–5), and Daniel (2:18, 4:34). First of all, if one does not assume the documentary hypothesis, the phrase appears in one of the

---

[45] Ibid., 158.
[46] Ibid., 152.
[47] Ibid., 163.

earliest books in the Bible in Genesis 24:3,7. Landes also cites evidence from the Zakir Steele that the phrase was used in Canaanite writings that date to the eighth or ninth century BC. He also notes that the phrase would have been known as a title for Yahweh as early as the tenth century BC in the Aramaic.[48] Thus, the use of the phrase "God of the heavens" does not provide enough determinative evidence to raise questions about the early date of Jonah.

The support for Aramaisms in Jonah is weak. The same can be said for the alleged late Hebrew words. The Hebrew expression אֱלֹהֵי הַשָּׁמַיִם/ is found in Genesis. At best, the linguistic arguments that support a late date for Jonah are based on presuppositions that cannot be proven Biblically.

The Alleged Historical Issues Regarding Nineveh

Another argument posed by critical scholars involves some statements about the historical situation that allegedly point to a late date for Jonah. First, critical scholars argue that Jonah 3:3 points to a past city that was very great. Second, they allege that the title "King of Nineveh" in Jonah 3:6 is anachronistic. Third, they say that the statement that the city required a three-day walk was not true of eighth century Nineveh. Fourth, they believe that the population described in Jonah 4:11 is too large. While these arguments are stronger than some of the others, they certainly can be explained without requiring a late date for Jonah.

Trible finds this argument to be fairly convincing. She writes:

> This argument seems cogent. Jonah is not concerned with historical Nineveh. The author draws upon memories of that once colossal place in order to portray a type of ancient city. It is not essential for historical Nineveh to

---

[48] Ibid., 155.

exist. The truth is quite the contrary. This story could hardly have been written while Nineveh was a historical reality. The writer knows of a city which *was in the past* very great (3:3). To this knowledge he adds imagination and thereby creates a legendary Nineveh. Surely this portrayal of Nineveh speaks for a time of composition long after 612 BC.[49]

Regarding the king of Nineveh, rather than reflecting a lack of knowledge of Assyrian politics, it may accurately reflect the historical situation in the eighth century BC. Page writes:

> According to G. Roux, "for thirty-six years (781–745 BC) Assyria was practically paralysed." W. W. Hallo observes that "even the central provinces maintained only a tenuous loyalty to Assyria, for the various governors ruled in virtual independence." This could explain the otherwise unknown expression "king of Nineveh" (rather than "king of Assyria" found elsewhere) in 3:6. Nineveh was at this time virtually the extent of the king's domain. It also could explain the unusual phrase in 3:7, "By the decree of the king and his nobles." As P. J. N. Lawrence has demonstrated, the precarious position of the king may have necessitated his acknowledging in his decree the power and influence of surrounding provincial governors.[50]

Furthermore, Stuart cites many situations in which a king may be designated by one city or region that he ruled. He gives Sihon as an example. In some places in Deuteronomy (1:4, 3:2, 4:46), Sihon is called "King of the Amorites" while in others

---

[49] Trible, "Studies in the Book of Jonah", 115. Emphasis hers.
[50] Billy K. Smith and Frank S. Page, *Amos, Obadiah, Jonah*, vol. 19B, 37 vols., New American Commentary (Nashville, TN: Broadman & Holman, 1995), 205.

(Deuteronomy 2:24, 26, 30) he is called the "King of Heshbon." Stuart also refers to Jabin who is called the "King of Canaan" as well as the "King of the Canaanites" in Judges 4:2, 23–24, but he is known as the "King of Hazor" in Judges 4:17. On this basis, Stuart concludes:

> A king could be associated, in other words, with a capital or main city within his empire, as well as with the empire itself (cf. 2 Sam 8:5; 1 Kgs 11:23, etc., where Hadadezer's kingship is associated with "Zobah" though his control extended considerably further).... Perhaps the closest OT parallel to "King of Nineveh" is found in 1 Kgs 21:1, where Ahab is called מלך שמרון "King of Samaria" in contrast to "King of Israel," the title used for him routinely elsewhere. If Ahab can be called "King of Samaria" in the OT there can surely be no valid objection to calling Aššur-dan III (or whoever was the king who responded to Jonah's preaching) "King of Nineveh" in Jonah 3:6... It is most probable that the narrator of Jonah chose "King of Nineveh" over "King of Assyria" (מלך אשור) simply because the story focuses on Nineveh per se rather than on the empire as a whole. However, since it clearly remained an option in OT narrative to speak of a king in terms of his capital or chief city, as the examples above illustrate, we cannot rule out the possibility that "King of Nineveh" was chosen according to this normal, not infrequent, idiom by a narrator and for an audience who would have considered it nothing other than a routine sort of option, as the writer (and presumably, audience) of 1 Kgs 21:1 did in the case of "King of Samaria."[51]

Page and Stuart both provide plausible explanations that overcome the arguments made by critical scholars against the

---

[51] Stuart, *Hosea–Jonah*, 440.

early date for Jonah.

As previously mentioned, scholars like Trible also focus on the past tense of Jonah 3:3. Based on the idea that "Nineveh was an exceedingly great city," Trible believes that the past tense of the verb decidedly shows that the book was written after Nineveh ceased to exist. However, Page rightly questions basing the dating on a stative verb that is used in direct speech, "Hebrew has only two so-called tenses, and they do not necessarily mark time, especially in the kind of circumstantial clause found here. The choice of verb form here is determined not by Nineveh's former greatness but by syntax and the past time of the surrounding narrative. It emphasizes the size and importance of the city in Jonah's day."[52] Citing Ogden, Stuart argues that the verb can be translated as "is" since "היה can be used to indicate a condition which began in the past and continues in the present, Isa 49:5, 'my God *is* (היה) my strength.'"[53] However, even if one were to concede the past tense of the verb, the question becomes how far in the past was it? In other words, arguing for the late date of Jonah based on the past tense of the verb is presuming much. Could it be, from the perspective of the narrator, that Jonah's visit occurred in the not so distant past from the time of writing?

With respect to questions regarding the size of the city, many critical scholars argue that the eighth century BC city of Nineveh would not have required a three-day walk as Jonah 3:3 indicates. However, this does not necessarily reveal how much time it would take to walk through the city but how much time would have been needed to be spent to prophesy in the city. As Lessing argues, the word מַהֲלָךְ is used in a wide variety of ways. It is used in Nehemiah 2:6 in order for the king to "ascertain when Nehemiah expects to return to his job, not the exact

---

[52] Billy K. Smith and Frank S. Page, *Amos, Obadiah, Jonah* (Nashville, TN: Broadman & Holman, 1995), 256.
[53] Stuart, *Hosea–Jonah*, 484.

distance he will travel."⁵⁴ He notes that the word is used in Ezekiel 42:4 as a passageway in the eschatological temple as well as in Zechariah 3:2 as the access he will provide to Joshua among those who stand by Yahweh.⁵⁵ Thus, the concept does not require the length of the city. If the city did have a population of at least 120,000 as Jonah 4:11 suggests, then it would not be surprising that it would take at least three days to reach that large of a population of people. Stuart suggests another reason for why it would have taken so long:

> Accordingly, Nineveh was undoubtedly a place Jonah, like any other "emissary," had to enter and leave according to accepted protocol. The story of course does not provide us with the details of how this was done. But we may assume that his first and third days involved meetings and explanations, perhaps even formal hearings. He may even have presented gifts to city officials upon his arrival, as was the custom in the case of official state visits, though his contacts may have been less formal and less high-level. The popular notion that Jonah, virtually unnoticed (except, as some have argued, for his skin stained or bleached by digestive juices!) wandered into Nineveh casually and then, at various stages of his trip, suddenly began shouting his message, would be far from a realistic portrayal of the events—and would have seemed as strange to the ancient hearer/reader as to the modern one. Rather, the narrator's point is that Nineveh was a "three-day visit city," a major diplomatic center of the ancient world, a city where a formal protocol was observed by official visitors, whose business could not easily be accomplished hastily, as if it were a small town. Another explanation is

---

⁵⁴ R. Reed Lessing, *Jonah*, Concordia Commentary (St. Louis, MO: Concordia Publishing House, 2007), 281.
⁵⁵ Ibid., 281.

also to be considered. A prophet might reach the populace of a small town with a word from God in a very short time. But in a major city, a prophet would have to travel to various sections, speaking to different crowds, over a period of time. "A three-day visit (city)" could imply simply that Nineveh's population and importance made it necessary for Jonah to preach there for at least three days, to be sure that God's message had been really heard by the bulk of the populace. One of these meanings must lie behind the nominal phrase מהלך שלשת ימים, used adjectivally to modify נינוה.[56]

Thus, Stuart rightly argues that the reason why Nineveh is called a city with a three-day walk may have much more to do with culture than geography. The key point of this section is that Nineveh was a very important city to God. This does not testify as much to its size but its importance in the eyes of a compassionate and loving God.

With respect to the size of the population, part of the problem is the critical assumption that the 120,000 must be infants. This would make the total population of Nineveh in the eighth century BC to be over 600,000 people. However, Stuart offers an alternate explanation for the size of the population and the statement that they did not know their right hand from the left:

> The speech goes on to point out that the people of Nineveh "do not know their right hand from their left," an idiomatic expression for a lack of knowledge, and/or innocence. The precise sense of the expression is hard to isolate. It does not seem to refer to infants per se (the closest OT parallel construction being Isa 7:15–16) as if the total population were so huge that just the infants

---

[56] Stuart, *Hosea–Jonah*, 487–88.

alone were more than 100,000 in number. The first two words, ידע בין ("know the difference between"), occur in the OT otherwise only in 2 Sam 19:36[35], where they clearly indicate an inability to discriminate ("between what is good and what is not"). An expression in Deut 1:39 (ידע טוב ורע "knowing good and evil"), sometimes cited in connection with Jonah 4:11, is actually a different idiom, essentially the same as is used in Gen 2:17 in the phrase "tree of knowledge of good and evil," i.e., "all sorts of knowledge" (good and evil being polarities which express totality in the Semitic merism).

This "lack of knowledge" displayed by the people of Nineveh probably means therefore that they could not make the kind of decision that would give them relief from the trouble (רעה) that had come to Yahweh's attention (1:2). The full expression ("who do not know their right hand from their left") might even be translated "helpless" or "pitiful" in keeping with Yahweh's announced intention to show the Ninevites concern in their plight. This is a profound point in light of the assumption of Jonah, and quite probably most ancient Israelites, that the people of Nineveh would surely be fully responsible in every sense for whatever miseries may have befallen them. It is *not* likely that Yahweh's words are to be interpreted as implying that the Ninevites are morally innocent, that they bear no guilt for their many crimes detailed in Nahum and other OT prophetical books. The people themselves acknowledge by their penitence that they have done wrong (3:5), and the royal decree categorically so states (3:8). Rather, these Assyrians are "innocent" and undiscerning in another sense: they are trapped by their troubles, not knowing how to escape them. Their troubles may not have necessarily been the result of any particular sin they have committed, especially since in other times they prospered while equally as evil. For most of its history, in other words, Assyria's fortunes were no more linked to its faithfulness to divine law than were Israel's fortunes. In the long run, sin against God was the cause for Assyria's destruction (Zeph 2:15) just as for Israel's (2 Kgs 17), but in the short run, i.e., at virtually any given point prior to the final destruction of these nations, they were not subject to punishments which correlated directly with the intensity of their sins (cf. 2 Kgs 17:14). Nineveh got away with a great deal of evil before Jonah's visit, and it would do so again for another century and a half until its downfall in 611 B.C.[57]

Stuart's explanation fits better contextually than the critical argument that God is pointing to the number of infants in Nineveh. As previously mentioned, the ignorant Ninevites provide a contrast to the Israelites who had been entrusted with the oracles of God (cf. Romans 3:2). However, despite their ignorance the Ninevites repented while those who had the truth refused to do so.

Rather than proving that the writer wrote long after the eighth century BC, each of these alleged inaccuracies actually demonstrates how familiar the writer was with that time period. Rather than proving a late date, these arguments provide evidence for the early date.

Genre and Historicity of Jonah

This historicity of Jonah was discussed in chapter two. In light of the historical accuracy of Jonah, chapter four evaluated some common arguments regarding the genre of Jonah and concluded that Jonah is not a parable, midrash, or allegory. Since those three genres were dismissed as possibilities, the argument for the late date based on the genre is inadequate.

A primary defense of the view that Jonah was likely

---

[57] Ibid., 507–08. Emphasis his.

written in the eighth century BC is that the book best addresses the historical situation in the eighth century BC. The later dates cannot prove how the message of Jonah would have connected to another group. Furthermore, the testimonies of Christ as well as Jewish and Christian witnesses demonstrate that the book was describing an actual historical incident. The message to the Israelites of their need for repentance in light of God's compassion would lose its force if Nineveh was destroyed when the book was written or if the event never happened.

Not only this, but the common critical arguments for a late date were inadequate to overturn the traditional early date of the composition of Jonah. The argument of reliance on other Old Testament literature was dismissed because the alleged connections are difficult to prove, and Jonah has more in common with Exodus and Joel than with later literature. The theological argument was rejected on the basis of the inaccurate assumption that Jonah is speaking of a universal love of God in order to overcome prejudice in the Ezra-Nehemiah era. Furthermore, one cannot prove that the actual theology espoused by the author of Jonah was not represented elsewhere in the early Old Testament canon. The linguistic argument was dismissed because of the identification of the alleged Aramaisms in the earlier writings in the Pentateuch or the connection with Ugaritic texts from 1200 BC. The historical inaccuracies argument was disproved on the basis that the alleged historical inaccuracies were misinterpreted by critical scholars. The argument from genre proved to be among the weakest for the late date. Since critical scholars cannot agree on the genre, one must question how this could positively prove a late date for the book. This argument is based on an anti-supernatural bias instead of a true representation of the text. Since the burden of proof was not fulfilled by advocates of the late date, the traditional early date should be upheld.

APPENDIX D

ALTERNATE VIEWS OF THE SIGN OF JONAH

Chapter five addressed the significance of the sign of Jonah for interpreting Jonah's prophecy. Merrill's arguments on the significance of the sign of Jonah defend the notion that Jonah was a sign of repentance to the Ninevites and destruction to the Jews who rejected Christ. This appendix addresses the different proposals for the correct interpretation of the sign of Jonah. Ernest von Dobschütz said that up until his time no one has been able to give a fair explanation of what the sign might mean.[1] While all possible interpretations cannot be addressed here, specific attention will be given to these six views of the sign of Jonah: the preaching of Christ, the sign of John, the *parousia*, different signs in different passages, the allegorical interpretation, as well as the death, burial, and resurrection of Christ.

The Preaching of Jonah

The first view of the sign of Jonah is that the sign was directly speaking of his preaching. This tends to be a popular view among New Testament scholars. According to Chow, advocates of this view include Manson, Perrin, Fitzmyer, and

---

[1] Ernst von Dobschütz, *The Eschatology of the Gospels* (Hodder and Stoughton).

Kloppenborg.² This view does justice to the fact that the Ninevites repented at the preaching of Jonah as described in Luke 11:32 and Matthew 12:41. Advocates of this view will quickly point out that the Lucan account does not have the description of Jonah's time in the belly of the fish that Matthew does. Consequently, they interpret Matthew in light of Luke.

A great challenge with this view is how Jonah's preaching is a sign. Rengstorf says:

> When all this is added up, the point of the demand is that Jesus should undertake to show thereby that God, in whose name He works, has unequivocally authorised Him. This authentication will take place when God does something or causes something to happen in relation to Jesus which will prove that any doubt concerning His divine authority is wrong."³

Thus, the sign must have been supernatural in nature since the Pharisees had already heard much of Christ's preaching and rejected it. Jeremias states, "it is highly unusual to describe the preaching of repentance as a → σημεῖον, since a sign consists, not in what men do, but in the intervention of the power of God in the course of events."⁴

Rengstorf argues against the sign of Jonah being Christ's preaching on the basis of Greek grammar since he takes Ἰωνᾶ as a genitive of apposition and finds in τὸ σημεῖον Ἰωνᾶ the sign which Jonah himself is in the singularity of his historical

---

[2] Simon Chow, *The Sign of Jonah Reconsidered: A Study of Its Meaning in the Gospel Traditions* (Stockholm, Sweden: Almqvist & Wiksell International, 1995), 17.
[3] Gerhard Kittel, Gerhard Friedrich, and Geoffrey William Bromiley, *Theological Dictionary of the New Testament*, vol. 7 (Grand Rapids, MI: W.B. Eerdmans, 1976), 234.
[4] Ibid., vol. 3, 408.

manifestation.⁵ Jeremias says that "the future ἔσται at [Luke] 11:30 rules out the possibility that Luke finds the renewed sign of Jonah in the present activity of Jesus as a preacher of repentance."⁶

Sign of John the Baptist

The second view argues that the sign of Jonah is the sign of John the Baptist. Chow lists Michael, Cheyne, Moxon, and Bacon as advocates of this view.⁷ Chow quotes Michael as saying that the confusion began with Q and that Q consequently did not accurately represent what Jesus said. Chow rightly eliminates this view because of its weak support and the clear statement that the sign of Jonah was originally to the Ninevites.⁸ The argument is fairly speculative since there is little textual evidence for it. Jeremias eliminates this view because "the linguistic basis of this hypothesis is insecure."⁹

The Parousia

The third view was proposed by Bultmann. According to Chow, he argues that the sign refers to the Son of Man coming as eschatological judge. Bultmann argues that just as Jonah came from a distant country to preach repentance, so Christ will come to judge. His primary defense of this is the use of ἔσται in Luke 11:30. However, Chow rightly disputes this view on the basis that the future tense can be used in a gnomic sense (as well as the fact that the death, burial, and resurrection is still future

---

⁵ Ibid., vol. 7, 233
⁶ Ibid., vol. 3, 408
⁷Chow, *The Sign of Jonah Reconsidered: A Study of Its Meaning in the Gospel Traditions*, 15.
⁸ Ibid. I do not consider the alleged lost Q gospel to have ever existed and I do not attempt to reconstruct Q within redaction critical analysis. For more information on this issue, please consult Eta Linnemann, "The Lost Gospel of Q—Fact or Fantasy? ," *Trinity Journal* 17, no. 1: 3–18.
⁹ Kittel, *Theological Dictionary of the New Testament*, vol. 3, 408.

when Jesus spoke these words) and "it will be too late to talk about repentance when the *parousia* comes."[10]

Different Sign of Jonah in Different Texts

Chow's thorough work *The Sign of Jonah Reconsidered: A Study of Its Meaning in the Gospel Traditions* provides a very detailed analysis of the background issues of the book as well as a redaction critical approach to the differences between Matthew, Luke, and Q. His ultimate conclusion is that the sign of Jonah in Q is likely the coming of the Son of Man in the *parousia*. Matthew understands the sign to be the death and resurrection of Jesus. According to Chow, Luke relates the sign to the preaching of the church in an effort to assure his readers that in the preaching of the name of the Messiah Satan is conquered.[11] While it is possible that Matthew and Luke had different intentions in addressing their audience, Chow's view should be discounted by the numerous similarities between the two accounts. Both accounts mention the preaching of Jonah, and the story of Jonah would have been readily understood by both audiences. If Matthew was the first gospel written, Luke likely incorporated Matthew's view into his research and possibly by this time it was commonly accepted that Jesus was referring to his death, burial, and resurrection as one aspect of the sign of Jonah. Irrespective of these possibilities, Chow focuses so much on the differences between Luke and Matthew that he does not seek to determine if there is one common denominator that links those passages as Merrill does.

Allegorical View

The next popular view among critical scholars is the allegorical view. Since they deny the historicity of Jonah, they

---

[10] Chow, *The Sign of Jonah Reconsidered: A Study of Its Meaning in the Gospel Traditions*, 16.
[11] Ibid., 211–12.

prefer to allegorize not only the story but the sign that accompanies it. Dom John Howton espouses this view in his article entitled "The Sign of Jonah."[12] He writes that "the 'sign of Jonah' has a deeper meaning than the one which was seized upon by the evangelists and the early church" and consequently argues that the sign of Jonah relates to his name which could be translated as dove.[13] He writes:

> The dove (or Jonah) was a sign to the Gentiles; the dove was the sign for Israel of whom the Son of Man was conceived as a remnant, he and Israel are both sons of God, although in different senses; the sign to this generation is again the sonship, represented by the dove; and so we have the comparison between the "Son of man" and the "sign of Jonah" or the dove. What our Lord is actually saying in a typical phrase pregnant with meaning is that as God of old worked out his purpose with Israel, whose sign was the dove, so now He works it out through Him who in His person unites all the earlier strands of thought. That purpose is still redemptive, and as old Israel refused to accept the mission of the dove, so now they can (and will?) reject Him.[14]

Howton justifies his view by relying on evidence from Jewish writings (especially depending on the Midrash) as well as some Old Testament references that compare Israel with a dove.

Allegorical views such as this one are full of problems. For one, since the full meaning of sign Jonah was not known by the earliest evangelists and the church, the intent of the author is

---

[12] Dom John Howton, "The Sign of Jonah," *Scottish Journal of Theology* 15 (1962): 288–304.
[13] Ibid., 288.
[14] Ibid., 304.

not the final determining factor in interpretation.[15] In light of the numerous possibilities of what a text could mean and little anchor for intended meaning in the hands of the original author, it should be no surprise that some like Adam have concluded:

> If, then, we adopt this Fish-eye view of interpretation, does the ideal of correct interpretation vanish? Yes it does; but only in the abstract, where it never did us any good anyway. "Correct interpretation" can still be invoked, but only in a limited way, by appeal to mutually recognized norms of interpretation; those who wish to judge interpretations will have to judge by standards to which those interpretations implicitly or explicitly appeal, or acknowledge the possible disjunction between the critic's and the interpreter's commitments. The fact is that we will find ourselves agreeing about many more aspects of a text than we disagree about. Just as no reader of this article really expected an ichthyological perspective on the text, so no reader will argue that "the sign of Jonah" was a placard which the prophet carried. If we limit the bases of our argument to commonly-held assumptions, if we use our terms and ideas in a common sense, way we will have mutually agreed-upon standards for correct interpretation, and on their basis we will be able to judge some interpretations of the sign of Jonah correct and others incorrect.[16]

Thus, since the intent of the author no longer leads to correct interpretation, the best one can do is determine what is not a correct interpretation (once the biased methodology is agreed upon), but there is no way of determining what is the correct

---

[15] As mentioned in appendix B, I agree with a Hirschian principle of interpretation that prioritizes the meaning as being determined by the intent of the original author.

[16] Adam, "The Sign of Jonah: A Fish-Eye View," 187.

interpretation.[17]

Getting back to Howton's view, the first major challenge is on his overreliance on Jewish sources with little or no attention to the clear statements in Matthew's gospel that contradict his claim. Additionally, if Jonah's name had any significance to the story of Jonah itself, it would not have the significance that he posits. The more likely parallel use of Jonah's name is found in Hosea 7:11 which says, "So Ephraim has become like a silly dove, without sense; They call to Egypt, they go to Assyria." Like Jonah, the Israelites discounted God's grace and rebelled against God.

Secondly, it is hard to understand how Jonah's name would be a sign that would bring the Ninevites to repentance. Throughout his article Howton criticizes others for not convincingly proving that their view is a true sign. Rather than giving σημεῖον the appropriate force as the *Theological Dictionary of the New Testament* does of it being "miracles and wonders by which God authenticates the men sent by him, or by which men prove that the cause they are pleading is God's,"[18] he apparently argues that the sign must be akin to a symbol which is not what the Greek word means.

Death, Burial, and Resurrection

The traditional view identifies the sign of Jonah as the death, burial, and resurrection of Christ. Justin the Martyr

---

[17] Appendix B noted the irony in Adam's closing footnote in which he writes on page 187, "My thanks to Richard Hays, for his helpful comments throughout my elaboration of this project, and to Stanley Fish, for emphatically (if not always successfully) correcting my misunderstandings concerning his work." The method of interpretation that Fish and even Adam would advocate of the Bible should not apply to any work written by Fish since he as the author has ultimate say about what the text should mean.

[18] Gerhard Kittel, Gerhard Friedrich, and Geoffrey William Bromiley, *Theological Dictionary of the New Testament*, vol. 3 (Grand Rapids, MI: W.B. Eerdmans, 1976), 409.

considered it to be so, "He replied to them, 'An evil and adulterous generation seeketh after a sign; and no sign shall be given them, save the sign of Jonah.' And since He spoke this obscurely, it was to be understood by the audience that after His crucifixion He should rise again on the third day."[19] In his article in the *Theological Dictionary of the New Testament* Joachin Jeremias says:

> M[atthew] 12:40 finds the *tertium comparationis* between the sign of Jonah and the sign of Jesus in the fact that Jonah stayed three days and three nights in the belly of the fish, the same period that the Son of Man will spend in the heart of the earth. For L[uke] 11:30, however, the *tertium comparationis* is that Jonah became a sign to the Ninevites, obviously as one who had been delivered from the belly of the fish, and that Jesus will be displayed to this generation as the One who is raised up from the dead. According to Lk., then, both the old and the new sign of Jonah consist in the authorisation of the divine messenger by deliverance from death.[20]

Merrill adopts this view and elaborates on it by arguing for Jonah's experience in the large fish having additional significance for the Ninevite audience. The sign of the death, burial, and resurrection best explains the data along with Merrill's points regarding the background circumstances that illuminate how Jonah himself was a sign.

---

[19] Alexander Roberts, James Donaldson, and A. Cleveland Coxe, *The Ante-Nicene Fathers Vol.I: Translations of the Writings of the Fathers Down to AD 325* (Oak Harbor, WA: Logos Research Systems, 1997) 252.
[20] Kittel, Friedrich, and Bromiley, *Theological Dictionary of the New Testament*, 409. Emphasis his.

BIBLIOGRAPHY

Achtemeier, Paul J., Harper & Row Publishers., and Society of Biblical Literature. *Harper's Bible Dictionary*. 1st ed. San Francisco, CA: Harper & Row, 1985.

Ackerman, Arthur W. "The Purpose of Jonah's Mission to Nineveh." *Biblical World* 12 (September 1898): 190–95.

Adam, A. K. M. "The Sign of Jonah: A Fish-Eye View." *Semeia* 51 (1990): 177–91.

Alden, Robert L. *Job*. Vol. 11. The New American Commentary. Nashville, TN: Broadman & Holman Publishers, 1993.

Alexander, T. Desmond. "Jonah and Genre." *Tyndale Bulletin* 36 (1984): 35–59.

Allen, Leslie C. *The Books of Joel, Obadiah, Jonah and Micah*. London, England: Hodder and Stoughton, 1976.

Allis, Oswald T. *Prophecy and the Church: An Examination of the Claim of Dispensationalists That the Christian Church Is a Mystery Parenthesis Which Interrupts the Fulfilment to Israel of the Kingdom Prophecies of the Old Testament*. Philadelphia, PA: Presbyterian and Reformed Publishing Co., 1972.

Augustine. *The City of God*. Translated by Henry Bettenson. Penguin Classics. London, England: Penguin Group, 2003.

Baker, David W., T. Desmond Alexander, and Bruce K. Waltke. *Obadiah, Jonah, Micah*. The Tyndale Old Testament Commentaries, ed. D.J. Wiseman. Downers Grove, IL: Inter-Varsity Press, 1988.

Barrick, William D. "The Openness of God: Does Prayer Change God?" *Master's Seminary Journal* 12, no. 2 (2001): 149–

66.

Ben Zehabe, Michael. *A Commentary on Jonah: Accidental Hebrew for Christians.* Los Angeles, CA: Shema Publishing Company, 2011.

Berkhof, Louis. *Systematic Theology.* 4th rev. and enl. ed. Grand Rapids, MI: Wm. B. Eerdmans Publishing Co. 1986 c1941.

Berlin, Adele. "A Rejoinder to John A. Miles, Jr., with Some Observations on the Nature of Prophecy." *The Jewish Quarterly Review* 66 (April 1976): 227–35.

Blaising, Craig A., and Darrell L. Bock. *Progressive Dispensationalism.* Wheaton, IL: BridgePoint, 1993.

Bob, Steven. *Go to Nineveh.* Eugene, OR: Pickwick Publications, 2013.

Boyd, Gregory A. *Satan and the Problem of Evil: Constructing a Trinitarian Warfare Theodicy.* Downers Grove, IL: InterVarsity Press, 2001.

_____. "Is the Open View the Only View Compatible with the Incarnation?" Christus Victor Ministries, Accessed November 15, 2008 Internet. Available from http://www.gregboyd.org/qa/jesus/is-the-open-view-the-only-view-that-is-compatible-with-the-incarnation/.

_____. "What Is the Significance of Jeremiah 18:7–11?" Christus Victor Ministries, Accessed November 22, 2008 Internet. Available from http://www.gregboyd.org/qa/open-theism/arguments-for-open-theism/what-is-the-significance-of-jeremiah-187%e2%80%9311/.

Brenton, Lancelot Charles Lee. *The Septuagint Version of the Old Testament. With an English Translation, and with Various Readings and Critical Notes.* Grand Rapids, MI,: Zondervan Publishing House, 1971.

Bright, John. *A History of Israel.* 4th ed. Louisville, KY: Westminster J. Knox Press, 2000.

Brown, Francis, S. R. Driver, and Charles A. Briggs. *The Brown-Driver-Briggs Hebrew and English Lexicon.* Peabody,

MA: Hendrickson Publishers, 2003. Reprint, Seventh.
Bullock, C. Hassell. *An Introduction to the Old Testament Prophetic Books*. Chicago, IL: Moody Press, 1986.
Cary, Phillip. *Jonah*. Brazos Theological Commentary on the Bible, ed. R.R. Reno. Grand Rapids, MI: Brazos Press, 2008.
Casanowicz, Immanuel M. "Paronomasia in the Old Testament." *Journal of Biblical Literature* 12 (1893): 105–67.
Chafer, Lewis Sperry. "Part 3 Biblical Theism: The Attributes of God (Concluded)." *Bibliotheca Sacra* 96, no. 381 (1939): 5–37.
Childs, Brevard. "Jonah: A Study in Old Testament Hermeneutics." *Scottish Journal of Theology* 11 (1958): 52–61.
Chisholm Jr., Robert B. *From Exegesis to Exposition: A Practical Guide to Using Biblical Hebrew*. Grand Rapids, MI: Baker Books, 1998.
_____. *Handbook on the Prophets: Isaiah, Jeremiah, Lamentations, Ezekiel, Daniel, Minor Prophets*. Grand Rapids, MI: Baker Academic, 2002.
_____. "Can God Be Trusted? Problems with Prophecy." Paper Presented at the Evangelical Theological Society Northwestern Regional Meeting. Tacoma, WA., March 2006.
_____. "Does God 'Change His Mind'?" *Bibliotheca Sacra* 152, no. 608 (1995): 388–400.
_____. "Making Sense of Prophecy: Recognizing the Presence of Contingency," Paper presented at the Far West Regional Meeting of the Evangelical Theological Society (Sun Valley, CA, April 2007).
_____. "When Prophecy Appears to Fail, Check Your Hermeneutic." Paper Presented at the Evangelical Theological Society National Meeting. Atlanta, GA. November 2003
_____. "Wordplay in the Eighth-Century Prophets." *Bibliotheca Sacra* 144, no. 573 (January 1987): 44–53.

Chow, Simon. *The Sign of Jonah Reconsidered: A Study of Its Meaning in the Gospel Traditions*. Stockholm, Sweden: Almqvist & Wiksell International, 1995.

Clements, R. E. "The Purpose of the Book of Jonah." *Supplement to the Vetus Testamentum* 28 (1974): 16–28.

Cole, Alan D. "The Purpose of the Book of Jonah." Th.M. Thesis, Detroit Baptist Theological Seminary, May 1989.

Danker, Frederick W., and Walter Bauer. *A Greek-English Lexicon of the New Testament and Other Early Christian Literature*. 3rd ed. Chicago, IL: University of Chicago Press, 2000.

Deere, Jack. *Surprised by the Voice of God: How God Speaks Today through Prophecies, Dreams, and Visions*. Grand Rapids, MI: Zondervan, 1996.

Dobschütz, Ernst von. *The Eschatology of the Gospels*. Hodder and Stoughton, 1910.

Dorsey, David A. *The Literary Structure of the Old Testament: A Commentary on Genesis–Malachi*. Grand Rapids, MI: Baker Books, 1999.

Durham, John I. *Exodus*. Vol. 3. 59 vols. Word Biblical Commentary. Dallas, TX: Thomas Nelson, 2002.

Elliott, Charles. "Jonah." *The Old and New Testament Student* 10, no. 3 (March 1890): 134–40.

Erickson, Millard J. *God the Father Almighty: A Contemporary Exploration of the Divine Attributes*. Grand Rapids, MI: Baker Books, 1998.

Faulstich, E. W. "Jonah: The Sign for Israel." Spencer, IA: Chronology Books, 1989.

Feinberg, Charles Lee. *The Minor Prophets*. Combined ed. Chicago, IL: Moody Press, 1976.

Freeman, Hobart E. *An Introduction to the Old Testament Prophets*. Chicago, IL: Moody Press, 1969.

Fretheim, Terence E. *The Message of Jonah: A Theological Commentary*. Minneapolis, MN: Augsburg Publishing House, 1977.

Frolov, Serge. "Returning the Ticket: God and His Prophet in the

Book of Jonah." *Journal for the Study of the Old Testament* 86 (1999): 85–105.

Gaebelein, Frank Ely. *Four Minor Prophets: Obadiah, Jonah, Habakkuk, and Haggai; Their Message for Today.* Chicago, IL: Moody Press, 1970.

Garrett, Duane A. *Hosea, Joel.* Nashville, TN: Broadman & Holman, 1997.

Garrett, Duane A., and Paul R. House. *Song of Songs.* Nashville, TN: Thomas Nelson Publishers, 2004.

Geisler, Norman L. *Inerrancy.* Grand Rapids, MI: Zondervan Publishing House, 1979.

———. "The Relation of Purpose and Meaning in Interpreting Scripture." *Grace Theological Journal* 5, no. 2 (1984): 229–46.

Gesenius, Friedrich Wilhelm. *Gesenius' Hebrew Grammar.* 2nd English ed., ed. E. Kautzsch and Sir Arthur Ernest Cowley. London, England: Oxford University Press, 1909.

Good, Edwin M. *Irony in the Old Testament.* Philadelphia, PA: Westminster Press, 1965.

Gordon, Cyrus Herzl. *Ugaritic Manual; Newly Revised Grammar, Texts in Transliteration, Cuneiform Selections, Paradigms, Glossary, Indices.* Roma, Italy: Pontificium Institutum Biblicum, 1955.

Gowan, Donald E. *Theology of the Prophetic Books: The Death and Resurrection of Israel.* 1st ed. Louisville, KY.: Westminster John Knox Press, 1998.

Green, Joel B., and Max Turner. *Between Two Horizons: Spanning New Testament Studies and Systematic Theology.* Grand Rapids, MI: W.B. Eerdmans, 2000.

Grice, Paul. *Studies in the Way of Words.* First Harvard University Press Paperback ed. Cambridge, MA.: Harvard University Press, 1991.

Grisanti, Michael A. "Conditional and Hyperbolic Language in the OT Prophets: Where Are We Now?." Paper Presented at the Annual Meeting of the Evangelical Theological Society, Washington, D.C., 15–17 November 2007, 1–9.

Grudem, Wayne A. *Systematic Theology: An Introduction to Biblical Doctrine*. Grand Rapids, MI: Zondervan Publishing House, 1994.

Halpern, Baruch, and Richard Elliott Friedman. "Composition and Paronomasia in the Book of Jonah." *Hebrew Annual Review* 4 (1980): 79–91.

Harris, R. Laird, Gleason L. Archer, Jr., and Bruce K. Waltke. *Theological Wordbook of the Old Testament*. Chicago, IL: Moody Press, 1980.

Hendriksen, William, and Simon J. Kistemaker. *Exposition of the Gospel According to Matthew*. Vol. 9, New Testament Commentary. Grand Rapids, MI: Baker Book House, 1953–2001.

Herzberg, Walter. "Polysemy in the Hebrew Bible." Ph.D. Dissertation, New York University, 1978.

Heschel, Abraham Joshua. *The Prophets*. 1st Perennial Classics ed. New York, NY: Perennial, 2001.

Hill, Andrew E., and John H. Walton. *A Survey of the Old Testament*. 2nd ed. Grand Rapids, MI: Zondervan Publishing House, 2000.

Hirsch, E. D. *Validity in Interpretation*. New Haven, CT: Yale University Press, 1967.

Hodges, Zane C. "Problem Passages in the Gospel of John Part 3: Water and Spirit—John 3:5." *Bibliotheca Sacra* 135, no. 539 (1978): 206–20.

Hoehner, Harold W. *Chronological Aspects of the Life of Christ*. Grand Rapids, MI: Zondervan Publishing House, 1977.

Howton, Dom John. "The Sign of Jonah." *Scottish Journal of Theology* 15 (1962): 288–304.

Johnson, Elliott E. *Expository Hermeneutics: An Introduction*. Grand Rapids, MI: Academie Books, 1989.

Joüon, Paul, and T. Muraoka. *A Grammar of Biblical Hebrew*. Rev. English ed. Vol. 2. Roma, Italy: Editrice Pontificio Istituto Biblico, 2003.

Kaiser, Walter C. *The Uses of the Old Testament in the New*. Chicago, IL: Moody Press, 1985.

Kittel, Gerhard, Gerhard Friedrich, and Geoffrey William Bromiley. *Theological Dictionary of the New Testament*. Vol. 3. Grand Rapids, MI: W.B. Eerdmans, 1976.
_____. *Theological Dictionary of the New Testament*. Vol. 7. Grand Rapids, MI: W.B. Eerdmans, 1976.
Klingler, David. "Jonah: A Call for Repentance." Th.M. Thesis, Dallas Theological Seminary, 2004.
Knight, G. A. F., and F. W. Golka. *Revelation of God: A Commentary on the Books of the Song of Songs and Jonah*. International Theological Commentary. Grand Rapids, MI: W.B. Eerdmans Publishing Co, 1988.
Koerbel, Leigh F. "The Historicity of the Book of Jonah." Th.M. Thesis, Capital Bible Seminary, 1985.
Köhler, Ludwig et al. *The Hebrew and Aramaic Lexicon of the Old Testament*. Study ed. Vol. 1. Boston, MA: Brill, 2001.
Laetsch, Theodore Ferdinand Karl. *Bible Commentary: The Minor Prophets*. Saint Louis, MO: Concordia Publishing House, 1956.
Landes, George M. "Linguistic Criteria and the Date of the Book of Jonah." *Eretz Israel* 16 (1981): 147–70.
Lessing, R. Reed. *Jonah*. Concordia Commentary. St. Louis, MO: Concordia Publishing House, 2007.
Lightner, Robert P. *A Biblical Case for Total Inerrancy: How Jesus Viewed the Old Testament*. Grand Rapids, MI: Kregel Publications, 1998.
Linnemann, Eta. "The Lost Gospel of Q—Fact or Fantasy? ." *Trinity Journal* 17, no. 1 (Spring 1996): 3–18.
Loken, Israel. *The Old Testament Historical Books: An Introduction*. Longwood, FL: Xulon Press, 2008.
Lubeck, R. J. "Prophetic Sabotage: A Look at Jonah 3:2–4." *Trinity Journal* 9, no. 1 (Spring 1988): 38–47.
Magonet, Jonathan. *Form and Meaning: Studies in Literary Techniques in the Book of Jonah*. Heidelberg, Germany: Herbert Lang, 1976.
Master, Jonathan. "Exodus 32 as an Argument for Traditional Theism." *Journal of the Evangelical Theological Society*

45, no. 4 (2002): 585–98.
Merrill, Eugene H. *Kingdom of Priests: A History of Old Testament Israel.* Grand Rapids, MI: Baker Book House, 1987.

———. "The Sign of Jonah." *Journal of the Evangelical Theological Society* 23, no. 1 (March 1980): 23–30.

Miles, John A., Jr. "Laughing at the Bible: Jonah as Parody." *Jewish Quarterly Review* 65, no. 3: 168–81.

Mitchell, Hinckley G. T., J. M. Powis Smith, and Julius A. Bewer. *A Critical and Exegetical Commentary on Haggai, Zechariah, Malachi and Jonah.* Edinburgh, Scotland: T. & T. Clark, 1971.

Nixon, Rosemary A. *The Message of Jonah: Presence in the Storm.* Downers Grove, IL: InterVarsity Press, 2003.

Oesterley, W. O. E., and Theodore H. Robinson. *An Introduction to the Books of the Old Testament.* London, England: Society for Promoting Christian Knowledge, 1960

Orr, James, John L. Nuelson, and Edgar Y Mullins, eds. *The International Standard Bible Encyclopedia*, Fully rev. ed., vol. 3. Grand Rapids, MI: W.B. Eerdmans, 1960.

Parunak, H. Van Dyke. "A Semantic Survey of NHM." *Biblica* 56 (1975): 512–32.

Patterson, Richard D., and Andrew E. Hill. *Minor Prophets.* Vol. 10. 18 vols. Cornerstone Biblical Commentary, ed. Philip W. Comfort. Carol Stream, IL: Tyndale House Publishers, Inc., 2008.

Perry, T. A. *The Honeymoon Is Over: Jonah's Argument with God.* Peabody, MA: Hendrickson Publishers.

Petrotta, Anthony J. *Lexis Ludens: Wordplay and the Book of Micah.* New York, NY: P. Lang, 1991.

Phillips, Richard D. *Jonah & Micah.* Reformed Expository Commentary. Phillipsburg, NJ: P & R Publishing, 2010

Pinches, Theophilus G. *The Old Testament in the Light of the Historical Records and Legends of Assyria and Babylonia.* 2d. ed. London, England: Society for Promoting Christian Knowledge, 1903.

Poythress, Vern S. *Understanding Dispensationalists*. Grand Rapids, MI: Academie Books, 1987.
Price, Brynmor F., and Eugene Albert Nida. *A Translators' Handbook on the Book of Jonah*. Stuttgart, Germany: United Bible Societies, 1978.
Radmacher, Earl D., Robert D. Preus, and International Council on Biblical Inerrancy. *Hermeneutics, Inerrancy, and the Bible: Papers from ICBI Summit II*. Grand Rapids, MI: Academie Books, 1984.
Rice, Richard. *God's Foreknowledge & Man's Free Will*. Minneapolis, MN: Bethany House, 1985.
Rodkinson, Michael L. *The Babylonian Talmud: Tract Sanhedrin* Whitefish, MT: Kessinger Publishing, 2004.
Roy, Steven C. *How Much Does God Foreknow?* Downers Grove, IL.: IVP Academic, 2006.
Ryrie, Charles C. *Dispensationalism Today*. Eighth ed. Chicago, IL: Moody Press, 1973.
_____. *Dispensationalism*. Rev. and expanded. ed. Chicago, IL: Moody Press, 1995.
_____. *Basic Theology: A Popular Systematic Guide to Understanding Biblical Truth*. Chicago, IL: Moody Press, 1999.
Saldivar, Samuel. "A Literary, Theological and Canonical Analysis of the Book of Jonah." Ph.D. Dissertation, Bob Jones University, May 2006.
Sandy, D. Brent. *Plowshares & Pruning Hooks: Rethinking the Language of Biblical Prophecy and Apocalyptic*. Downers Grove, IL: InterVarsity Press, 2002.
_____. "Plowshares and Pruning Hooks and the Hermeneutics of Dispensationalism." Paper presented at the annual meeting of the Evangelical Theological Society, San Diego, CA, 14–16 November 2007).
Sasson, Jack M. *Jonah: A New Translation with Introduction, Commentary, and Interpretation*. 1st ed. New York, NY: Doubleday, 1990.
Scott, R. B. Y. "The Sign of Jonah." *Interpretation: A Journal of*

Bible and Theology 19, no.1 (January 1965): 16–25.

Simon, Uriel. *Jonah*. JPS Bible Commentary. Philadelphia, PA: Jewish Publication Society, 1999.

Smith, Billy K., and Frank S. Page. *Amos, Obadiah, Jonah*. Nashville, TN: Broadman & Holman, 1995.

Smith, John Merlin Powis, and Julius August Bewer. *A Critical and Exegetical Commentary on Haggai, Zechariah, Malachi and Jonah*. New York, NY: C. Scribner's Sons, 1912.

Stallard, Michael D. "A Dispensational Critique of Open Theism's View of Prophecy." *Bibliotheca Sacra* 161, no. 641 (2004): 27–41.

_____. "An Essay on Liberal Hermeneutics." *Conservative Theological Journal* 3, no. 10 (1999): 290–303.

_____. "Literal Interpretation, Theological Method, and the Essence of Dispensationalism." *Journal of Ministry and Theology* 1, no. 1 (Spring 1997): 6–37.

_____. "Literal Interpretation: The Key to Understanding the Bible." *Journal of Ministry and Theology* 4, no. 1 (Spring 2000): 14–35.

_____. "The Open View of God and Prophecy" Paper Presented at the Annual Meeting of the Conservative Theological Society. Fort Worth, TX, August 2001.

_____. "Why are Dispensationalists so Interested in Prophecy?" Paper presented at the annual meeting of the Conservative Theological Society, Fort Worth, TX, August 2005.

Stanton, Gerald B. "The Prophet Jonah and His Message Part 1." *Bibliotheca Sacra* 108, no. 430 (1951): 237–50.

_____. "The Prophet Jonah and His Message Part 2." *Bibliotheca Sacra* 108, no. 431 (1951): 364–77.

Stuart, Douglas K. *Hosea–Jonah*. Vol. 31. 52 vols. Word Biblical Commentary. Waco, TX: Word Books, 1987.

_____. *Exodus*. Vol. 2. 37 vols. New American Commentary. Nashville, TN: Broadman & Holman Publishers, 2006.

Theological Dictionary of the New Testament. Translated by

Geoffrey William Bromiley. Vol. 7. 10 vols., ed. Gerhard Kittel and Gerhard Friedrich. Grand Rapids, MI: W.B. Eerdmans, 1985.

Trible, Phyllis. "Studies in the Book of Jonah." Ph.D. Dissertation, Columbia University, 1963.

──────. *Rhetorical Criticism*. Old Testament Series, ed. Gene M. Tucker. Minneapolis, MN: Fortress Press, 1994.

Trumbull, H. Clay. "Jonah in Nineveh." *Journal of Biblical Literature* XI, no. Part I (1892): 53–60.

Tucker, W. Dennis. *Jonah: A Handbook on the Hebrew Text*. Baylor Handbook on the Hebrew Bible Series. Waco, TX: Baylor University Press, 2006.

Waltke, Bruce K., and Michael Patrick O'Connor. *An Introduction to Biblical Hebrew Syntax*. Winona Lake, IN: Eisenbrauns, 1990.

Walvoord, John F. *Prophecy Knowledge Handbook*. Wheaton, IL: Victor Press.

──────. *The Prophecy Knowledge Handbook*. Wheaton, IL: Victor Books, 1990.

──────. "Interpreting Prophecy Today Part 1: Basic Considerations in Interpreting Prophecy." *Bibliotheca Sacra* 139, no. 553 (January 1982): 4–12.

──────. "Millennial Series: Part 13: The Abrahamic Covenant and Premillennialism," *Bibliotheca Sacra* 109, no. 433 (1952): 42.

Watson, Wilfred G. E. *Classical Hebrew Poetry: A Guide to Its Techniques*. 2nd ed. Edinburgh, Scotland: T & T Clark, 2005.

Watts, John D. W. *Isaiah 1–33*. Waco, TX: Word Books, 1985.

Wendland, Ernst R. "Text Analysis and the Genre of Jonah (Part 1)." *The Journal of the Evangelical Theological Society* 39, no. 2 (1996): 192–207.

──────. "Text Analysis and the Genre of Jonah (Part 2)." *The Journal of the Evangelical Theological Society* 39, no. 3 (1996): 374–409.

Wilson, Ambrose John. "The Sign of the Prophet Jonah and Its

Modern Confirmations." *The Princeton Theological Review* 25, no. 25 (1927): 630–42.

Wiseman, Donald J. "Jonah's Nineveh." *Tyndale Bulletin* 30 (1979): 29–51.

Wolfe, David L. *Epistemology, the Justification of Belief.* Contours of Christian Philosophy. Downers Grove, IL: InterVarsity Press, 1982.

Wolff, Hans Walter. *Obadiah and Jonah: A Commentary.* Translated by Margaret Kohl. Minneapolis, MN: Augsburg Publishing House, 1986.

Wood, D. R. W., and I. Howard Marshall. *New Bible Dictionary.* 3rd ed. Downers Grove, IL: InterVarsity Press, 1996.

Woodard, Branson L. "Death in Life: The Book of Jonah and Biblical Tragedy." *Grace Theological Journal* 11, no. 1 (1990): 4–17.

Youngblood, Kevin J. *Jonah: God's Scandalous Mercy.* Edited By: Daniel I. Block. Grand Rapids, MI: 2013.

Zlotowitz, Meir, and Nosson Scherman. *Yonah = [Sefer Yonah] = Jonah: A New Translation with a Commentary Anthologized from Talmudic, Midrashic, and Rabbinic Sources.* 2nd ed. The Twelve Prophets. Brooklyn, NY: Mesorah Publications, 1980.

Zuck, Roy B., Eugene H. Merrill, and Darrell L. Bock. *A Biblical Theology of the Old Testament.* Chicago, IL: Moody Press, 1991.

www.ingramcontent.com/pod-product-compliance
Lightning Source LLC
Chambersburg PA
CBHW071734150426
43191CB00010B/1571